Modes of Learning

Whitehead's Metaphysics and the Stages of Education

George Allan

Published by State University of New York Press, Albany

Printed in the United States of America

For information, contact State University of New York Press, Albany, NY
www.sunypress.edu

Production by Kelli W. LeRoux
Marketing by Fran Keneston

Library of Congress Cataloging-in-Publication Data

Allan, George, 1935–
Modes of learning : Whitehead's metaphysics and the stages of education / George Allan.
p. cm.
Includes bibliographical references (p.) and index.
ISBN 978-1-4384-4187-0 (hardcover : alk. paper)
ISBN 978-1-4384-4188-7 (paperback : alk. paper)
1. Whitehead, Alfred North, 1861–1947. 2. Education—Philosophy. I. Title.

LB775.W4642A45 2012 2011021200
370.1—dc23

10 9 8 7 6 5 4 3 2 1

Disinterested scientific curiosity is a passion for an ordered intellectual vision of the connection of events. But the goal of such curiosity is the marriage of action to thought. . . . Education should turn out the pupil with something he knows well and something he can do well. This intimate union of practice and theory aids both. The intellect does not work best in a vacuum.

—Alfred North Whitehead, *The Aims of Education*

Whatever is found in 'practice' must lie within the scope of the metaphysical description. When the description fails to include the 'practice,' the metaphysics is inadequate and requires revision. There can be no appeal to practice to supplement metaphysics, so long as we remain contented with our metaphysical doctrines. Metaphysics is nothing but the description of the generalities which apply to all the details of practice. . . . No metaphysical system can hope entirely to satisfy these pragmatic tests. At the best such a system will remain only an approximation to the general truths which are sought.

—Alfred North Whitehead, *Process and Reality*

Contents

Introduction

There is nothing more important than a good education—the kind of education needed in order to become a good person and a good citizen, a responsible adult member of political, cultural, and natural communities. In this book I will explore, by means of the process philosophy of Alfred North Whitehead, these interrelated notions and their metaphysical conditions.

Although the specifics have changed over the centuries, a key claim about a good education has been that it has two stages. First, students should be taught the basic skills necessary for learning about anything, no matter what it is. Then, second, they should be taught a specialized field of inquiry. In the medieval European universities, students first learned the trivium—the general subjects of grammar, logic, and rhetoric—and then the quadrivium—the basic sciences of arithmetic, geometry, astronomy, and music. This two-stage sequence is echoed today, although only faintly, in the distinction between elementary and secondary education, or at the university level between general education courses and those that constitute a major field of concentration.

Process philosophers of education, following Whitehead's suggestions in two short chapters from *The Aims of Education*, re-express this traditional sequence as a cyclic rhythm of three learning stages rather than as a two-stage linear development. These chapters, a 1922 essay on "The Rhythm of Education" and an essay the next year on "The Rhythmic Claims of Freedom and Discipline," run to a total of only twenty-six pages. Yet they develop what is probably the most frequently mentioned of all Whitehead's ideas: that education has a rhythmic structure to which teachers should be sensitive.

In his first essay, Whitehead cites the "truism" that "different subjects and modes of study should be undertaken by pupils at fitting times when they have reached the proper stages of mental development" ("Rhythm" 15), then parses the "fitting times" as having to do with "rhythmic" stages of a pupil's "mental growth." He organizes these stages into a "threefold cycle," which he likens, tongue in cheek, to Hegel's dialectic of thesis-antithesis-synthesis, labeling them as the stages of Romance, Precision, and Generalization (17).

Education, Whitehead argues, "should consist in a continual repetition of such cycles" (19). He then applies these three cyclical stages to infant and adolescent learning, and makes some comments about university education. He concludes with a warning that the stages are not linear but concurrent: each stage marks merely "a distinction of emphasis, of pervasive quality"—an "alternation of dominance"—in a process where all three are "present throughout" (28).

In his second essay, Whitehead elaborates these same points with a few minor differences. He characterizes the three stages as marked respectively by "freedom, discipline, and freedom" ("Rhythmic Claims" 31). Then he emphasizes that the cycle of stages recurs in differing ways in different educational situations, as "minor eddies" in ever wider contexts, "running its course in each day, in each week, and in each term" (38), as well as composing the way by which a formal educational curriculum should be organized and, indeed, by which a person's whole life should be structured. "Education," Whitehead concludes, "is the guidance of the individual towards a comprehension of the art of life" (39).

Romance, precision, and generalization. These Whiteheadian notions have taken on a significance all out of proportion to the few oracular pages in which they are presented. Indeed, most people know of Whitehead only through secondhand versions of these notions, along with a treasure trove of phrases he used in explicating them, phrases that are cryptic enough to make wonderful epigrams for books or papers on educational practices, or as titles for conferences on current issues in education. I suspect this interest is a function of their vagueness, their utility as a way to suggest a wide variety of ideas about the dynamics of learning, enough to generate an interesting exchange of differing views. This suggestiveness is especially attractive for those who reject the excessively modular ways in which contemporary education is imagined and implemented, and who are looking desperately for a few countervailing quotes with which to indicate their distress.

These opportunistic uses and misuses of Whitehead's ideas about education raise a serious question. Are his ideas merely so much rhetorical bling, a convenient way to add a bit of glitter to one's substantive discussion of important educational issues? Or do they get us to the heart of such issues, cutting through the dross of tired ideas and the cant of the standard educational jargon they spawn? Is Whitehead's philosophy a new way of saying the same old things about teaching and learning, or does it offer a transformative fresh insight into the nature and function of education?

For those who know Whitehead's philosophy well, the quotability status that the rhythm of education has among educators raises this same serious question in a different manner. The antidote to the ineffectiveness of schools and universities that is proposed by educators influenced by Whitehead's thought is the admonition to think holistically; to embrace relational theories about facts, ideas, and persons, and about how intellectual understanding and mature selfhood develop. It is not quite clear, however, how these relational approaches are connected to Whitehead's philosophy of education, except for the minimalist observation that the iterated rhythm of romance-precision-generalization is indeed relational. What is the relation of Whitehead's educational notions to his metaphysics? Are the two little talks in *The Aims of Education* marginalia of no concern to the serious work of attempting to understand Whitehead's metaphysics? Or are his metaphysics and his philosophy of education intimately connected, each an implication of the other?

The aim of this book is to provide plausible, and I think interesting, answers to both these kinds of questions. I will argue that a careful examination of Whitehead's metaphysics reveals aspects of his views about the stages of learning that we are not otherwise likely to notice. And conversely, I will suggest ways in which Whitehead's stages of learning reveal aspects of his metaphysics often misconstrued or ignored by Whiteheadian scholars. I hope to show that Whitehead's ideas about the modes of learning can and should be educationally transformative because they reflect a transformative metaphysical understanding of the world and how it functions.

Chapter 1 presents the standard understanding of romance, precision, and generalization developed in Whitehead's two chapters in *The Aims of Education*. The conversation between this standard view and Whitehead's metaphysical writings begins in chapter 2, with a comparison of the stages of learning and the notions of Beauty, Truth, and Art developed in *Adventures of Ideas*. This inquiry suggests a further comparison, explored in chapter 3, between his three stages and the theory of knowledge explicated in *Symbolism: Its Meaning and Effect*. From there we turn to the dynamics of world history, exploring in chapter 4 how the tension between romance and precision that generalization resolves is like the tension between speculative and practical reason that in *The Function of Reason* is resolved by what Whitehead calls the "Greek Discovery." We then embrace the whole of our cosmic epoch in chapter 5 by relating the stages of education to implications of the interplay between the ultimate notions of matter-of-fact and importance discussed in *Modes of Thought*. In chapter 6, the developmental implications of the cycles of learning, how they create the conditions necessary for achieving a good education, and hence for becoming good persons and forming good communities, are explored through a consideration of the development of a sense of Peace that Whitehead articulates in the last section of *Adventures of Ideas*. Chapter 7 recollects the key educational and metaphysical claims of the earlier chapters, emphasizing the similarities among the different sets of similarities that have been explored.

I have purposefully omitted any consideration of *Process and Reality*, widely considered Whitehead's most important book and treated by many Whiteheadian scholars as though it were his only metaphysically significant book. I have omitted it even though Whitehead's account there of the concrescence of actual occasions can with little difficulty be mapped analogically onto the stages of education. My reason is that I think *Process and Reality* obscures important features of Whitehead's metaphysics, features emphasized in the four books I will be discussing, one written just before *Process and Reality* and the others written after it. They all interpret reality as fundamentally temporal and human good as fundamentally a process of learning how to think and act pragmatically.

I hope that by the time readers finish this book, they will have gained a holistic sense of the way in which Whitehead's philosophy of education is both a source and a fruit of his metaphysics. It is a source, because the processes of human learning are one of the specific kinds of experience from which his metaphysics arises. It is also a fruit, because learning to understand and put to good practice the ways by which we can develop into civilized human beings is one of the most obvious and important applications of that metaphysics. This accords with Whitehead's famous airplane metaphor: "The true method of discovery is like the flight of an aeroplane. It starts from the ground of particular observation; it makes a flight in the thin air of imaginative generalization; and it again lands for renewed observation rendered acute by rational interpretation" (*Process* 5). In this book, education provides the observational departure ground and metaphysics the thin-aired flight. My hope is that by book's end those who have made this journey with me will find their grasp of the modes of learning rendered acute by rational interpretation.

My presentation is rife with examples: those of Whitehead and quite a few of my own invention. These are not window dressing, not crutches to assist those unused to abstract ideas, not ladders to be tossed aside once one has climbed up to the realms of metaphysical discourse. The function of the examples is to tether Whitehead's philosophical ideas to the specific learning experiences those ideas generalize. A philosopher should not be someone whose feet are both firmly planted in midair. If the flight of the philosopher's metaphysical airplane is from the ground into the thin air of speculation, it is important that the pilot know at all times from where the flight departed and to where it must eventually return. In other words, the examples with which I work throughout the book are concrete intimations of the philosophical ideas that are developed from them, just as those ideas turn out to be, if they are effective, abstract intimations of the specific realities they interpret. Neither the examples nor the ideas can stand alone, for our experiences are functions of our interpretations and our interpretations functions of our experiences. Since, however, our experiences are not generic but unique to each of us, the examples, both Whitehead's and mine, invite readers to provide the imaginative substitutions and embellishments needed to make them their own. By doing so, readers can begin to see themselves from within the perspective Whitehead's theory offers, to understand as he would have us understand why how we learn is so important for who we are and who we might become.

I have written this book for that mythical kind of person, the "intelligent reader." The category may be mythical, but its members are very real. They include professional educators—college professors and schoolteachers—who are looking for the stimulation of fresh ideas about the nature of human learning, about the conditions for becoming good learners, and who realize that they may need to alter their assumed metaphysical perspective to find it. Among these educators, of course, are philosophers whose aim is the inverse of this: those who are looking for the stimulation of fresh ideas about what the character of metaphysics should be if its understandings are to be both warranted and relevant, and who realize that they need therefore to rethink their ideas about the function of learning in the nature of things.

The intelligent readers I have in mind also include parents, no matter what the age of their children, who are concerned about the ways in which their sons and daughters are taught and whether what they learn will serve them well not merely in the development of their marketable skills but more importantly in the development of their character and the moral quality of their commitments. And of course, we have all been students ourselves, and I would hope still are, and we are all philosophers despite our protestations to the contrary, and I hope would like to be self-critically aware of our metaphysical assumptions. So the question of how we might be better learners is reason enough for any lively minded person to join me in this book's explorations.

My intention is to provide a carefully grounded presentation of Whitehead's metaphysical and educational ideas. I have cleaved to Whitehead's text throughout, but in trying to explain what he is saying, and to justify my claims concerning the import of what he says, I have constantly ventured freely into considerations and arguments of my own invention. My personal interests and professional proclivities result in a selective bias to my presentation—a bias not a prejudice, in that I think it is solidly grounded in the texts. Even the most faithfully objective exposition of a text, however, even the most loyally ingratiating interpretation of its significance, like even the most accurate translation of a poem into another language, is unavoidably selective. The innovative selectivity is a given; the question is whether it is true or not, whether it is fruitful.

My interpretation of Whitehead's views is innovative simply because it is made from a standpoint other than that of the original author. Whitehead wrote his two education essays in the early 1920s for British audiences. As I now come to them, as I now bring my readers to them, we are separated from Whitehead and those he was trying to influence by the wide Atlantic Ocean of our cultural divergence; by the collapse of all the European and most of the Asian colonialist, fascist, and communist imperialisms, and by the rise of new kinds of imperialism; by nearly a century of changes in educational practices and reflection; by the publication of Whitehead's metaphysical books, all of them written after the two education essays; and by a vast library of Whiteheadian metaphysical and educational interpretation.

It is fitting that we must take seriously the transformations effected by time and tide when attempting to explicate the ideas found in the writings of a philosopher who argues that the most fundamental realities are transformative processes and that individuals are complex unities emergent from ever-changing contexts. In believing it important for our cognitive and moral nurture that we understand what Whitehead once said, we will reach as best we can toward a reality the full richness of which is forever lost in the mists of the past, hoping that we have touched the heart of what he meant while recognizing that it is no longer a living heart. In this sense, faith is a hope grounded in love. The pages that follow are an attempt to be faithful to Whitehead's texts but not slavishly, and in so doing to enrich the standard view of their meaning.

***

Chapters 2 through 6 have genetic antecedents in published essays that I would like to acknowledge. The progenitors are briefer explorations and have been considerably altered subsequently in detail, sometimes altered enough in focus and implication that their genetic claims are not obvious. They are:

Chapter 2: "The Wand of the Enchanter." In Michel Weber and Pierfrancesco Basile, eds., *Subjectivity, Process, and Rationality* (Festschrift honoring Dr. Reiner Wiehl). Frankfort/Lancaster: Ontos Verlag, Process Thought Series XIV, 2007, pp. 249–61.

Chapter 2: "Helical Learning." In Adam C. Scarfe, ed. *The Adventure of Education: Process Philosophers on Learning, Teaching, and Research*. Amsterdam: Rodopi, 2009, pp. 31–40.

Chapter 3: "Whitehead's Modes of Experience and the Stages of Education." In Franz Riffert, ed., *Alfred North Whitehead on Learning and Education: Theory and Application*. Amersham, UK: Cambridge Scholars Press, 2005, pp. 59–87.

Chapter 4: "Solomon's Dream and Whitehead's Stages of Learning." *Process Studies* 34(2): 224–39 (2005) [2006].

Chapter 5: "Creating the Future." *Process Studies* 38(2): 207–27 (2009) [2010].

Chapter 6: "On Learning to Be Good." In George Allan and Malcolm D. Evans, eds., *A Different Three Rs for Education: Reason, Relationality, Rhythm*. Amsterdam: Rodopi, 2006, pp. 21–42.

Although I have received helpful comments from many people on drafts of these chapters, the earlier essays, or related presentations, or on ideas expressed more informally face-to-face or via e-mail, I would like to especially thank the following: Malcolm Evans, for his careful reading of the last two drafts of this book, and for his comments and encouragement throughout regarding the educational ideas I explore; Frederick Ferré, for his helpful criticism of most of the book's ancestral essays; Pam Crosby, for her suggestions about issues and initiatives in current education relevant to my arguments; and Stefan Schindler, for his critiques of both the style and substance of my arguments. My thanks also to the two anonymous outside readers of the manuscript I originally submitted to SUNY Press, both of whom liked what I had to say, but not so well that they didn't find important difficulties I needed to correct, and who made valuable suggestions for improving my argument that I have often if not always followed.

Modes of Learning is dedicated to four Dickinson colleagues, all emeriti like myself: Daniel Bechtel, Harry Booth, Truman Bullard, and Gordon Bergsten. None are philosophers but all are educators delightfully grounded in the liberal arts. We comprise a weekly book group that through our choice of readings and our lively discussions of them has widened my cultural horizons significantly and thickened my understanding in ways that often to my surprise have found expression in the examples and arguments of this book.

CHAPTER ONE

The Rhythm of Learning

I begin with an account of Whitehead's three stages of education. My approach is not to provide a close reading of first one and then the other of the two relevant essays, first "The Rhythm of Education" and then "The Rhythmic Claims of Freedom and Discipline." Rather, I draw freely from them both in offering an interpretation of each stage sequentially: first Romance, next Precision, and finally Generalization.

Brave New Worlds

Whitehead argues that the first stage of learning should be that of Romance, in which students are encouraged to explore in as wide ranging and adventurous a way as possible the natural and cultural worlds in which they live. The mood is appreciative and inclusive.

The stage of romance is one of "first apprehension" ("Rhythm" 17), says Whitehead. It is marked by our initial "awakening to the apprehension of objects" (19), to an awareness of the objects of immediate experience comprising the content of our world. As newborns, this world is narrow, composed of our aching hunger, an offered nipple, and softly cradling warmth. That inchoate world slowly expands as we grow, coming to include the noise of our own crying, flashes of movement, cold touches and smooth textures, smiles and hugs. Eventually it encompasses the sticks and stones, chairs and tables, cats and dogs, fathers and mothers of the everyday commonsense world. Romance is an occasion for delighting in this world immediately around us, savoring its flavors, basking in its sunlit embrace.

Openness to the world as we find it is only a partial characterization of what apprehension involves, however. For Whitehead's world is profoundly holistic, its individual objects internally related to each other. So romance is more than an awakening to things; it is also an awakening to an "appreciation of their connexions" (19). There is more to the familiar than meets the eye. The objects of our experience, we come to realize, have an "import": they come redolent with "unexplored relationships" (18). What we apprehend "holds within itself unexplored connexions with possibilities half-disclosed by glimpses and half-concealed by the wealth of material" (17). For everything we encounter, there is a "more" it conceals, a terra incognita still to be disclosed, a world vivid with novelties, a world of such unbounded plenitude that nothing can be noticed without whatever is next to it catching our attention and evoking our response.

Hence "interest is the *sine qua non* for attention and apprehension" ("Rhythmic Claims" 31), and so education at all levels should constantly root and reroot itself in the same fertile soil—the inherently interesting, wonderfully alluring thises and thats of the world around us.

As an infant, I turn my head toward jingling noises and circling movements, cooing at their presence and crying when they stop. I reach out for an object myopically glimpsed and bring it to my mouth, taste what it's like, and from the resulting sensation discover that it can be delightfully sweet or unexpectedly bitter, deliciously slippery or repulsively rough. At first, I don't generalize: I experience this-here-now sweetness and then this-here-now bitterness. I suck the world in or spew it out, and remain as curious as ever about how it might taste when next I get it to my mouth. As I become a toddler and sense the permanence of objects, I look for the bird to whose morning song I have awakened, wondering when the sound stops where it has gone and why it is hiding from me. Perhaps if I fall back to sleep, when I reawaken it will have returned. Or perhaps it only sings when I have arranged my stuffed animals in a circle properly attentive to the magic of its melody.

While playing alone in my backyard, an unturned stone becomes a mystery I must set about solving. Its smoothly rounded visible surface promises a smooth completion on the unseen portion of its circumference. But this promise comes with a titillating hint that the underside might have a different shape altogether and might even afford access to creepy-crawly worms or pale curled tubes of plants it has been holding prisoner. At least that's what a stone's underside disgorged the last time I turned one over, even though, come to think of it, that wasn't so for the stone before that one. And thereby is kindled the mystery of the stone I now approach with delightfully anticipated disgust.

My father gives me a big white-and-black ball with which to play. I sit down and a playmate sits facing me, each with our legs spread apart, so that we can roll the ball back and forth, trying to guide it between the other's legs. Soon we get good enough for our little game to grow tiresome, and so I purposefully miss, requiring my friend to get up and retrieve the ball in order to take her proper turn. Then she tries to miss as well, and we end up kicking the ball, racing after it, kicking it again, racing and kicking until we fall exhausted and laughing on the grass. In kindergarten, my teacher takes us for a stroll in the nearby park where we run after a bird we see hopping across the grass. We then climb in the rocks, throw pebbles into the stream, and play catch-me among the trees. I go running to our teacher in momentary fright when an unfriendly bird scolds me raucously from somewhere above us, and I am glad to walk back to the familiar safety of our school hand-in-hand with my classmates.

I am given a new book to read in first grade, each page of which is fraught with the unknown pages still to come. I am tempted to peek ahead, to learn where I am about to go before going there. And when I succumb to this temptation, I thereafter enjoy the smug godlike satisfaction of knowing what the characters in the story cannot yet know because for them it has not happened. Ahead of spoken words I cannot peek, however. Which is the drawback of having my teacher or aunt or older brother read to me, or of listening to the story on an audio disk. Some of my classmates prefer hearing a story, comfortably surrounded by friends, the characters in the story incarnated by a reader's familiar voice. I prefer, however, the solitary silence of reading a book to myself, with no constraints on where my imagination can take me, even when it takes me so far and fast that I become lost in my fantasizing and the book falls unnoticed to my lap.

On a summer vacation to the beach after second grade, I build a castle in the sand, struggling unsuccessfully in the growing dusk to buttress it against the rising tide by surrounding it with a moat. To ease my unease, I imagine myself somehow transported to a castle in the sky where no tide ever threatens and the sun always shines benignly on my projects. I sign up with a third-grade Y-Club soccer team and learn that a black-and-white ball can be used to play a game which involves me being on a team, wearing a blue T-shirt, and trying to kick the ball down the field into a net while other kids in yellow T-shirts are trying to kick the same ball into a net at the other end of the field. This is good fun, although sometimes I forget about the net part and am content just to kick the ball before a yellow shirt can, no matter where I kick it. This can often be difficult, what with all twenty or so of us gathered around the ball at once.

By sixth grade, I am reading adventure stories and imagining myself as a participant in them. I am Arthur as he grasps the sword in the stone and as the ladies bear his wounded body across the lake to Avalon. I am Guinevere as she wrestles with her impossible love for both Arthur and Lancelot, and as she withdraws at the end into a monastery castle surrounded by a moat. I come up with a new idea, an idea of my own invention, about how the Round Table should be formed and how the Quest for the Holy Grail should be pursued, and lying in bed at night I spin out its exhilarating implications.

In all the phases of our lives—as babies, toddlers, kindergartners, and grade-school pupils, but also as adolescents and adults for whom childhood is never merely a memory—the stage of romance is a time when "ideas, facts, relationships, stories, histories, possibilities, artistry in words, in sounds, in forms and in colour, crowd into the child's life, stir his feelings, excite his appreciation, and incite his impulses to kindred activities" ("Rhythm" 21). In romantic experiences, the world "stirs" our imagination, "excites" our curiosity, and "incites" us to respond in kind, to make ourselves "kindred" spirits with it, and through it with each other. We learn to delight in the multifarious gifts of the world, delighting in them for their own sake and responding to those gifts in all the ways they invite response.

Whitehead offers an example of how this adaptive exuberance works in his account of reading DeFoe's *Robinson Crusoe* for the first time. Crusoe is just a character in a story, an imaginary man stranded on an imaginary island. I come to the story with a repertoire of everyday knowledge. I know about men and women, my parents and adult friends. I know about their busy comings and goings in the cities and towns where I live. I know about my own experiences in the home, at school, around the neighborhood. And I know about islands, about their beaches, and about how walking on them leaves footprints in the sand. "But the sudden perception of the half-disclosed and half-hidden possibilities relating Crusoe and the sand and the footprint and the lonely island secluded from Europe constitutes romance" (18). Aspects of my everyday world, taken for granted because they are so everyday, so boringly commonplace, are brought together by the story in such a manner that something more than their everyday meaning rises to the foreground, shimmering with import, with unexplored implications that whet my imagination.

I wonder about what it might be like to live so far from civilization, to be forced to seek food and shelter on my own, to have the courage and craft it would take to survive. I worry about what the dangers might be, what carnivores might be lurking on such an island, wanting me for their evening meal. And then, amid these unsettling questions—behold, that footprint in the sand. A simple fact, unexpectedly adding mystery to danger, the uncanny to the unknown. There are no fortresses ready at hand to offer me protection, no obvious path along which I might escape. Even Excalibur would not be enough, nor Lancelot riding to my rescue. And yet if I were Crusoe I could surely manage. And, ah yes, look: it seems he manages quite well indeed. He has the right stuff, that guy, and so would I.

The "natural mode" for stirring our imagination, for exciting our interest, for inciting us to explore the undiscovered import of our immediate experiences, is "enjoyment" ("Rhythmic Claims" 31). Whitehead doubts the efficacy of birch rods. They work, to be sure, but only as long as an authority figure is wielding them. "Undoubtedly pain is one subordinate means of arousing an organism to action. But it only supervenes on the failure of pleasure." A person's education is best furthered "along a path of natural activity, in itself pleasurable" (31).

In another of Whitehead's striking examples: a teacher assigns me the task of looking at the stars through a telescope, but unless my experience is marked by the "transfiguration of imposed routine" that romance cultivates, unless for me this is not an assignment to be carried out but rather an opportunity to gain "free access to the glory of the heavens" (33), no genuine educational growth will occur. "Without the adventure of romance, at the best you get inert knowledge without initiative, and at the worse you get contempt of ideas—without knowledge" (33).

I am more likely to eat my brussels sprouts because I enjoy eating a good meal—in the company of friends, or attended by my favorite stuffed animals, or hand-in-hand with some young prince whose destiny may be entwined with my own—than because I have been told that without eating dark leafy vegetables I will die of a heart attack in my forties or because I am dutiful to my parents' insistence that I eat everything on my plate. Babies will spit out the spoon of spinach mush, and who can blame them, unless we transform the spoon into a speedboat and their mouth becomes its safe harbor.

Every soccer player wants to be a striker, for it is from that position that a person is best able to score goals, and surely no one would voluntarily pass up the glory and satisfaction this entails. Yet a team has eleven positions, many of which involve a basically defensive role, so one of the tasks elementary school coaches have is assigning most of their players to unglamorous positions. A poor coach might tell me in a take-it-or-leave-it authoritarian voice: You play sweeper or you don't play. Good soccer coaches, however, will lure me into discovering the excitement and satisfaction of playing defense, discovering skills I didn't realize I had, and coming to appreciate how the strikers are dependent on us defenders for their success. It's our ability in preventing an opponent from scoring goals that turns a striker into a hero for putting the game's only goal into the net. How exhilarating it is to discover the joys of being a team player, to sense the deepening character that comes from recognizing my intrinsic even if unsung worth.

We are more likely to read a philosophy book, maybe even Whitehead's horridly difficult *Process and Reality*, if some of his epigrams from *The Aims of Education* have pricked our imagination and set us wondering about what vision of the nature of things might lie behind his clever turns of phrase. Whitehead says, for example, that "The present contains all that there is. It is holy ground; for it is the past, and it is the future" ("Aims" 3). Our rational imagination is likely to be titillated by this assertion, for how could we not wonder what he could possibly mean, this philosopher who is said to take time seriously, when he not only sanctifies the present moment but claims that's all there is. We might be drawn by this curious claim of his to struggle willingly with such obscurities as his assertion "that the potentiality for being an element in a real concrescence of many entities into one actuality is the one general metaphysical character attaching to all entities, actual and non-actual; and that every item in its universe is involved in every concrescence" (*Process* 22). Better the lure of the quote from *The Aims of Education* than the threat of a poor grade on the next hourly exam, if the aim of education is to nurture a love rather than a contempt for ideas, to bring ideas alive rather than, finding them inert, to bury them as soon as the hour exam is over and they have begun to putrefy.

Whitehead calls the path of natural learning "discursive" because it is "a process of discovery, a process of becoming used to curious thoughts, of shaping questions, of seeking for answers, of devising new experiences, of noticing what happens as the result of new ventures" ("Rhythmic Claims" 32). Romance, in other words, has a trajectory. It involves not only apprehension, appreciation, and interest but also their iteration until they become habits of the heart and mind. In the stage of romance, we are not only learning about whatever our inquiries happen to turn up but also developing a habit. We are becoming used to asking questions and seeking new experiences, imagining novel possibilities and ferreting out their implications. Romance begins in wonder and develops a wondering disposition. Under its aegis students develop a discursive openness to things, a predisposition to follow the story wherever it might lead and to revel in the amazing adventures that thereby ensue.

A predisposition is a habit, and thus in classrooms at every level the most important task of a teacher is helping students develop a habit of being curious. The wise pedagogue teaches romance best by not getting in the way of a student's natural curiosity, but that curiosity needs to be pricked until its exercise becomes a habit. Laissez-faire is not enough. "Now undoubtedly," says Whitehead, "this stage of development requires help, and even discipline" (32). A teacher should therefore intervene, although light-handedly, creating an appropriately stimulating environment, one "chosen to suit the child's stage of growth" and "adapted to individual needs" (32), setting tasks and challenges, encouraging and suggesting, admonishing and redirecting. These interventions have to be done in such a way that students respond out of their own kindled interests and not because they feel compelled to do so, eventually responding because of their inquisitive proclivity, their habitual curiosity, their cultivated wonderment. Any such intervention is "in a sense" an "imposition from without; but in a deeper sense it answers to the call of life within the child" (32–33).

Some events thrust us willy-nilly into their enthralling mystery, force us to question their significance, even to wonder about their intelligibility. But romantic education should teach us to ask questions of even what is apparently obvious or trivial, to be curious about what is deemed irrelevant or threadbare. We should be interested not only in exploring the unexplored dimensions of our known world but also in poking around for other unnoticed or hitherto unknown dimensions, and wondering about what lies beyond even all of that. The romance stage of education has done its work when "there has been plenty of independent browsing amid first-hand experiences, involving adventures of thought and of action" (33).

The habit of looking under rocks, imagining how sand castles might survive the tide, conjuring imaginary friends to help eat our brussels sprouts—they are all ways in which we do not take the way things are as necessities to which we must bow down. We cannot change what is the case, but we can imagine it as only a part of something grander, a portal into a fairyland or an alternative universe or a better tomorrow. We can develop a habit of presuming that there is more here than it would seem, and that it is a wondrous more, alien and threatening perhaps, but fraught enough with bright possibilities that uncovering it seems well worth the risk. We will never discover the golden fleece hidden in a land just beyond the farthest edge of the known sea, unless the prospect of encountering dragons along the way lures us into setting sail from the comforts of our familiar hearth, thrilled more by the adventuring than by the goal, excited more by the likelihood of storms and pirates than by the placid harbor to which we might eventually come.

The attraction of stories is that they take us through such mysterious portals and across such ranging seas while we are curled in a chair by the fire. And yet these imaginative tales are every bit as dangerous as actual journeys because they also take us beyond the boundaries of our accustomed imaginings into what had been for us not only unknown, not only unbelievable, but hitherto simply unimaginable. "O wonder!" gushes Miranda, seeing for the first time human beings other than her father and Caliban,

> How many goodly creatures are there here!
> How beauteous mankind is! O brave new world
> That has such people in't. (Shakespeare, *Tempest* Act 5, Scene 1)

It's quite a sorry group of men at which she looks, that shipwrecked duke and his entourage, but she finds them "brave"—handsome, noble, wondrous—because her knowledge of humans is so limited, the boundary of her world so narrow. Calm down, says Prospero, you overstate things; they are really not so brave, it's just that "'Tis new to thee."

We are intrigued by the possibility of new beings of which we are as ignorant as Miranda was of us and our kind—Chewbacca, R2-D2, and Yoda; Frodo, Gimli, and Elrond. And yet in seeking them out as our friends and allies, we run the risk of meeting instead Emperor Palpatine or Darth Vader, Gollum or Sauron. Even Miranda's brave new world of handsome men might be transformed for us, as for Aldous Huxley, into a dystopian nightmare. Romancing our world opens it out, pushes back its boundaries, and does so in often surprising ways, disturbing our familiar comforts, bringing us into the presence of more things than we imagined possible—things that sometimes are for the better, sometimes for the worse, but that are always transformative.

Masterpieces

Whitehead says that the stage of romance in our educational development should in due time pass over into a stage of precision, a stage in which "width of relationship is subordinated to exactness of formulation" ("Rhythm" 18). We have a natural "aptitude for exact knowledge" (22), says Whitehead, for a shift in our way of learning from one rooted in appreciation to one that is critical and analytic. Without the prior interest stirred up by romance, however, the exact knowledge we achieve will be merely "a series of meaningless statements about bare facts, produced artificially and without any further relevance" (18). Yet although the romance is crucial, it is important that it give way to precision. The right time for this shift is when the freshness of romance has begun to wane, when our initial curiosity has been satisfied and we grow restless with the limitations inherent in appreciative apprehension, thinking of it increasingly as superficial. When we come to it in this timely fashion, "precision will always illustrate subject-matter already apprehended and crying out for drastic treatment" (25).

Descartes is the patron saint of precision because in his *Discourse on Method* he provides a set of instructions for arriving at the exact truth. He is upset by the conflicting claims made by scientists and philosophers, by kings and priests, that they alone know what is true. Refusing to accept any of these warring claims simply on the authority of their advocates, he decides to find out for himself how to distinguish genuine truths from supposed truths. He resolves to be "like a man who walks alone in the darkness": he will proceed in step by step fashion, "slowly and circumspectly," sacrificing rapid movement in order to be "at least safe from falling," until he arrives at conclusions he can trust to be true (*Discourse* 11).

Descartes proposes a method that involves four simple steps. First, "never to accept anything as true unless I recognize it to be evidently such," which means that it presents itself "so clearly and distinctly to my mind" that there can be "no occasion to doubt it" (12). Second, "divide each of the difficulties which I encountered into as many parts as possible," each one of which because less complex than the initial difficulty will make for "an easier solution" (12). Third, "think in an orderly fashion," moving from the "simplest and easiest to understand" to what is "more complex" (12). Fourth, "make enumerations so complete, and reviews so general, that I would be certain that nothing was omitted" (12). Identify, analyze, synthesize, and then check your work.

Attaining the exactness to be cultivated during the stage of precision involves, first of all, grasping particular facts clearly and distinctly, specifying precisely what each one is and is not by analyzing it into its simplest components. Such precision is best achieved by quantitative measurements, so the educational examples that come immediately to mind are scientific ones—determining rates of motion in a physics class or identifying precipitates in a chemistry lab. Sometimes, however, the only kind of precision initially available to us, even in the sciences, is nonquantitative, a matter of careful perceptions judged by reference to exemplary instances.

The birds we saw when my classmates and I took a nature walk in the park stimulate our interest in finding out their names. So we return to the park, but this time equipped with binoculars and copies of a field guide, Kaufman's *Birds of North America.* Before long, I spot a winged creature perched on a nearby branch. We use Kaufman's "pictorial table of contents" to get an initial fix on the sort of bird we are seeing by noting its general size and shape. Not waterbirds, not birds of prey, larger than hummingbirds or warblers, smaller than pigeons and parrots. Among the vast array of the medium-sized birds remaining, our bird's thick beak becomes a first key identifier, pointing us to the part of the field guide for "finches and buntings." Color now begins to be important, and once we have eliminated birds not found in our part of the country, the reddish color around our bird's head suggests it is most likely either a male House Finch or a male Purple Finch. We opt for the latter identification because its head is drenched in the reddish color whereas the top of a male House Finch's head is capped in brown and it has dark stripes on its sides that a Purple Finch lacks. As a clincher, the bird's rich mellow warbling lacks the rough notes with which a House Finch typically ends its song.

We may well have overlooked some important distinguishing feature, especially since some of our judgments were based on the absence of House Finch features rather than the presence of those belonging distinctively to a Purple Finch, and we did not pay attention to subtle issues like the possibility of local variations that would obscure the differences between these two kinds of finch. If we could subject our bird to the quantitatively precise analysis a laboratory dissection would offer, the likely accuracy of our identification would increase dramatically. But given our handy field guide and ample opportunity to compare its pictures and text to what we can see of the bird in the tree, our claim that it's a Purple Finch and not a House Finch is reasonable. And so we cheerfully add it to our classroom's Year List.

One of us picks up a grayish rock during our new stroll in the park and wonders what kind of rock it might be. Our teacher suggests that we take it back to our science lab for testing. Close inspection under bright laboratory lights shows that its grayish color is not uniform but a mix of lighter and darker colors, including various bits of what look like shell fragments. It can be scratched easily and when a hammer and chisel are used it splits along fault lines that suggest the rock is sedimentary, built up over time by layer after layer of these materials. There are signs that water has leached grooves in its surface, and at our teacher's suggestion we drip some hydrochloric acid on the rock, which to our delight bubbles on contact.

We take down from our library shelves *Peterson's Field Guides: Rocks and Minerals* and discover that what we have observed suggests the rock is limestone. It could be dolomite, however, which the book says is quite similar except that it has to be ground into powder before hydrochloric acid will make it bubble. We would like to be more confident that the rock isn't dolomite, and so we increase the technical precision of our inquiry by undertaking a chemical analysis, following standard laboratory procedures for doing so. The results indicate that the rock is composed mainly of the mineral calcite: calcium carbonate, $CaCO_3$. That makes it limestone because dolomite includes magnesium as well as calcium, in the form of calcium magnesium carbonate, $CaMg(CO_3)_2$. Thus the precision of our analysis allows us both to be clear about what the rock is and to be able to distinguish it from what it is not, to identify it as limestone rather than dolomite.

The sciences, of course, are not the only areas of learning in which precision emerges out of romance. There comes a time when I and my friends grow bored with bumblebee soccer and want to acquire the skills at which the older children are adept. We have begun to notice that they are always beating us not because they are bigger and stronger but because they can kick the ball more accurately, anticipate our moves better, and sense more quickly when a teammate has become open. Our coach explains that such skills are acquired by practicing them and that the best form of practice is running precise repetitive drills until our feet and not merely our brains know how to do what needs doing. So we kick the ball at the goal from a variety of different angles, with or without a goalkeeper attempting to block our shot, sometimes from a set location and sometimes after receiving a pass while running an approach pattern—again and again, accompanied by the coach's never-ending words of complaint and praise. And eventually we get better, and after a while move up to a level of play where our newly learned skills are crucial not only to succeed but even just to keep up.

My fascination with the King Arthur legends leads me to wonder if such a king ever lived, if Camelot was a real place and Mount Baden a real battle. A little historical research online and in the local library makes it clear that the legends have some connection to what is known about the ancient Britons. They were conquered in the last century BCE by Roman legions, but in the fourth century CE the legions were withdrawn and the civilized order they had assured disintegrated. In desperation, the Britons invited Saxon mercenaries to help defend against invading Picts to the north. The Saxons then stayed, however, settled on the land with their families, and slowly but inexorably expanded their presence, killing or enslaving whoever stood in their way. The Britons resisted as best they could, and in the fifth century fought a series of battles against the Saxons.

Contemporary reports from these times, I discover, and even relevant archeological findings, are practically nonexistent. The earliest account of the battles makes no mention of a special battle-leader, much less one named Arthur. Only in the ninth century is he mentioned by name and his role described in a single terse sentence. Three centuries later, in 1135, Geoffrey of Monmouth published a history of the kings of Britain, the climax of which is an account of the exploits of the high king Uther Pendragon and his successor King Arthur. According to Geoffrey, Arthur was a skilled military commander and political ruler who extended British hegemony throughout most of western and northern Europe, only to be mortally wounded while suppressing a local rebellion and who, dying, surrendered his crown to Constantine of Cornwall in 542.

By Geoffrey's time, however, legends of Arthur's life and achievements were in plentiful supply and so the factual accuracy of Geoffrey's account is hardly trustworthy. Hence, in trying to be clear about who Arthur really was, I end up needing to distinguish the Arthur of history from the Arthur of myth—and I discover there is little of the former and a great deal of the latter. My interest may then shift to asking about the origins and development of these legends, and I end up tracing them from Celtic tales through their spread to Normandy and into France, their linkage to Christian myths, and their literary apotheosis in the twelfth-century poetry of Chrétien de Troyes and the fifteenth-century prose of Thomas Malory.

When I build sand castles at the shore, I find myself thinking of them as replicas of Camelot. This leads me to researching the character of medieval castles and discovering that the fourth-century earthen embankment crowned by a timber stockade that Arthur would have built is quite different from the Romanesque structure Geoffrey probably imagined him fashioning or the gothic castle Malory presumably had in mind. I am struck by the architectural and engineering advances that made this shift possible, and begin tinkering with how I make my sand castles to see if by using piers sunk into the sand and by both thickening and doubling the walls I might make them more resistant to the ebb and flow of the waves. And I begin tinkering with the possibility of using flying buttresses instead.

Precision involves not only specifying what a fact is and isn't but also, as Descartes's third step instructs us, specifying its relationship with other facts. Typically, the best way to depict relationships among facts is by organizing them into a coherent and consistent hierarchy. Magnesium and calcium, for instance, are both alkaline earth metals, comprising along with beryllium, strontium, barium, and radium the elements in group 2 of the periodic table. They are all similar in color, hardness, and density, and they all react readily with halogens to form ionic salts and with water to form strongly alkaline bases.

The Purple Finch is one of the twenty-one species of finch comprising the *Carpodacus* genus, which is one of the twenty-two genera that make up the *Fringillidae* family of true finches (some birds are called finches, like the Darwin's Finches of the Galapagos, but are not *Fringillids*). The finch family are passerines, members of the Order *Passeriformes*—perching birds, songbirds—which is the largest order of the class *Aves*, those bipedal, warmblooded, egglaying vertebrate animals that evolved from theropod dinosaurs during the Jurassic period and have flourished from the subsequent Cretaceous period to the present. So *Tyrannosaurus rex* and the *Carpodacus purpureus* are cousins, although *T. rex* and all its other dinosaur relations, excepting the birds, perished in the mass extinction that ended the Cretaceous period sixty-five and a half million years ago.

In my King Arthur explorations, having shifted my focus from the historical facts on which the legends rest to an account of the development of the legends, I might next return to matters of historical fact and trace the influence of the Arthur myth on British politics and cultural self-understanding. Henry VII, for instance, was trying to solidify the legitimacy of the Tudor dynasty by naming his first son Arthur. I could also move in a quite different direction, however, by exploring how the Arthur legend is a species of a genus of story, that of the culture hero.

Joseph Campbell in *The Hero with a Thousand Faces* argues that Arthur is one of those faces, his story unfolding in accord with the generic account of the culture hero. This story has three main phases: (1) *departure*, in which the hero is called from his everyday life into a perilous adventure, accompanied by a wise helper and possessing a protective talisman—young Arthur called by Merlin from his idyllic life on Hector's farm, drawing Excalibur from the stone as the emblem and instrument of his kingship; (2) *initiation*, in which the hero is faced with many trials, through which he matures and reaches an apotheosis of power or influence—Arthur's foolish affair with Morgause, his battles against pretenders to the throne, his victories over the Saxons, the building of Camelot, and the formation of the Round Table; and (3) *return*, in which the hero's successes lead to a final battle where the hero bestows a special gift on his people—Arthur's battle against Mordred at Camlann, his grievous wound, and his removal by the Lady of the Lake to Avalon with the promise that he will return at some future time should his people need him.

Insofar as the Arthur's story can be interpreted as an instance of the hero myth, Arthur can be compared to other mythic heroes, from Achilles to Luke Skywalker. My understanding of the meaning of the Arthurian legend is thereby deepened, as reciprocally is my understanding of those other legends. Soon I begin asking questions about such legends. They seem so very definitely a product of particular cultures and times, and yet their similarities are so striking and so widespread that it seems unlikely they would have been passed from one culture to another by itinerant bards carried along in the wake of trade or war. Perhaps the hero myth is an archetype, a structural feature of the human mind or, as Jung argues, of the unconscious, a necessary universal core of meaning clothed in the contingent particularities of various cultural tellings of it.

Precision thus provides "both a disclosure and an analysis of the general subject-matter of romance" ("Rhythm" 19). The vagueness is penetrated; boundaries and differences are specified; an ordered system of relationships is imposed, deploying a unitary coherent structure on a raucous multiplicity of particular experiences.

We tend to think of these impositions as cold and impersonal, the subordination of our vital feelings to the formalisms of linguistic grammars and mathematical functions. However, after claiming that a child's "first stage of precision" is "mastering spoken language as an instrument for classifying its contemplation of objects," Whitehead adds that precision is also an instrument "for strengthening its apprehension of emotional relations with other beings" (19). Our emotional as well as our cognitive worlds are strengthened because the generalized patterns of the relationships imposed by precision become tools for linking and then expanding the boundaries of both. As a result, new and sometimes startling connections are discovered and predicted. Who would have thought that *Star Wars* is a retelling of the Arthur myth or that birds evolved from dinosaurs. If birds have feathers, then its ancestral dinosaurs may have been feathered also and not lizard-skinned. If Arthur's story fits Luke Skywalker, maybe it fits us as well, living as we do in these times when our democracy seems especially vulnerable to being transformed into an empire.

New facts will be acquired and our horizons expanded through the analysis and systematizing of vague facts. These facts must be acquired, however, not in the meandering manner of romantic inquisitiveness but methodically: "in a systematic order" (19). Method for Whitehead is "a given way of analyzing the facts, bit by bit," and of accumulating new facts insofar as they "fit into the analysis" (18). Birding can be a serendipitous activity, as it was when our class visited a park and tried to identify whatever bird happened to catch our attention. Ornithologists take a more systematic approach, however, as when they make a survey of bird populations in a given geographic area by mapping the area onto a grid and locating a scientist at each node of the grid for a specified length of time, with instructions to record all the different kinds of birds and the numbers of each that can be seen or heard from that position. This sampling technique lacks the precision available to us in identifying the chemical composition of our rock, but the information is accurate enough to provide, when part of an extended longitudinal study, important facts about increases and declines in species populations.

Just as the stage of romance culminates in the development of habits of imaginative inquisitiveness, in similar fashion precision culminates in accepting the discipline of an established method. We have learned to think and act precisely when we have acquired "the habit of cheerfully undertaking imposed tasks" ("Rhythmic Claims" 35), and thereby have come to realize "the inescapable fact that there are right ways and wrong ways, and definite truths to be known" (34). Not only do we need to learn how to think systematically and rigorously with regard to any specific area of knowledge, but we also need to learn what constitutes "the best practice" already accepted by experts in that area. "Knowing the subject exactly" means "retaining in the memory its salient features," becoming familiar with "the fundamental details and the main exact generalisations" of that subject area, and "acquiring an easy mastery of [its] technique" (34).

The Art of Life

Whitehead was dissatisfied with the traditional two-tiered approach to education—romance followed by precision, general education courses followed by work in a disciplinary major, breath followed by depth, first the trivium second the quadrivium. He added a third stage to the process of becoming educated, which he calls the stage of generalization.

This third stage is the "fruition" of the other two, "a return to romanticism with added advantage of classified ideas and relevant technique" ("Rhythm" 19). We are back in the world of romance, a world redolent with important matters for our consideration, significant problems requiring our attention. But now we come furnished with the tools needed to address these issues effectively. Our mind is now "a disciplined regiment instead of a rabble" ("Rhythmic Claims" 37); our forces are ready to be sent into combat. The abstractions of precision, the well-established theories and methods of systematic inquiry, need to be cashed out. "The pupil now wants to use his new weapons. He is an effective individual, and it is effects that he wants to produce" (36–37). The freedom generalization offers a person is "the active freedom of application" (37).

By this recurrent emphasis on activity, Whitehead takes us beyond the academy into the world of practical affairs. The focus is now on using the methods of precision to address the important concerns uncovered in our romantic explorations. My curiosity about limestone led me to analyze its chemical makeup, which I discovered was primarily calcium carbonate. Well, then, to what uses might I put limestone other than for constructing stone fences and the walls of my home or castle? I learn—in an engineering class, perhaps, or as part of on-the-job training, or even, as must have originally been the case, by trial and error—that heating limestone in a kiln to a very high temperature produces a clinker that when ground up yields cement. Cement is the key ingredient in concrete, which is used in creating barrier fences on highways and constructing the foundations and walls of buildings. These structures are less expensive, more enduring, and more easily formed than if made with slabs of limestone rock.

I can't fulfill my dream of taking part in a field research project in the Montana high prairie digging for dinosaur remains until I have become familiar with the characteristics of the Jurassic and Cretaceous periods with respect to Montana's geology and with the emergence and dispersal of *Theropoda*. This paleogeology and paleobiology also will be helpfully supplemented by what I know about calcium carbonate, because the fossils I seek are calcified organic matter. In the fossilization of an organism's skeletal remains, hard water—water with a high calcium content—typically seeps into the bone structure, slowly replacing the bony material with a precipitate of calcium carbonate. Eventually, the bone is fully replaced by a calcified replica. In extracting a fossil from the ground and in cleaning away the material surrounding it, I would be helped by knowing that I am working with something no longer organic, with rock rather than bone.

My enchantment with Arthurian legends led me to the library where I sought verified knowledge about both the history of Britain during the time when Arthur supposedly flourished and the history of the Arthurian myths themselves. Now the time has come for me to use that research as a tool in my own enterprise. I might write a scholarly essay about one of the Arthurian stories, or a monograph attempting a new assessment of Malory's literary importance, or a book on the quest for the historical Arthur. Alternatively, I might write a novel that re-presents Malory's original story in a contemporary idiom, with or without the magic, or one that transforms it imaginatively by telling it from Merlin's standpoint—or Mordred's. Or I could climb up further on the generalization ladder and become a political theorist, exploring the importance to a people's self-understanding of its myths of national origin. Climbing even higher, I might philosophize about the nature of mythic symbols and their foundational role in the development of other forms of symbolization.

As we move beyond romance and precision into generalization, we find our earlier naive enthusiasms chastened by a recognition that things are more subtle, complicated, and conflicted than we once had thought. In addressing those old romantic concerns, we are more effective because we are clearer about the facts, and because this clarity has uncovered far more facts than we had previously appreciated. But the important contribution of precision to the effectiveness of generalization is not the facts as such but the systemic structures—the general ideas—by which they are organized.

There is an important difference between accumulating information about a subject and understanding it. The one can be accomplished by rote memorization; the other involves recognizing the principles by which the subject is organized, its cognitive framework. To understand a subject is to see its forest and not just the trees. William Perry tells about a student who wandered into an anthropology class when a test was about to be given, and decided in a fit of whimsy to take it ("Examsmanship"). Asked to discuss two contrasting assessments of a book he knew nothing about, he did so with aplomb and received an A– for his effort. He lacked what Perry calls "cow"—a command of the relevant details—but he was very good at "bull"—seeing or inventing structural relationships that are able to organize the details usefully. Seeing the facts—the trees, the cows—as features of a system that explains them—the forest, the bull—is what makes the difference between a data collector and a scientist, a chronicler and an historian, a diarist and a lyric poet.

In the stage of generalization, "concrete fact" ceases to be in the foreground of our interest, serving primarily "as illustrating the scope of general ideas" ("Rhythm" 26). Likewise, theories cease to be uninterpreted abstractions, serving instead as instruments for guiding our understanding and hence our action, making it possible for us to identify ends worth pursuing and then effectively to achieve those ends. Putting general ideas into practice takes practice, however. Generalization involves "comprehension of a few general principles with a thorough grounding in the way they apply to a variety of concrete details" (26).

Whitehead wants us to be so thoroughly at home among both particular facts and general ideas that seeing their interdependence has become a habit. He defines a general principle as "rather a mental habit than a formal statement." It is "the way the mind reacts to the appropriate stimulus in the form of illustrative circumstances" (26). This active application of principles involves "shedding details" in the sense that we cease to focus on the specific technical terms, the individual steps in a procedure, the mathematical formulae by means of which the principle is formally expressed. Instead, we adapt its essentials in fashioning directly relevant contextualized interpretations with "the details retreating into subconscious habits" ("Rhythmic Claims" 37). Learning should culminate in the achievement of "active wisdom," which is "a preparation for battling with the immediate experiences of life, a preparation by which to qualify each immediate moment with relevant ideas and appropriate actions" (37).

On our stroll toward the park, none of us is able to identify a bird high in the sky over a nearby open field because it is too far away, appearing as little more than a black dot. Our teacher, more skilled than us in identifying birds, calls it a Red-tailed Hawk. Not because she can see the dot any more clearly than we can, but because she can read very subtle clues provided by its shape and flight style, and because she knows that Red-tails are the predominant raptors in our area this time of year. She brings to the identification an orienting sense of location probabilities and behavior patterns that is lacking in us novices whose birding skills are limited to a handful of good looks at a few birds and a mental list of a dozen or so bird species with the four or five distinguishing color and shape features of each.

This generalization skill is also illustrated in an athlete's awareness of the whole field of play. The ability of a center midfielder in soccer to see opportunities developing as teammates and opponents quickly alter their relative positions and likely trajectories involves having what seems often to be a fish-eye view of the total dynamic field of interactions. It's one thing to know how to execute effectively a tricky heel kick or to bend a shot accurately into the far upper corner of the net; it's another thing to see the split-second opening that calls for just such actions. This constant alertness to contextual relevance is what the stage of generalization means: an integration of information and interpretation, of technique and timing, into an effective game-tested style of problem solving.

So once again, the development of a habit is key to the stage of learning. In this case, however, the habit is explicitly dynamic, and necessarily so. Generalization is "the habit of the active utilisation of well-established principles" (37), "the habit of active thought, with freshness" (32). The practical world of our daily lives is dynamic, constantly rendering old truths uncouth, constantly requiring the deployment of new methods, better theories, and more relevant facts. So the habits of romance and precision, when yoked in the service of the habit of generalization, effectively putting our knowledge to work to solve important problems, must be a habit of transcending old habits toward more adequate ones. Generalization involves the habitual reformative critique of established habits.

Thus, for Whitehead, general principles are not mental habits in a sense that would suggest they are unthinkingly utilized. The habit crucial to generalization is the habit of using principles that are themselves altered as they are used to alter things. Confronted with a task, whether a problem or an opportunity, our more particular principles will be brought into play as part of our habitual use of a repertoire of workable ideas; but this application will be done critically, the particular relevance of the principles routinely under scrutiny, their coherence and consistency always open to revision. Similarly, the retreat of details into subconscious habits is not a process by which the details become unimportant but one in which their importance lies not in their isolated features but in their relevance to the applicability and adequacy of the principles they putatively illustrate and so constantly test.

Generalization is "active mastery" of knowledge, "knowledge so handled as to transform every phase of immediate experience" ("Rhythmic Claims" 32). To be attempting always to frame afresh some suitable interpretation of facts, which facts are always then being brought forward to be tested afresh against that interpretation, is to attain the apotheosis of "mental cultivation." It is "the satisfactory way in which the mind will function when it is poked up into activity" ("Rhythm" 27). The habit of generalization is a way of life, a style of engagement. It has to do not with what we know but with how we put our knowledge to use, so that it both achieves our immediate ends and, by criticizing our way of doing so, improves the chance for achieving our subsequent ends.

Generalization's practical orientation does not mean it has no place in formal education, that it belongs solely to the world beyond the walls of academe. Rather, Whitehead identifies university education as "the great period of generalisation" ("Rhythm" 25), chastising professors for constantly succumbing to the temptation to turn it into an extension of secondary school where romance and precision predominate. For the task of a university is to give students the opportunity to practice generalization until it becomes their second nature. "The ideal of a University," Whitehead argues, "is not so much knowledge, as power. Its business is to convert the knowledge of a boy [or girl] into the power of a man [or woman]" (27).

In the practical contexts of classroom instruction and curriculum design, helping students learn how to become effective generalizers can most readily be implemented through some form of interdisciplinary effort. Take, for instance, a university course in which our professor has me and my classmates investigate an issue that has not been predefined by a traditional expertise—a so-called real world problem, a public issue of local or national or international importance, a perplexing task commonly agreed to be worthwhile but for which there is no agreed-on method for approaching it. Addressing such a topic requires the collaboration of various disciplinary perspectives, making use of the richly varied repertoire of concepts, information, and skills they collectively possess. No single mode of precision is sufficient, but many are necessary. The academic discipline I have majored in, and think that I am well on the way to mastering, is brought into a context wider than the one within which its narrowed focus is competent. I quickly become aware of my discipline's limits, its need for the complementing disciplines in which the others in the class have majored, for its use to be collaborative rather than definitive.

Environmental issues provide obvious examples of what such a problem-oriented interdisciplinary course might tackle. I join a group of faculty and students in conducting a longitudinal study of bird populations in our area, and in doing so we discover that there has been a decline in waterbird populations due to the draining of wetlands for agricultural purposes or suburban expansion. A problem immediately presents itself: What is the situation with wetlands habitat in this area, and if it is in decline what can be done to prevent irreversible damage, in particular, to the waterbirds who use it and, more generally, to our regional environment?

We ornithologists need community ecologists to help us identify which organisms other than birds have been put at risk by draining the wetlands and which have benefited. We need wetland ecologists to help us understand why a wetlands environment is the natural condition and why draining some of the wetlands has changed the rest of it as well. Chemists are needed to identify the character and dispersion of the agricultural runoff, and economists to explain the financial advantages of suburban expansion.

Sociologists might help us appreciate the reasons people have been moving away from the cities, preferring to live in areas so far removed from where they work. The reasons for those preferences can usefully be deepened by seeking the help of a surprisingly wide range of further kinds of expertise, including insights from anthropology, evolutionary psychology, history, literature, religious studies, and philosophy. My recommendation to the group is that we read William Pogue Harrison's book *Forests: The Shadow of Civilization*, where he tells us that

> [t]he global problem of deforestation provokes unlikely reactions of concern these days among city dwellers, not only because of the enormity of the scale but also because in the depths of cultural memory forests remain the correlate of

> human transcendence. We call it the loss of nature, or the loss of wildlife habitat, or the loss of biodiversity, but underlying the ecological concern is perhaps a much deeper apprehension about the disappearance of boundaries, without which the human abode loses its grounding. (247)

When precision hits an impasse, we can press on dogmatically but ineffectually, continuing to combat a problem with practices that have become ineffective, until the problem becomes virulent and we find ourselves overwhelmed. Or precision can return us to the wider buzzing blooming world of romance out of which it was honed, and we begin to pay attention to some of those things we had previously neglected. In the stage of generalization, the limits of accepted forms of precision are recognized and alternatives are suggested by thinking outside the boxes of tried but no longer true methods.

One of the important consequences of being able to function at the level of generalization is that we come to realize that the technical and scholarly disciplines we use have limits. In order to systemize our knowledge, we must exclude certain aspects of experience from consideration. This price for attaining precision is worth paying, given the trustworthy results a systematic approach achieves—but nonetheless, in pushing romance aside a price has indeed been paid, and it is crucial that we realize this is so. In the stage of generalization, I can recover my appreciation for the importance of what my disciplinary training ignores.

The novelties created are necessarily limited because while generalization enlarges our vision to include the wider regions of the experience that romance embraces, it also remains respectful toward the now faltering precision to which we have long entrusted ourselves. The novel solution, the fresh new precision we devise, is not so much something new as something renovated, the old methods refashioned in the light of marginalized or overlooked possibilities. The new ways to which generalization leads us are versions of the old ways—adaptations, modulations, extensions. If all goes well, the result is the creation of new sorts of precision and new applications of old ones, methods creative and adaptive with which to tackle afresh the problems our old ways were failing to address.

Whitehead's emphasis, however, is not on how generalization functions in the university curriculum, nor on its relevance to job preparation, but rather on its role in the furthering of the general good. The business of the university is to prepare men and women to become active, contributing citizens. Its task is to empower us not merely by broadening our interests in the natural and cultural world we inhabit, or merely by training us in the socially useful technical skills needed to succeed in that world, or merely by doing both. The work of the university, already presuming the educational stages of romance and precision, is "the guidance of the individual towards a comprehension of the art of life. And by the art of life," says Whitehead, "I mean the most complete achievement of varied activity expressing the potentialities of that living creature in the face of its actual environment" ("Rhythmic Claims" 39).

The full expression of a person's potentialities calls for "subordinating the lower to the higher possibilities of the indivisible personality" (39). It involves more than simply developing one's capacities. We engage in the art of life when we try to fashion from the varied activities in which we engage some unified whole—an indivisible personality, a moral character. The art of life is to make of our life a work of art, to craft for ourselves a whole self, a self with integrity. In discussing the art of life, Whitehead turns to science, religion, morality, and the fine and practical arts. For they all "take their rise from this sense of values within the structure of being." Whatever the resources and techniques used in crafting an identity, "each individual embodies an adventure of existence. The art of life is the guidance of this adventure" (39).

Generalization so understood has a moral dimension, for it holds us responsible for what we make. We are moral agents in the sense that we give things value, or detract from their value, by what we understand them to be and by how we engage them. Their worth is in part what we make of them, and we are answerable to ourselves and others for those valuations. Disdaining a friendly gesture as insincere rather than genuine, preferring one possibility over another, encouraging a course of action while railing against its competitor, joining forces with one group of people but not with others—in such ways we create or destroy values, and validate or invalidate others' values. These are all moral actions, constructing or deconstructing things worth our while, realizing utility or violating right.

Because our character is composed of the pattern of these choices and of how we go about making them, because our character is a matter of our preferential habits, we thereby create ourselves and our worth as selves. As moral agents, we fashion the private world of our immediate experience, externalize that world through our engagement with the material environment, and interlace our world with others' worlds through our interactions with them, transforming personal goods into a common good, private utility into altruism, immediate satisfaction into a sense of duty toward ancestral practices and toward future generations.

Games are an excellent pedagogical strategy for introducing us to these moral dimensions of how we think and act as generalizers. Most obviously, competitive team games thrust us into a world where the team's success depends on teamwork, but we need also to learn about a less obvious yet more important moral dimension to our game playing, for the competing teams compete because they both subscribe to the rules of their game, rules both sides must embrace as constraining them in their pursuit of sharply divergent goals. We have to fashion a wider common good concerning the rules of engagement as the context for the narrower common good of our team's victory, just as our own personal success as a hero for the winning side or a valiant defender for what proved to be the losing side depends on our prior acceptance of the team's importance. Altruism and self-interest are interdependent goods. Generalization needs always to draw us from the narrower to the broader dimensions of our responsibilities, helping us glimpse the gyre of nested goods that comprise the moral import of any world we might enter.

The trivium, as I noted in the "Introduction," was taught in the medieval university as the necessary foundation for attaining knowledge and securing well-being. The Latin word, *trivium*, means literally a place where three roads meet, a "tri-via." It is the same root from which the English word *trivial* comes, which means something common. The trivium is the place we have in common—the crossroads where we meet, despite the different roads we are taking, despite the different metaphysical traditions and commitments from which we have set out and the different metaphysical visions toward which we are headed.

The foundation of a good education should include romance, teaching us to appreciate all the myriad travelers who were once and are even now passing through the world. A good education can then build a school of precision on this foundation, teaching us to appreciate with particular intensity and subtlety our own cultural pathways, the alphas and omegas of our religions, governments, scientific enterprises, artistic creations, and philosophies—of our familiar memories of where we have come from and our expectations of where we should be heading. But this love for a particular pathway should be constantly brought back to the crossroads, to be chastened and enlivened by the work of generalization, teaching us to share what we have learned with those who are traveling different routes, who have learned different truths and are oriented by different values. If we can learn to appreciate the babble of our disparities, perhaps we can fashion as a result of these exchanges the trailheads for new practical pathways, including novel kinds of pathways—ones that will be needed in the future if we are someday to live together peacefully on this planet.

CHAPTER TWO

Learning Helically

In the previous chapter, I have presented Whitehead's ideas about the rhythm of learning as they are found in *The Aims of Education.* I have ranged far beyond his few examples in attempting to illustrate what his ideas mean, and my arguments on behalf of those ideas are obviously of my own invention, or where they are others' arguments their relevance is of my own fashioning. All of what I've done is nonetheless carefully grounded in Whitehead's two brief texts and offers, I think, an accurate re-presentation of his views for readers whose great grandparents might have heard or read their original presentation.

With this new chapter, I now begin an exploration of some striking similarities between these ideas of Whitehead's about education and his metaphysical ideas, his speculative theories about the general nature of things. Readers will discover, I hope, that these comparisons will for the most part confirm what has been learned from chapter 1. But I venture the further expectation that they will also widen and deepen that learning, and on occasion transform it.

In discussing Whitehead's three stages of education, our tendency is to focus on the inadequacy of pedagogies that emphasize precision at the expense of romance. We are rightly angered by those whose teaching is exclusively about facts and systems of facts, about things we can observe with a bare or instrument-assisted eye and theories that organize those experienced particulars into intelligible wholes.

We attempt to correct this bias by extolling the importance of romance, encouraging students to explore aspects of their world that are not certified facts and that escape the confines of any particular system. We want students to immerse themselves in the unsystematized wonders of the concrete and to let their imaginations wander adventurously. Our argument is that students will gain from those romantic experiences the healthy motivation they need in order to undertake the rigors of precise analysis and systemic interpretation. Generalization, Whitehead's third stage, is then taken to involve a return to the world initially explored in romance, but now coming to it equipped with the tools of precision. We claim that our students so prepared will be able to penetrate the worldly mysteries that had originally stimulated their curiosity, to solve the problems they had posed.

Notice how this standard scenario, explicated in the previous chapter, is a linear progression. Romance is about our naive responses to a confusing cacophony of sights and sounds; it is a time of surprise and bewilderment. The point of precision is to carry us beyond such things, to set aside our childish ways for the sophistication provided by systemic understanding and control. Generalization is the capstone, the theorizing put to work in solving real-life problems. Our educational trajectory is upward and onward. From romance through precision to generalization; from primary education through secondary education to higher education; from the general basics to a disciplinary specialization to the mastery of a career vocation.

Whitehead is partly to blame for this linear view. He refers to the stages of education as "first apprehension," "precise progress," and "final success" ("Rhythm" 17–19), and associates them with, respectively, early education, middle schooling, and the university. However, he explicitly rejects interpreting the stages as a simple linear progression, arguing as I made clear in the "Introduction" that they have a cyclical rhythm, and that "education should consist in a continual repetition of such cycles" (19). Each cycle is composed of a linear triplet: romance, followed by precision, followed by generalization. But the cycle is then repeated, and therefore the new romance will not be a repetition of its predecessor but will be a different kind of romance, one rooted in the generalization that concluded the prior cycle, and the new precision and new generalization will similarly be different from the earlier precision and generalization.

Romance is a stage of elementary school learning, but it is also a stage of secondary school and university learning. It is a important stage in mastering an academic discipline but also an important stage in the first course taken in that discipline and in the last course taken. The three stages apply to each individual classroom session, to how the teacher fashions his kindergarten lesson plan for Thursday or the university professor designs her weekly graduate seminar. The cycles are what are repeated, not their content. The stages of education are helical in the sense that they transform as they return, spiraling into learning contexts that are always different and, when effective, more adequate. Learning is an adventure spiraling down into and therefore out beyond the known.

I think we can best appreciate why the stages of education should be understood in a helical rather than linear manner by associating them with what Whitehead in the closing chapters of *Adventures of Ideas* identifies as the five conditions of civilized life: Truth, Beauty, Adventure, Art, and Peace. Aristotle says there are four factors relevant to a thing that we must know in order to understand what it is—its material, formal, efficient, and final conditions. To know what the rock is that we are holding, we need to know its tangible qualities, its molecular structure, the geologic history of its formation, and the uses to which it can be put. To realize who this Arthur is that has pulled the sword from the stone, we need to know that, although his physical strength is not unusual for a strapping young man, his character is surpassingly strong, that he is in fact Uther's rightful son, and that his destiny, as what he has just done shows so decisively, is as the Britons' next High King.

These four conditions of understanding can be identified, respectively, with Whitehead's notions of Truth, Beauty, Adventure, and Peace—the brute fact that something actually exists, the structure that defines what it is, the process that gave rise to it, and the end that justifies its emergence. But Whitehead adds a fifth condition: Art. He does so because for him, in contrast to Aristotle, the conditions of a thing are not ontological givens but temporal constructions. There are no necessary realities, no natural kinds, no fixed conditions, no predetermined outcome to things. Adventure needs Art to formulate the Peace at which it ought to aim and the Beauty by which to pursue it in fashioning each moment's Truth, in determining ever and anew what can and should and eventually must be made.

Closed Systems

Let us begin with precision, Whitehead's second stage of education, which I propose we associate with the notion of Truth, since precision and truth are both about the careful correlation of symbols with what they symbolize. A theory, in Whitehead's somewhat idiosyncratic terminology, is an Appearance, an image that purports to be a photocopy of Reality. An Appearance is True if it actually mirrors Reality, as it claims to do.

My perception of an attractive pebble noticed just in front of me as I walk along the beach is a true perception if it really is the case that a distinctive bit of ocean-rounded rock is located where I think it is, that my mental image correlates with a physical object. "Truth is the conformation of Appearance to Reality" (*Adventures* 241). This image I have of the pebble is a very simple theory about the way the world is configured. It's a claim that I'm looking at an actual feature of my surroundings, one that justifies my interest in it and thereby influences what I am likely to do. Theories of any sort, no matter how complex, are images: an idea about how things are, a perspective on them, a point of view, a description of some portion of the world. So for an Appearance to conform to Reality, for an image to be True, means that it provides us with a coherent and consistent portrait applicable to some identifiable region of the world and provides an adequate depiction of its features.

Notice the adjectives in my previous sentence: coherent, consistent, applicable, and adequate. These are the four standards for judging a metaphysical theory famously identified by Whitehead at the beginning of *Process and Reality* (3). My theory is consistent when if something is true its denial cannot also be true; that pebble cannot at the same time be both on the beach and in my hand. My theory is coherent when all the truths I assert fit together so that they are in some manner interdependent; my little piece of rock and the much larger one from which Excalibur protrudes are constrained by the same laws of physics. These two "logical" criteria are complemented by two "empirical" criteria. My theory is applicable when there are aspects or regions of human experience that it interprets; I see the pebble at a place on a beach where I often walk, and consider using it as an ornament for the ramparts of the sand castle I'm building. My theory is adequate to experience when there are no regions or aspects to which it is not applicable; there are no places where that pebble is located other than right here, no other pebble that is like it in all respects.

Consistency and applicability are the weaker of the four criteria for truth, the ones with which we begin in constructing a theory. At minimum, we want to make sense of some specific set of circumstances, to say something directly applicable to the world as we are experiencing it, and as we develop what we have to say about those circumstances we try to avoid contradicting ourselves. That's a pebble I've come across, and not a piece of wood; it would be interesting, however, were it fossilized wood or even better a fragment of a dinosaur bone; no other sand castles I've ever seen had a dinosaur on their ramparts.

Our ultimate aim, however, the ideal toward which we strive, is to devise a theory that brings all known and conceivable circumstances together within a single systematic framework of understanding. I begin by noting the pattern of high and low tides along the seashore because of its relevance to the security of my castle in the sand, and I end with Newton's laws of motion and the patterns of galactic ebb and flow that they disclose. I begin with a pebble and end with Darwin's laws of evolution and the possibility that the seashore might contain remnants of forms of life extinct for millions of years.

So a true theory is a well-ordered concept, an image—an Appearance—that meets all four of Whitehead's criteria. Theories of every sort, including but not limited to metaphysical ones, are rational systems that claim to clarify by their unambiguous precision the vaguely felt world around us, to represent it as it truly is. In learning how to think systematically, we become skilled at distinguishing theories that are apparently true from those that are actually true, distinguishing mere Appearances from True Appearances. The stage of precision is where we acquire the tools for making accurate maps of the world, intellectual road atlases that we trust will guide us truly toward what is truly important and will thereby give meaning to our thoughts and purpose to our actions.

Languages are powerful tools of precision, far better than iconic images or bodily gestures or other sorts of nonlinguistic symbols in creating an Appearance that refers without distortion or confusion to its correlative Reality. Scientific language is the apotheosis of this truthful correlating. Consistency and coherence are typically achieved by attending solely to the quantifiable features of the world, features that can be measured unambiguously and therefore can be precisely described. Quantitative expressions can then be substituted for qualitative ones, and these quantities then re-expressed in terms of mathematical symbols or in terms of a strictly denotative technical vocabulary.

For example, upset and crying at the news of my father's death, I take a walk by myself that leads to a lilac bush that engulfs me unexpectedly in its shout of purple colors and sweet fragrances. In a scientific description, this moment becomes an organism of the species *Homo sapiens* showing certain characteristic fluctuations in its brain wave patterns, which are caused by sensory stimuli that are governed by laws concerning the propagation of refracted light and scent molecules from a plant of the species *Syringa vulgaris*, occurring at latitude 40°15'49" N, longitude 77°02'03"W, and 16:37.20 hours GMT, on 09 April 2011 CE.

The value of the truth science achieves, so powerfully subtle, accurate, and usable, is obvious. It provides the control over nature that makes possible production of the abundant resources that have transformed the quality of human life in its shift from hunter-gatherer tribalism to urban-centered industrialized society. Any such rational scientific system is necessarily inadequate, however. No matter how well organized and useful it may be, it leaves things out. It involves a double constriction of experience. A system of scientific truths creates a vertical constriction, because its truths are abstractions from the unsystematized and often unquantifiable complexity of the concrete. It also creates a horizontal constriction, because those abstracted truths are derived from a narrow slice of the whole of that concreteness.

A scientific theory, like any abstraction, is adequate only with respect to some purpose. In describing my moment among the lilacs in terms of neural impulses and fractions of a Greenwich Mean Time hour, a scientist's interest is in general considerations that my experience illustrates. The scientist can legitimately ignore what for me is most important, my feelings: my melancholic mood that fateful morning, my sense of personal loss and how I had associated it because of the lilacs with Walt Whitman's sense of America's loss at Lincoln's death that fateful day of mourning "When Lilacs Last in the Dooryard Bloom'd." Such meaning is simply outside the physicist's purview.

A roadmap leaves out vast riches of fascinating information about an area, limiting itself to just the minimum things we need to know in order to drive through it without confusion. If everything were somehow included on the map—the color and height of the road signs, whether the highway was asphalt or concrete, the square footage of the buildings, the species of the trees in the forests—the result would be an unintelligible and therefore useless mess. The coherence essential to any well-ordered system requires the elimination of factors incommensurate with its objective. Absolute Truth is an oxymoron. The squiggles on paper that form a scientific description of events achieve what Whitehead calls "anaesthesia": a confined perfection, perfect "in its type of finiteness with such-and-such exclusions" (256). Its propositions are part of a system of symbols that because of its clarity and coherence achieves immense effectiveness. A theory can be coherent and adequate only in the limited sense achieved by deliberate anesthesia, by including some things while excluding the rest.

Scientific truths are closed systems. Their Appearances are True only of what has been herded into their vertical and horizontal confines. The perfection of such truths is constrained within boundaries based on a decision to exclude certain kinds of things in order to achieve a systematic understanding of what remains. In doing so, however, a system sows the dragons' teeth of its undoing. What it excludes does not go away; it is merely ignored. As novel conditions emerge, drawing their power in part from what has been ignored, the closed system cannot cope with them adequately. If it continues to ignore what it can no longer afford to ignore, retreating behind the walls within which its methods work, it may still function usefully, but less effectively than an alternative more adequate system. The old system, increasingly stubborn and inflexible, will under the pressure of the cultural equivalent to natural selection eventually collapse. Acquiring the skills of precision is a wondrous accomplishment but also a dangerous one, because those skills embraced uncritically are instruments that can destroy their users.

The precursor to Truth is Beauty. It is akin to romance because it has to do with imagination, with exploring untried possibilities, unearthing unnoticed or previously uninteresting facts and novel patterns of relatedness. "Beauty, so far as concerns its exemplification in Appearance alone, does not necessarily involve the attainment of truth" (267). It is an Appearance appreciated just for what it is, without any regard for whether or not it is true. The romantic stage of learning has this character of direct appreciation—reading an Arthurian novel without filtering it through the lens of some literary theory, delighting in the twinkling little stars without asking for a scientific explanation of why they twinkle, taking part in a march to protest the war or one to support our troops without having weighed the moral and prudential reasons for doing so. We respond spontaneously to the Beauty of the occasion, to its vivid and vital immediacy. Our imaginative engagement with the bounty of the world in which we are immersed comes first. The analysis, the theorizing, the rational account come later.

Generalization, understood in the standard way in which I presented it in the prior chapter, understood, that is, as part of a linear sequence, is a return to romance armed with the tools of precision. In turning our attention back to the concrete world and its delightful experiences, we put to work the methodological techniques learned from our disciplined training in a specific science. We come ready to explore the uttermost limits of the world as our science defines it, to uncover new facts and fashion new theories—but only those that presume the boundary conditions scientific inquiry requires. Our task is to test these theories under practical conditions, and to undertake the reforms and improvements suggested by these applications. We engage in what Thomas Kuhn in *The Structure of Scientific Revolutions* calls "normal science."

Having been taught the familiar theories of literary interpretation, we are invited by our teachers to apply one of those theories to the Arthurian legend. Our resulting term papers will be judged by how well we demonstrate our knowledge of the theory and how insightfully we apply it to the legend. The importance of the theories is presumed, however, denying us the possibility of writing a paper that spoofs any of the literary interpretations, as Frederick Crews does in *The Pooh Perplex*. In having us observe the four main moons of Jupiter through a small telescope, our teachers will likely save us from a too great reliance on book learning, returning us to firsthand observation. We will walk in Galileo's footsteps, seeing the moons as he saw them, and thereby will avoid substituting an unquestioned acceptance of the teachings of Galilean science for the unquestioned authority Galileo's prosecutors found in the teachings of the Church. Our interpretation of what we see, however, our account of how the moons move around Jupiter, will remain decidedly Galilean. Our teachers will ask us to reflect on the divergent marches in which we participated, some of us opposed to the war and some of us supporting it, and they will be content if we account for these differences among us as the result of partisan convictions, as expressions of incompatible moral and political ideals that even when opposed should be respected.

Generalization in this sense is the way by which we are able to perfect a limited perfection, even to expand the umbrella of its theory, the extent of its application, to new subject matters and concerns. It carries us to the apex of adequacy, providing us with a complete and fully sophisticated understanding of the world. But this understanding is of the world as our closed system discloses it. We remain bound by its boundary conditions. Generalization taken as the final stage of learning may perfect our accepted ways of thinking and acting, but it does not transform them. It is not able to guide us through a paradigm shift from one form of normal science to a successor form.

Returning to romance, guided by generalization of this linear sort, we might even be able to recover the affective aspects of experience from which the quantified precision of a scientific system abstracts. But these recovered emotions are then easily bound to that system, clothing its presupposed worldview in vivid but circumscribed intensities of belief and commitment. The clarity and convenience of a well-ordered system of ideas or a smooth-running social institution is invested in this way with an unjustifiable significance, an import and value it does not deserve and cannot control. Emotions bound to closed systems are blind. They are most familiar to us in the form of religious fanaticism and political jingoism, which are instances of the fallacy of misplaced concreteness at its most virulent. Whatever Whitehead may have meant by generalization, surely it was not this.

The Enchanter's Wand

We can escape this capstone view and its negative implications if we think of Art as crucial to the move from the stage of precision to that of generalization. Whitehead's discussion in *Adventures of Ideas* of the function of Art with respect to Truth and Beauty shows us a way to understand generalization as not merely a process by which we take the fruits of some precise system-building effort and put them to work in the wider concreteness from which they were initially derived. It reveals how generalization also discloses the limits of that precision and provides us with the resources and motivation for building a better system to replace it. It also tells us how generalization discloses the limits of our original romantic experience, critiquing the scope and depth of our imaginative powers as well as our rational skills, questioning the adequacy of our feelings as well as our concepts. By means of Art, generalization becomes a transformative stage of learning.

Artistic symbols are like scientific symbols—both of them abstract from concrete reality. However, Whitehead argues, an artistic symbol intensifies rather than eliminates our felt sense of that reality's significance. It captures a complex concatenation of emotionally overwhelming events in a single contour of color, distills years of struggle into a single phrase. It even abstracts completely from the representational function of its symbols in order to express meanings too subtle or too inchoate to be represented. "It unlooses depths of feeling from behind the frontier where precision of consciousness fails" (*Adventures* 271).

Scientific symbol systems such as Newton's laws and philosophic symbol systems such as Whitehead's categoreal scheme pare away the details of what we experience in order to emphasize useful patterns of systemic relatedness. For instance, the rich diversity of physical objects populating the universe interact with one another in richly diverse ways. A billiard ball set in motion by the thrust of a cue stick strikes a stationary ball, setting it in motion and simultaneously altering its own direction. The moon is pock-marked with craters created by meteors burying themselves in its surface during the 5 billion years of its existence. The head-on convergence of the Indian and Eurasian tectonic plates about 10 million years ago pushed up the Himalayas to heights found nowhere else on Earth, although the gentle hills marking the boundary of Pennsylvania's Cumberland Valley are the stubby remains of mountains that once had been even higher than the Himalayas. In a galaxy far, far away, the interactions of a white dwarf sun with its red giant neighbor causes it to explode into a supernova, and centuries later our ancestors marvel at the sudden appearance of a bright star in the eastern sky. The sniper presses the hair trigger on his rifle and smiles with satisfaction at the revenge he has exacted from those who shot his father for having shot theirs.

When we study Newton in our physics class, we learn that all these interactions illustrate the simple general rule that for every action there is an equal and opposite reaction. Similarly, when we study Whitehead in a philosophy class we learn the importance of what he calls "the principle of relativity," which is "the one general metaphysical character attaching to all entities, actual or non-actual": that "it belongs to the nature of [any] 'being' that it is a potential for every 'becoming' " (*Process* 22). Whitehead thus offers a simple metaphysical hypothesis interpreting the complexly multifarious interactions among whatever is. The interactions between moons and meteors or tides and castles, like those between Hatfields and McCoys or Britons and Saxons, between utopian dreams and the collapse of civilizations, always and necessarily involves internal relations like those between Arthur and his son Mordred, *T-rex* and the Purple Finch, birth and death, even though they may appear to be related only externally. Thus for both science and philosophy, we learn that the Appearance—the theory expressed in unambiguous words or, wherever possible, expressed mathematically—is a sleekly simple symbol that elegantly tells the Truth about some aspect of Reality that is neither sleek nor simple.

In contrast, in an arts class we discover that when an artist formulates a specific symbol it is done in such a way that the symbol manages to coalesce various particulars into one concretely unique whole. The work of art integrates its components in a way that discloses within a specific integral quality the fuller reality it symbolizes, rather than separating that reality into essences and accidents, into first principles and their derivative instances.

We learn how Mahler organizes sounds into symphonies and that what is important about each of them is its unique particularity, not the form it shares with his other symphonies or symphonies more generally. His work is not illustrating a truthful theory but creating a truthful experience. It is not simply a particular experience, however, but one that in its particularity has as much universal meaning as a theory. The lines of paint dripped across a Pollock canvas, because they have been freed from their usual role of indicating the boundary of a concrete or abstract shape, invite us to appreciate them as the two-dimensional realities they are intrinsically. However, the chaotic character of Pollock's paintings also anticipate chaos theory, so that in viewing them in all the immediacy of their two dimensions an unnerving shiver of recognition runs up our spine, the realization that his creations are representational after all, images of nature as it really is. In reading Malory, we find toward the end of his book the statement that "many men say that there is written upon his [Arthur's] tomb this verse: Hic Jacet Arthurus, Rex Quondam Rexque Futurus" (2,519). We tremble at the thought. Could it be that he who was once our king might somehow yet be our king again? And in a twinkling, the sad ending of a story of a great king suddenly expresses hope beyond the death of hope, hints at meanings too breathtaking for us to dare comprehend.

The artistic Appearance, the Beauty that an aesthetic symbol not merely manifests but existentially is, evokes a fuller Reality than does the scientific Appearance because its symbols are the means not by which to order that reality but by which to experience it more completely. In hearing a story, viewing a painting, listening to an orchestral performance, we experience that wider reality more profoundly, appreciate better its subtleties and nuances, its hidden depths and complexities.

We need to learn in our art, music, and literature classes the disturbing truth that artists fashion open symbols rather than closed ones. They create symbols that call our attention to neglected features of what we experience, inviting us to embrace a world more complicated than any finite system could ever encompass. Art invites discord rather than excluding it. Not only are contrasting incommensurable elements retained in its unity, each with its own distinctive uniqueness, but the mode of their integration retains the emotional intensity accruing to them by virtue of that uniqueness. The created Appearance that is a work of art, says Whitehead, "summons up new resources of feeling" lying "below the stale presuppositions of verbal thought," lying "beyond the dictionary meaning of words" (*Adventures* 266–67). An artistic symbol is an individual thing, "detailed from the vague infinity of its background," that sends us a "message from the Unseen" (271). There is no way to design machine-graded test questions that indicate whether or not we have received such messages and have been shaken by their import.

To appreciate Whitehead's point, we need to understand why he says that an aesthetic symbol is a "bare *It*" (254; 262–64). Works of art achieve their intensely valuable harmonization of diverse elements by inventing a significant individual, an aesthetic symbol—a bare "*It*"—that stands for those elements but is not abstracted from them, and consequently to which a profound aura of importance comes to be attached. "The emotional significance of an object as '*It*,' divorced from its qualitative aspects at the moment presented, is one of the strongest forces in human nature" (262).

In creating such symbols, art imitates life, for our everyday experience is rife with these distillations. I have interacted with a favorite aunt thousands of times over the years of our acquaintance, from my earliest memories to the present day. I remember the tilt of her head when she smiles, the aroma from her kitchen as she bakes a batch of chocolate chip cookies, her loving embrace that afternoon she visited me in the hospital, my embarrassment at her chiding admonition after I did something stupid, my anticipation of her arrival for my twenty-first birthday party, the clever congratulatory present she sent on the birth of my first child. I remember her not as an indistinct amalgam of all those particular interactions, however, not as an instance, not even a paradigmatic one, of what a Platonist might call the Form of Aunthood. Instead, I imagine my aunt as a single enduring concrete reality, this particular "*It*," to whom I then attach the whole parcel of my memories about her, as well as my expectations about how she will behave the next time I see her, what she does in my absence, who she was before I knew her.

In this way, I have created a particular symbol, an enduring reality I call my aunt, and have invested it with a special significance, an importance that is composed of a lifetime of particular experiences, each with its own distinctive emotional flavor, distilled into one reality. Each time I see my aunt again, or think of her, I take these events as further thickenings of my beloved aunt's importance, as contributions to my sense of the intrinsic value of who she has been and is and will become.

Furthermore, I also associate other more general values with her. In thinking of my aunt, I think of my other aunts and uncles, of family gatherings fondly remembered and of my resolve to begin planning for our next gathering. I imagine what her parents, my grandparents, might have felt and thought about her and about their own aunts. I imagine what it was like to have lived a hundred or a thousand years ago and to be loved by the aunt of an ancestor of whom I have no knowledge, her origins lost in the mysterious past, yet without whom I and my aunt would not be who we are. My aunt bears these vaguely felt values as well as the vivid ones, her presence thus redolent with the importance of those communities that I intuitively know give my life meaning, that provide the continuities that are my salvation. I have fashioned an enduring "*It*" that I call my aunt and have filled it with a wealth of significance far greater than the mere sum of the values of our interactions.

Our national flag is another example of an aesthetic symbol, a bare "*It*" not only displaying a distinctive pattern of bright colors as it flutters in the wind but also displaying the story of our nation. Americans pledge allegiance "to the flag" and "to the nation for which it stands." The symbol, made of cloth rather than words, concentrates in its stars and stripes the full sweep of our country's history. It reminds us of colonial origins and rebellious defiance, of a founding constitution in Philadelphia and a refounding speech at a graveyard near Gettysburg, of immigrants fleeing religious persecution and immigrants seeking fame and fortune, of the denial of entangling foreign alliances and their celebration. Our flag is not a triumphalist symbol, however, for it reminds us also of our willingness to enslave Africans and exploit foreign workers for commercial advantage, of our turning members of the settled Indian nations into homeless refugees and reneging on our treaties with them when it suited us, of excluding Jews from our universities and women from the executive offices of our corporations. And so we salute our flag both proudly and humbly, because it reminds us of the nation for which it stands, our nation, its victories and defeats, its glorious ideals and its betrayal of those ideals, evoking emotions and beliefs far above the poor power of our words to add or detract.

One of Whitehead's examples of an enduring "*It*" is that of a cenotaph in a museum exhibit that intrigues us so much we want to touch it, a two-millennia-old "inscribed stone, executed at the command of and under the very eyes of Sennacherib" (262). We will learn many important things in history class without ever going on museum tours, but we will never have the transformative encounter with the past that Whitehead imagines us having in the presence of Sennacherib's cenotaph. We prize the stone because of its historical uniqueness, its having been fashioned at a very particular time and place. Seeing it, touching it, evokes our emotional engagement with this powerful monarch, and through him with an ancient empire that once flourished. We participate intimately in a sense of glorious achievements won and lost, and we are overwhelmed by an ontological sense of the hard truth that all things, even monarchs who have come to bestride the world like a colossus, soon perish.

Sennacherib's stone is precious to us not only because of the importance of the original reason for its having been inscribed and because of its direct influence on events at that time, but also because of the long centuries of human history that have elapsed since then, across which we reach when we stretch out our hand to touch it. By comparison, "a really admirable replica by a modern workman lacks interest" (262), for it does not exude the history with which the actual stone is imbued. The replica is just a piece of rock on which someone has carved things, whereas the cenotaph is an aesthetic symbol brimming over with historical significance. Sennacherib's stone is a priceless "*It*"; the replica of it has accreted nothing of significance and so is sold for a few euros in the museum gift shop.

We live amid such concrete particulars, ones fraught with transcending importance. Works of art are intentional efforts to create symbols designed to function in this significance-invoking manner. In the most archaic form of artistry, the created symbols were probably bodily movements. "The origin of art lies in the craving for re-enaction," argues Whitehead. "In some mode of repetition we need by our personal actions, or perceptions, to dramatize the past and the future, so as to re-live the emotional life of ourselves, and of our ancestors" (271; see also his *Religion in the Making* chap. 1, sec. 3). Early humans, for example, gathering to share among themselves the results of a successful hunting expedition, applaud one of their number as he mimics the hunt by stalking around in a crouched position, rearing back and pretending to throw a spear, making knife-cutting gestures, loading an imaginary carcass on his back and dumping it on the ground in front of his appreciative audience. The original actions are mimed, not mimicked. Irrelevant details are omitted and key moments exaggerated so that the contour of the sequence from departure to return might be evident. The day's effort by these particular hunters to find meat for themselves and their families becomes a graphically told hunting story.

The next hunting story told, although unique in so many salient ways, will share some features with the earlier story, and eventually the hunting story will become a generic account involving stylized steps and gestures standing for typical kinds of hunterly actions, exhibiting overall a characteristic quest-struggle-celebration pattern. Eventually, the dance performed in celebration of a successful hunt, although still a concrete particular dance, will no longer refer to a particular event. It will offer a form, a formulaic bare "*It*," designed to evoke memories of old hunts and prior dances, designed to convey a sense of their endless extent, of hunts more ancient than those remembered by even the eldest members of the tribe, hunting stories that have been told so many times they must first have been told by the gods to the tribe's progenitors, and of hunts and stories yet to come, ones that will occur and recur for as long as the tribe endures, and beyond that for as long as the immortal gods tell each other the story of the heroic exploits that were that peoples' glory.

The polyglot richness of the familiar world of our experience, including its remembered and anticipated aspects, and also its forgotten and neglected aspects, are unified and intensified by the artist's craft into a Beauty that in its uniqueness knows no bounds. The richness of our experience is melded spatially into the bare beautiful "*It*" of a painted canvas or a formed piece of baked clay, shaped temporally into the bare beautiful "*It*" of a musical trajectory or a pattern of ritual enactment. The closed frameworks created by our scientific and commonsensical symbols have not eliminated this richness. They have only hidden it, pushed it into the background. They have constructed boundary walls over which we cannot see in order to see more clearly what lies within those walls. But what lies beyond them is not thereby nothing.

These familiar aesthetic symbols that dominate the foreground of our everyday experience, although creatures of our established ways of thinking and feeling, often exude a whiff of something more, a hint of their limited effectiveness. Those "*Its*" condensing our individual and collective memories and hopes—a dear aunt, a revered flag, treasured bits of memorabilia—are so very important for us because they manage to preserve the emotional features not only of that foreground but also of what has been relegated to the background. They embody not only the explicit meanings crucial to the framework governing them but also the intangible meanings associated with realities lurking in the background, just beyond the reach of our comprehension.

Science makes sense of the world by enclosing it within a system; art discloses the limits of that making and invites us to embrace a world more richly diverse than any finite system can encompass. Art is susceptible to closure, however. Like science, it too can seek perfection within a type—although the consequences of doing so are unfortunate. In the scientific use of symbols, where only denotative meaning is relevant, this arbitrariness is a powerful tool in fashioning a coherent system. A new linguistic symbol can be invented, for instance, or an old one given a new definition, in order to create a technical term that refers unambiguously to a specific referent. Artistic symbols, however, retain their connotative penumbra of emotional significance, and so when their denotation is shifted from one reference to another the value intensities appropriate to the old are transferred, inappropriately, to the new.

For instance, the cultural heritages of various tribal groups have each been concentrated by the symbolically rich accounts they cherish of their ancestral heroes, the great events that took place under the leadership of those heroes, and the hallowed ground where victories were won, where martyrs perished, and where guiding hopes for the future were first envisioned. As these peoples are brought under the aegis of a newly emerging nation state, their varying heritages need to be further concentrated. This can be done by bringing them together around new symbols such as a national flag, arbitrary symbols only recently invented that stand nonetheless for a reality that those who have just now become the new nation's new citizens feel must have the same deep historical roots their tribal symbols have, and that therefore have immense present worth. More profoundly, these heritages can be brought together not around new symbols but around old ones given new meanings, such as when the tribal heroes are taken as the various manifestations of a single national hero.

How easy it is, however, for the intensities of value clothing the "*It*" of these symbols to be taken as bounded, for the referent of the symbols to be restricted to specified individuals, those belonging to only one of the original cultural traditions or those of a particular race or gender or skin color or religious belief. That the nation should be restricted to a portion of the people encompassed by its political authority is an arbitrary decision, abusing the scientific method of horizontal constriction by using it as a tool of political rather than intellectual inquiry. Equally arbitrary is an imposed restriction that includes all the nation's citizens but misuses the vertical constriction of scientific abstraction to cut off the nation's unifying symbols from their transcending power, from their capacity to reach beyond the nation and its cultural heritages to other nations and cultures. Its citizens are blocked by the limiting exclusiveness of such national symbols from being able to glimpse, however fleetingly, their values as flowing into the values of the human species, the planet, and even the whole cosmos.

The transformation of patriotism into jingoism is achieved by closing the aesthetic symbols of a nation's identity, converting their self-transcending openness into instruments of exclusion. The restriction of values of profound importance to a special group justifies treating those who lack those values as inferior, as unimportant people whose worth is only their utility for the special group's ends, or treating them as threats to the privileged group and therefore as needing to be isolated or exterminated. When the governing elite, or a single individual, becomes the symbol for all those other symbols, when the nation is thought to be incarnate in the Party or the Leader, the resulting totalitarian subjugation brings this closure to its nihilistic apotheosis.

Art ceases to fulfill its proper educational function of showing us the limits of our systems of institutional organization and scientific knowledge when it marshals its connotative powers to indemnify one of those systems against criticism. Living within an aesthetically closed system, we lose any awareness that our familiar boundaries could be transcended and so we have no motivation to push against their limits. Confined to the familiar, we grow progressively incapable of recognizing changes that are rendering the familiar inadequate. As the strong timbers of old truth grow weak from the rot of neglected maintenance, we nonetheless cling to them as though to a life raft in a gathering storm, hanging on in blind loyalty and with increased desperation to fundamentally important meanings for which we can imagine no alternative. Our romance loses its adventurous energy and slips into an inertial aestheticism, a love for only what is familiar and authorized, pretty and proper.

Art can therefore lead us to the same impasse that science does, to a closure from which there is no escape. The aspirations and ideals fostered by Beauty, just as easily as willful selfishness, can become the executioner of Truth. It is the shame of our educational system from kindergarten to university general education courses that the arts are typically taught as closed systems, fostering either vapid aestheticism or blind jingoism, and so fail to nurture the imaginative energy we need to break out of our conformist prisons. However, if that fuller reality can be evoked by a new aesthetic symbol in a particularly efficacious manner, its forgotten possibilities will rise to the surface and become available for fashioning novel perspectives, innovative systems of interpretation, a new ideal of perfection. The unity of a vibrant aesthetic symbol, of a good work of art, is expressed in terms of balance and contrast rather than coherence and consistency, in terms of intensity and importance rather than adequacy and applicability. And so it invites us to overrun the boundaries of the established systems in which we have been comfortably dwelling. A great artist crafts symbols in paint or marble, in words or gestures—and on our seeing or hearing them, their impact can be transformative. Our eyes are opened, our ears scoured, our emotions shaken. For behold, all things have been made new.

A great work of art, "as if by the wand of an enchanter," calls into being "a beauty beyond the power of speech to express" (283). Its Beauty suddenly makes present the deeper contextualizing Reality on which the regnant system of established Truth rests, from which it has been abstracted. The artistic masterpiece releases a tidal wave of novel feeling along with a conflicting welter of previously unnoticed particular facts and possibilities, all of them become resources on which our imaginations can draw. Art liberates us from the old and increasingly stifling boundaries of our familiar world with its familiar sense of what counts as a Truthful Appearance. We are plunged headlong into aspects of Reality previously beyond our imagining, free at last to draw on these exhilarating novelties in order to create a different Appearance, one never seen before on land or sea.

This novel Beauty may also be True in a way we had never before understood or even imagined. If so, it beckons us and our collaborators to fashion some new scientific system able to harmonize effectively the facts and possibilities it has revealed. We are impelled by the Beauty that Art crafts to undertake a new Adventure in order to conceive of a system the Truth of which is more adequate to experience than its predecessor—and, imagining it, to set about attempting to bring it to some kind of concrete actualization. We are empowered to give systemic organization to our new sense of reality, to create a new way of understanding and of action, one more adaptively adept—one that works. But of course in doing so, we will have to exclude a cacophonous welter of other things, pushing them into the background. Unavoidably, therefore, our success will eventually prove inadequate to its task, and our successors will need once again to fashion fresh artistic symbols capable of transgressing the constraints of that better Truth we had worked so hard to establish.

Spiral Weaving

Art, understood as functioning in this way, explains why generalization is not the final stage of a linear progression. Rather, it is a crucial phase in the open-ended cyclings of a helix. Learning is a process that begins with romance, with exploring unfamiliar facts and novel possibilities. It matures into the phase of precision where closed interpretive systems are proposed and deployed, where their implications are tested and their usefulness fully exploited. Generalization then emerges as the critique of these systems, the recognition that their boundary conditions are too constricting. Art is the way by which the positive side to this critique is accomplished. It provides us access to the resources able to occasion a new round of exploration, interpretation, and evaluation. The openness of romance leads to the closure of precision, but generalization fosters with the aid of Art a freshly insightful openness, making possible the creative invention of a new closure more adequate to the existing conditions. Open, closed, reopened more insightfully, closed again in a more effective way, and so on and so on.

The practical implications of this interpretation of Whitehead's stages of education are manifold. Most obviously, the helical character of learning suggests that the arts and sciences always need each other. We must reject the debilitating dichotomy between subjective and objective, mental and physical, emotional and rational, that underlies how most curricula are organized. Based on these dichotomies, the arts are traditionally associated with things subjective, intuitive, and intangible; the sciences, with what is objective, rational, and material.

The purview of the arts, however, is not limited to expressions of personal feeling and subjective preference—its concern is not solely with truths of the heart. The purview of the sciences is not limited to publically verifiable hypotheses about the objective world—its concern is not solely with truths of reason. Rather, science has to do with closed symbols and systemic hierarchies of interpretation that are immensely useful, the arts with open symbols and boundary-transgressing concrete particulars of immense importance. Both kinds of symbols encompass the subjective and the objective dimensions of experience and reality, both use reason and feeling, both inquire into the nature and meaning of things.

My sand castles by the sea led me to dream of building a wondrous magical cathedral to the glory of God. And this childhood dream as I matured has become a more realistic truth of the heart, but my task now as a fully credentialed and widely experienced architect is to create an actual building that expresses that truth rationally. My task is to utilize the sciences of architectural design and engineering in order to construct from wood and stone a place of worship able to endure for a thousand years or more. I need to fashion a building not only well constructed to withstand the forces of nature that would undermine it but also well constructed to exhibit the divine glory it would honor. The cathedral needs to be a physical environment within which anyone, not just myself, can sense both its emotional and its rational power. My aim is not merely to externalize a personal feeling but rather to objectify a feeling others have as well, to display in public a significant public value, to help a group of people celebrate a particularly important communally felt good.

For our class to study the cathedral at Chartres, we need to investigate not only the features of the building—its shape, the materials used in its construction, the striking array of statues along its facades—but also the meaning of those features for those who built it. Why is its shape cruciform, why wasn't it built of less expensive, more easily worked material, what persons or types of persons do the statues represent and why were those and not others chosen? These investigations carry us far beyond objective facts and subjective feelings, into matters of religious belief, political judgment, ethical values, aesthetic taste, and historical tradition, into questions about a society's worldview and the ways it liberates and controls our imagination. In studying the Chartres Cathedral, we will find ourselves studying the culture that made it possible, and in doing so wondering also about our own culture's practices and what we build these days that we think has a glory deserving a collective effort to give it public expression.

Some truths of reason are as saturated with feeling as a mother's kiss; some truths of the heart are as solidly objective as trees. Indeed, the landscape around Chartres has the character it has because of the hearts of its human inhabitants, who shaped the natural order to suit their cultural proclivities. These two kinds of discipline, the arts and the sciences, need each other. They are intellectual Siamese twins, polar tensions in a single dialectic. To be properly educated, we need to study art history as much as economics, to spend as much time in studios learning how to paint still-life compositions as we spend in laboratories learning how to conduct chemistry experiments, and to be taught in each of these milieus the relevance to it of its twin.

More subtly understood, the helical character of learning means recognizing that both the arts and the sciences are composed of disciplines, each of which has a tradition of acceptable standards regarding methods and results. Therefore each in its way is a closed system, successful within its boundaries and so resistant to having them challenged. The cathedral at Chartres, after all, is just another Gothic cathedral conforming to the standard procedures of its era, relying uncritically on such tried and true techniques as the use of flying buttresses to prevent its high graceful walls from buckling outward under the pressure of its wide-vaulted ceilings. It would be strange to suggest that the walls could be supported using other materials or thickened or built into a mountainside. It would be stranger still—or rather, it would be sacrilegious—to suggest that places of worship need not lift themselves toward heaven, need not aspire to the infinite, in order to express God's glory, much less to suggest that heaven is not above nor God infinite. Closed systems have an integrity and an authority based on their coherence and established success that make them difficult to escape. They have no doors or windows, and their walls are immensely high and well buttressed.

Obversely, however, both the sciences and the arts are creative endeavors, each of them nurturing practitioners who become impatient with the constraints of their discipline, who break through its conventions, who invent new disciplinary paradigms and whole new disciplines. The arts and the sciences, each in its own way, are open systems. The use of flying buttresses was a bold departure from the Romanesque cathedral design, a brilliant insight into how to dispense with the massively thick walls and countless interior pillars that detract from the sense of grandeur that a vast open interior space creates. Populating the cathedral facade at Chartres with a host of disparate statues was also a bold innovation, expressing grandeur in a startlingly different way, although one that was not emulated elsewhere, its novelty too bold to give it effective leverage against the then reigning truths of heart and reason.

Hence, each academic field of study, each course in a program of study, each classroom session of a course, in a way appropriate to the occasion, needs to have a romantic moment, a period of precision, and a generalizing critical transcendence. Students need constantly to experience in their education the cyclical rhythm between openness and closure that lures them into learning in a helically developmental manner. Information-imparting courses and the multiple-choice-exam questions in which they delight are almost unavoidably about precision at the expense of romance. Discussions in which everyone's viewpoint is eagerly encouraged and equally treasured, and which delight in daily thought-diaries as the basis for evaluation, are almost unavoidably about romance at the expense of precision. Only when these first two stages of education are modulated so that they interact will it be possible for generalization to emerge, and thus for our learning to become adaptively mature—to become helical.

We should be encouraged in our literature courses to read joyously, to delight for its own sake in the world to which an author has introduced us. We need also to learn rigorous procedures for sorting out sloppily subjective readings of that author's text from warranted interpretations. We should learn from these experiences how to glimpse in the shortcomings of a text the fresh possibilities other authors have explored, innovations in content and style to which we too might aspire. In our biology courses, we should become familiar specifically and concretely with the organisms we wish to study, well-informed about their behaviors and the ecologies that support and threaten them. We should then learn the theories that explicate the nature of those organic processes and the methods by which these theories have been formulated and validated. However, we also need to find ourselves perplexed by serious problems about these matters, for which the available formulae and methods of inquiry are seemingly inadequate and for which new lines of research by others, ourselves included, might be undertaken.

In short, every academic discipline should be taught as a helix dialectically weaving its closed and open features into an interesting, because constantly self-transforming, adventure. The romance provided by an artful intrusion of other disciplines into this process is an effective way, maybe a necessary one, for prodding a discipline into generalization when it begins to be blinded by the closure inherent to its precision phase. The pernicious consequence of the isolation of the disciplines is obvious when courses of study are fashioned, as they are in most of our colleges and universities, so that entering an academic major means bidding good-bye to other ways of learning.

So the rhythm of education for Whitehead is helical. And thanks to the function of Art, which constantly speaks Beauty to the currently reigning Truth, we should no longer think of generalization as the capstone to mastery of a discipline. It is rather the transformative realization that this mastery always comes at an unacceptable price, that there is more to truth than that discipline can ever conceive. Generalization is the recognition that truly to master a discipline is persistently to rethink its conditions, to reconceive its theories and redesign its methods. To master a discipline is to perfect the world it fashions by surpassing it, and to do so again and again, worlds without end.

CHAPTER THREE

Learning to Be Free

In this chapter, I will shift our focus from aesthetics to epistemology, mapping Whitehead's stages of education onto the theory of knowledge he develops in *Symbolism: Its Meaning and Effect*. The parallels are to be expected; learning, after all, is a process of coming to know things.

Whitehead is an empiricist insofar as he argues that the sole sources of our knowledge about the world are our sense perceptions. The ways in which we experience reality—seeing, hearing, touching, tasting, smelling—tell us not only about the external realities we perceive, however, but also about ourselves as perceivers. We learn something about who we are and what it is to be human in learning about how we come to know the things around us. This connection is captured in the commonplace metaphors we use in characterizing what we know about people. We say, when we think them ignorant, that they are blind to the truth; when arrogant, that they lack a common touch; when boorish, that they are culturally tone-deaf; when deceitful, that what they are doing smells bad. The better we are at understanding the character of our sensory experiences, the more they tell us truths about the character of reality and our own character. Learning and perceiving are closely related enterprises, and if this is so then comparing them should be a useful undertaking.

Under normal conditions, looking at a rock or listening to a bird is so familiar and spontaneous an experience that we take what we are doing for granted. Physical disabilities, difficult environing conditions, emotional intrusions, or mental distractions, however, often force us to pay attention to what we are doing, to wonder what we are seeing or what we just heard. What are these things in our world such that sometimes they are as plain as the nose on our face and sometimes incomprehensibly mysterious? Who are we such that we can know so much and yet fail to know so much more? To what extent are these skills teachable and to what extent innate? And what are their limits?

In the previous chapter, we have seen how the romance of Art, functioning within the stage of generalization, opens pathways that take us beyond the boundaries of our conventional and usually trustworthy understandings. This chapter makes a similar journey, but uses the more prosaic language of the stage of precision to describe how truth is ascertained and how the increase in competence and judgment thereby acquired enhances a different kind of art, one key to the creation and sustenance of free individuals in a free society.

Experience

The clichés of common sense celebrate the certainties of direct experience. You assure me that a Cassin's Finch has been seen in a nearby park, but I'm skeptical about such a bird being in our neighborhood, so far from its usual range—until I race over to the park and get a good look myself at it perched in a spruce tree. Seeing is believing. I can put on a dramatic presentation for the garage mechanic about the strange thumping sound that appears whenever I drive my car above sixty miles per hour, but until he hears the sound himself he is likely to dismiss it as merely road noise. For the mechanic, hearing is believing. The proof of the tastiness is in the pudding, the justification for judging the one wine better than the other is its bouquet. We are all doubting Thomases until we have ourselves touched once more what we have loved and yet had thought we lost.

Then along come the philosophy professors, undermining this confidence. Our sensory experiences are in our heads, they argue. Images, sounds, tastes, smells, textures are brain states. We think that these mental sensations, these sense impressions, are caused by external realities. We believe that when a Cassin's Finch vocalizes, it sets in motion vibrations in the air that travel from its beak to my ears and stimulate an auditory sensation in my head that I recognize as a snatch of birdsong. But we know nothing directly about these external causes; we have no way to justify the claim that what we see is like its cause, that our mental image is a snapshot of a portion of the external world. Nor can we even claim that the causes of our sensations are outside our minds. Sometimes we confuse seeing a bird with imagining we saw it, or just dreaming we did. When I hear crickets, the cause may be my tinnitus.

So our philosophy professors lead us into the dark wood of skepticism. They tell us that direct experience is awareness only of the content of our minds. Inferences from that content to knowledge about the external world is unjustified. Since what we know of the past is a matter of memories that derive from previously direct experiences, our inferences to what was once the case are as problematic as our inferences to what is now the case. Indeed, the only way we can distinguish present perceptions from remembered perceptions is by means of yet another unjustified inference, arguing that the less vivid images are the elder ones. Our skepticism ends in a Pyrrhic triumph over rational common sense. It strands us, as Santayana famously puts it, in "solipsism of the present moment" (*Scepticism* chap. 1).

Whitehead escapes this dead-end by arguing that our direct experiences come in two modes, not one. They are of external intrusions as well as of mental states. He calls the first mode of direct experience "causal efficacy," the second "presentational immediacy." Perception in the mode of presentational immediacy is derivative from the more primitive perception in the mode of causal efficacy. It "is an important factor in the experience of only a few high-grade organisms," whereas "for the others it is embryonic or entirely negligible" (*Symbolism* 23). Instead of our emotions being reactions to information provided by our senses, Whitehead inverts the relationship, arguing that sense-data are specialized abstractions from our vague feelings of an impinging elsewhere.

Sense-data—the "colours, sounds, tastes, touches, and bodily feelings" (25) that comprise the deliverances of presentational immediacy—are "vivid, precise, and barren" (23). Because they are therefore "definite in our consciousness," they are "handy" to use and "easy to reproduce at will" (43). When I catch sight of a bird, especially when that look is augmented by a pair of binoculars, the image is easily remembered, easily enough at least for me to have time to compare it with images in my *Kaufman Field Guide*, until I find a good match and recognize it as some kind of finch, most likely a Purple but just maybe a Cassin's.

The vivacity and precision of these remembered images allow me to match them by reference to minor differences, such as the brightness of the red on the bird's cap or the length of its bill. The images are barren frozen snapshots of complex activity, devoid both of the bird's movements in its restless perching and of mine as I strain to bring it into focus and register as many of its features as I can before it departs or my arms grow tired holding the binoculars. This barrenness is precisely what makes the images useful. The unchanging images of superficial features are simple enough to be remembered and thus compared with Kaufman's fits-in-aside-pocket repertoire of possibly similar images. An experience composed of sense-data "halts at the present, and indulges in a manageable self-enjoyment derived from this immediacy of the show of things" (44).

In contrast, the causally efficacious experiences from which sense-data are abstracted are "vague, haunting, unmanageable" (43), "heavy with the contact of the things gone by, which lay their grip on our immediate selves" (44). Because the show of things is both mesmerizing and immediately useful, we easily overlook the more primitive mode of experience underlying it. Whitehead notes, however, that "certain emotions, such as anger and terror, are apt to inhibit the apprehension of sense-data" (42), and that when this happens we become sharply aware of "the pressure from a world of things with characters in their own right, characters mysteriously moulding our own natures" (44)—an often "terrifying sense of vague presences, effective for good or evil over our fate" (43).

A shadow passes across the open space where I am peering into my binoculars. My finch and all the other nearby birds fall silent. Something sinister has come this way: perhaps a hawk after its prey; or no, perhaps it is the angel of my death; or please, oh please, perhaps just clouds piling up toward a storm. I shake off the shiver running down my back and return to my binoculars as the birds resume their chirping, chastened by the sudden recognition that there are more important things in life than birding. "For all their vagueness, for all their lack of definition, these controlling presences, these sources of power, these things with an inner life, with their own richness of content, these beings, with the destiny of the world hidden in their natures, are what we want to know about" (57).

Whitehead uses the motto typically found on traditional sundials, a line from the poet Martial, to suggest the contrast between these two modes of direct experience: *Pereunt et imputantur*—They [the hours] pass away and are reckoned on [our] account. " 'Pereunt' refers to the world disclosed in immediate presentation, gay with a thousand tints, passing, and intrinsically meaningless. 'Imputantur' refers to the world disclosed in its causal efficacy, where each event infects the ages to come, for good or for evil, with its own individuality" (47). Martial's poetic phrase links the two, conveying through their contrast, through "the imagined fusion of the two perceptive modes by one intensity of emotion," the "pathos of the lapse of time" (48). We normally experience the world neither as a collection of clear and distinct sense-data, nor as a congeries of vague but yet hauntingly intrusive efficacious realities, but as a merging of the two. Whitehead calls this natural ability we have to link the two modes of perception "symbolic reference." We take the immediately presented sense-data as symbols referring to the causal efficacy of what lies beyond us. The sense-data are abstracted from the efficacy and then projected outward, providing us with information about their cause: where it came from and what its features are. "Symbolism from sense-presentation to physical bodies is the most natural and widespread of all symbolic modes" (4).

I become aware of something changing in my visual field, a sudden shift in color altering slightly the character of the landscape at which I've been looking, a flash of purple over there in the tree branches. It must mean that the unlikely finch I so want to see is here after all. My eyes follow after the flash, searching for more color by which to confirm the meaning of the initial glimpse, attempting to specify more precisely its point of origin and to find what other color patterns it exhibits, what shape it has, in what direction it is moving. If all goes well, I will soon be confident enough to claim that the flash was of a bird, the red was the coloring of its cap, and the movement was it hopping to a higher branch where I now have it clearly in my binoculars and know for sure that it is a finch, which given its size and hefty bill is probably the Cassin's!

The awareness of something important out there, important because seeming to impinge in some way on my purposes, gives aspects of my visual sensations a special salience that I use to identify their location and their features. I pay attention to the reddish patches and spatial coordinates because I want to know what's out there. And I want to know because my interests are at stake: my endeavor to identify a bird, to feel yet again the satisfaction I find in birding, and through it to confirm my sense of who I am and what it is for me to live meaningfully.

The barren sense-data and the rich loam of my concerns are separated only in unusual circumstances. Their correlation is the default mode, the natural way of our experiencing the world. Where the vagueness predominates, we normally attempt to augment how we characterize it; where the clarity predominates, our tendency is to plumb for its significance. We need the symbols to find the meaning, but we need the meanings to want the symbols. We understand the world and ourselves through the interplay of symbolic reference.

The content of experience in the mode of presentational immediacy is derivative, an abstraction from the reality concretely experienced in the mode of causal efficacy. The truth of the abstraction is a matter of its adequacy, its satisfactory correlation with the concreteness from which it was derived. This is the familiar correspondence theory of truth mentioned in the previous chapter—but with a transformative difference. The correlation is between two versions of our experience of the same reality. We are not inferring from what we know firsthand to what we do not know at all. Our inference is from one form of firsthand knowledge to another form, indeed from a derivative to a primary one. Insofar as they purport to tell us truths about the world, the vivid colors and sounds, textures and tastes of immediate awareness are constrained by the less vivid but more vital sense we have of that world's influence—"The *how* of our present experience must conform to the *what* of the past in us" (58).

Since the qualities of a perception are abstractions from the emotionally richer experience of causal efficacy, it would seem that perceptions should be devoid of emotional content. Yet obviously they are not. A mathematical idea or a daydream lack the vivid immediacy, the aura of importance, that sense perceptions have. My castles in the sky are pale shadows of the actual castle I'm patting into shape as I squat awkwardly in the sand. When our sense perceptions are veridical, we are aware of their fit with our emotionally charged feelings. Seeing the bird as a Cassin's Finch is more thrilling than a thousand pictures of a Cassin's or a hundred imagined moments of seeing it. We find the fit satisfactory, preferring the adequacy of our perceptions to their mere coherence.

When lilacs last in my dooryard bloomed, I step outside for a close look at the green-leafed bushes with their purple flowers swaying gently in the spring breeze. I feel a massive presence, a movement of planes and angles, and I feel it in a greenish-purplish way—soothingly, fresheningly. What I feel directly is a vague presence; how I feel it is greenishly and purplishly. Certain aspects of what I have experienced are transformed by various abstraction habits into its quantitative features: ovoid shapes with flexible surfaces, relatively unvarying on one side but corrugated on the other, shifting this way and that on their tubular stems. Other aspects of my experiencing are transformed by similar abstraction habits into perceiving those quantitative features as having a delicate green color and a subtle acidic fragrance, as being both smooth and rough to the touch. Although it is true for the quantitative data, the so-called primary qualities, it is vividly true for the secondary qualities that their display bears witness to the power of their origin.

Thus, although our sense-data are abstractions, they retain the emotional import of the concrete efficacies from which they arose. The sense of importance conveyed by that from which they have been abstracted is transformed into the secondary qualities we naively attribute to objects, until philosophers mislead us into thinking they are actually features of our mind. Whitehead is arguing that red and loud, sweet and rough, as well as long and large, thick and double, are indeed mental qualities projected onto external objects, but that these qualities are derived from those external objects in the first place. The qualities comprising the content of experience in the mode of presentational immediacy, taken as definable features of a specific region of the external world, are actually derived from the indefinite but strongly felt experience of that region in the mode of causal efficacy and then projected back onto it. As a result, the felt power of the world infuses our sense of its qualitative features. My sense of the lilac bush is not only of an interesting harmony of moving shapes of various colors but also of a real thing important for me to take account of.

A perceptual image, however, does not necessarily describe the felt reality to which it refers. My lilac bush may not actually be as robust as it looks because my point of view obscures the curled leaves on the side away from me. My despondent self-absorption, derived from events having nothing to do with the bush, may obscure my appreciation of its fresh fragrance. Yet we are typically not misled if we take the symbolic reference correlating the two modes of perception as a truthful characterization of reality; it usually works for us to do so. Whitehead has a pragmatic theory of truth: the correlated perceptions need not mirror reality to be true of reality. It suffices that the immediacies and the efficacies share enough in common for us to be able to interact in a satisfactory way with the world they present to us. If it quacks like a duck, it's reasonable to think it's a duck.

Causal efficacy, presentational immediacy, and symbolic reference: Whitehead's tripartite characterization of perceptive experience might seem at first blush to provide likely parallels to the educational stages of romance, precision, and generalization. Causal efficacy is "the primitive element in our external experience," its content "vague, haunting, unmanageable" (43), "heavy with the contact of the things gone by, which lay their grip on our immediate selves" (44). Similarly, the stage of romance is "the stage of first apprehension" ("Rhythm" 17), in which we open ourselves appreciatively to the boisterous world around us, accepting it for what it is and reveling in its surprises and possibilities. Romance is in this sense naive: uncritical, uncalculating, unconstrained. Our education begins when we discover this world, the world simply as a felt impingement.

In contrast, presentational immediacy involves "our immediate perception of the contemporary external world" as "a community of actual things" (*Symbolism* 21) related "by reason of their participation in an impartial system of spatial extension" (23). This systemic whole is "effected by the mediation of qualities" (21) called sense-data, "generic abstractions" (22) that are "vivid, precise, barren," and largely "controllable at will" (23). Similarly, the stage of precision teaches "exactness of formulation" ("Rhythm" 18), achieved through the deployment of systems of order, whether grammatical, legal, or scientific.

Symbolic reference is then the synthesis of causal efficacy and presentational immediacy, the way by which "the various actualities disclosed respectively by the two modes are either identified, or at least correlated together as interrelated elements in our environment" (*Symbolism* 18). Similarly, the stage of generalization is synthetic; it is "the final success" whereby romance is transformed by the addition of "classified ideas and relevant technique" ("Rhythm" 19), whereby "concrete fact" is "studied as illustrating the scope of general ideas" (26).

These apparent similarities are at best superficial, however. The fundamental problem is that perceptive experience—experience involving the two modes of perception and their symbolic correlation—is our spontaneous way as higher organisms for becoming aware of and dealing with our world. It is how human beings instinctively know things. The stages of education, however, are how we acquire cultural enhancements to our instinctive way of knowing, how we develop artfully sophisticated modes of experiencing.

Our bodily feelings of the world and their correlation with sense-data are biological capacities. They are the way we construct a meaningful world from the double deliverance of direct perception, a way sufficiently adapted to the exigencies of circumstance to have allowed our species reproductive success over its various competitors. We are born with these capacities and we survive as well as we do because of them. Perceptive experience, therefore, is what education presupposes and where it therefore begins.

Perception

The epistemological package composed of causal efficacy, presentational immediacy, and symbolic reference thus finds its educational parallel in the stage of romance. Both are initial moments in an increasingly sophisticated development. By linking romance to perceptive experience, hence making symbolic reference one of its important features, dimensions of romance that are far too often neglected come into focus.

We can better appreciate now why romance is a stage of discovery. It is effected by encouraging the enlargement of perceptive experience through the enlargement of symbolic reference. Because perception is active not passive, it can be improved. We can train our eyes to see more sharply, our ears to hear more acutely, our touch to be more sensitive—to abstract sense-data from causal efficacies that allow us to interpret those felt importances in ways more adaptively relevant to our changing needs and aspirations because more attuned to the penumbra of the obvious, to the borderlands of the known world. The symbolic reference we take as just plain common sense leaves out all those aspects of our feelings that aren't relevant to our getting on with our lives in a normal manner. Our sense of the "circumambient efficacious world of beings" (*Symbolism* 55), however, cries out for interpretations that are adequate to it, that do not suffer unnecessarily this diminution in our feelings of importance.

Walking in the park with our teacher and classmates, if we take the stone we stumble over as just another stone in a dreary expanse of similar stones, we may grumble briefly about its inconvenient location but our attention will be elsewhere, perhaps focused on a bird we are attempting to identify. If, however, we begin to wonder why there should be a stumbling block in the middle of a well-traveled park trail, if our grumpy exclamation becomes an interrogative, our focus will shift from the sky to the ground; our effort to identify something will be transferred from bird to rock. We become interested in learning about the rock when our awareness of its presence takes into account neglected feelings of the circumambient efficacies it evokes but to which we are not accustomed to pay attention.

As our sense of the rock's presence deepens into a sense of the mystery of its reality, the puzzling origin and character of its having intruded into the private space of our familiar world, we become interested in sharpening what we are perceiving so that our sense-data will prove adequate to the occasion. Wondering if the rock is sedimentary and if so whether it is limestone, we flake off a piece and rub it between our fingers while looking to see if it is a composite. Our feelings of mystery and wonder, our puzzlings about what tripped us up and how it could have and why, drive our effort to determine what kind of thing it is and therefore how it is likely to behave, where it fits in with the things we already know about. Our sense of a thing's importance is the mother of our knowledge of it.

And, reciprocally, the specific information we acquire about something provides a way to rescue from irrelevance its neglected or obscured meanings. Wanting to become an expert on the King Arthur legend, I dutifully set about collecting all the information I can find about Britain after the withdrawal of the Roman legions. The result is just a pile of random facts nor worth remembering, unless I organize these data chronologically. I may then begin to see faint suggestions of how the historical events are implicit in the legend. In an attempt to get the facts of the Saxon expansion straight, an exciting idea comes to mind, the possibility that Arthur is an actual Briton warlord whose brief career became a lodestone for the remnants of a defeated people's proud heritage—a way to hold it together, to preserve its coherence and hence its meaning, and therefore its power, in the hope that someday defeat might be transformed into victory. The historical facts about Arthur, scant though they be, make visible a mythic hero who not merely reflects the glory of the ancient Britons but is modern Britain's deepest truth about itself. A firm grasp of the facts is the mother of our awareness of their importance.

If I aspire to be an outstanding striker for our soccer team, I need all the virtues appropriate to that sport—physical stamina, quick acceleration, adept ball handling, a sense of field, shot control, and the like. But I need in addition an acute awareness of the complementary virtues of my teammates, and how they dovetail with mine in all the subtle and unpredictable ways that fashion those great imponderables in sports: team spirit and the effective teamwork it nurtures. Our experience is always of yesterday's and yesteryear's opponents, challenges met and opportunities lost. To get from this clatter of data to an understanding of soccer and of myself as a soccer player, the data must be integrated into a portrait of a team that is more than what it has done and more than what it hopes to do. It must reveal to me the spirit those data imply in a way that adds my virtues as fuel for its fire, and thereby grounds my aspirations in its nurturing power.

So we are all the time spontaneously striving for an adequate and coherent fit between our feelings and our perceptions, our intentions and our thoughts, between our dim intuitions of what is vital for us and our bright shining systems of interpretation. Therefore, we should not understand the appreciative apprehensions key to Whitehead's first stage of education as merely affective, as simply a matter of passive visceral responses to external and internal stimuli. Romance is not a "touchy-feely" way of learning. It involves the interplay of two modes of perceiving: the one vague, haunting, unmanageable; the other precise, vivid, barren. Romance encompasses both efficacious power and presentational pattern, and it involves integrating these contrasting features of experience by taking those at one pole of the contrast as referring to those at the other pole.

The wet sand on a lonely beach stirs my imagination, so that I begin to see it as though strewn with the wreckage of an ancient castle, and I soon find myself attempting to shape the sand into a replica that does it homage. The idea of the castle was not something I concocted out of whole cloth and imposed arbitrarily on the sand. Rather, it was the beach that evoked the feelings for which the idea was an interpretation, as then the castle I shaped from the sand was an interpretation of the idea. Paleontologists do a similar thing, but in ways marked by greater technical prowess, when they imagine how the petrified dinosaur bones, emerging in the cleaning laboratory from the rock that contained them, might look when clothed with flesh and blood, and then construct a model of it as an interpretation of what it must have been like to see *Tyrannosaurus rex* when it was alive. The bones suggest to the informed eye their interpretation, so that the model of the dinosaur can claim to truly represent the real *T-rex*, whereas the bones, although truly its remains, do not.

Hence "growth in mentality" ("Rhythm" 19)—growth in the scope and power of our appreciative apprehension of the world—occurs as we hone our capacity for symbolic reference, exploring new ways in which our sense-data are taken as signs of the impinging world, a world to which we attribute ever-expanding spatial and temporal horizons and an ever more complex landscape. The abstractions derived from presentational immediacy are used with increasing subtlety and detail to organize the feelings resulting from causal efficacy around frameworks of connection by means of which those feelings can be understood and acted on. These frameworks are linguistic and behavioral—concepts and gestures, grammatically complex sentences and shared enterprises, myths and rituals, systemic theories and law-abiding actions. They are the many and varied ways by which we apprehend appreciatively what our world is like and by which we engage it.

The romantic phase of education, therefore, involves more than passive appreciation. We are insufficiently romantic if all we do is sit in libraries, labs, and lecture halls enjoying the sounds and colors of our surroundings, taking note of what comes our way and packaging it for whatever future use we think it might have. Our romanticism is equally insufficient if we spend our time wallowing enthusiastically or snidely in the flow of passion that tries to fill our every moment. Passivity of either sort, the merely factual and the merely emotional, is anemic. The one is a mere beholding of our direct and incorrigible experiences without seeking their import, the other a mere reveling in our feelings without seeking their meaning. Romance delights in both features of our experience, not for their own sake but for ours. We enjoy the play of our senses and our emotions for their relevance, for the way they fulfill our lives. Our apprehension is active not passive. We use what we perceive to transform our inchoate feelings into a world of meaningful objects and events, into a context within which our yearnings make sense, where our hopes and our worries have a point, where meaningful things are taking place and we have a part to play in them.

We stand before Sennacherib's cenotaph, sensing its antiquity, and we spontaneously begin to spin a story for ourselves that gives our feeling content. The story may at first barely differ from the feeling, a once-upon-a-time notion of when the world was far different than our own. The more we attend to the object, however, the more we fill out its story, and the more we know about the world, the more resources we have for doing so. The story grows increasingly coherent and adequate as it shifts from our private musings to our embellishing of half-remembered tales of olden times, and as it eventually shifts from a mythic to a historical account, its development stopping only as our curiosity is sated or our imagination fatigues or our interest shifts elsewhere. Our teachers when they take us to museums should remember that there is more for us to learn there than moldering facts, that there are sermons in stones for us to hear, stories that will add breadth and depth to our personal story, a story we had naively thought private and so no wider than our head or older than our birth.

We apprehend the world by engaging it; we appreciate it by appropriating it. We apprehend the world as useful or dangerous, we appreciate it as rife with opportunities for enjoyment or as beset with threats to our present or our possible enjoyment. We thus make a meaningful storied world for ourselves by using our experiences, our feelings and perceptions, to fashion something relevant to our needs—and indeed to discover what those needs are or might better be. The stage of romance, in each of its helical reappearances, its increasingly sophisticated manifestations throughout a person's education, is always a busily active time as we attempt to dress out our feelings with perceptions that make sense of them and to ground our perceptions in feelings that give them worth. That's why it was as though we had entered a sacred place when we walked up to that cenotaph, that's why the beach seemed haunted that afternoon, that's why the protruding edge of a petrified bone sent such a shiver down our spine.

Our propensity to actively engage the surrounding environment is innate, a part of our genetic inheritance. We are born to be world-makers, but how we make those worlds, how we interpret our experience, how we correlate by symbolic reference the data of presentational immediacy with the deliverances of causal efficacy, is by no means genetically determined. There are many ways to interpret experience, to decide how best to construe what our sense-data signify. In construing them as we do, we therefore exhibit ourselves as free. Not as arbitrarily free, for we have no choice over what impinges on our senses, but as creatively free in our ability to interpret what has impinged, making it into an intelligible world, a world we can understand and shape. Romance, says Whitehead, is the "first period of freedom" ("Rhythmic Claims" 31). It is that stage of learning in which the focus of our classroom activities should be on encouraging the expansion of our freedom, broadening the range of facts experienced, deepening those experiences through exploration of their import—augmenting the opportunities for refurbishing and remaking the worlds with which we have become familiar.

So the appreciative character of romance is not solely or even primarily receptive. It is also and more fundamentally pragmatic. We are aware that our experience is an artifact, that we have fashioned its specific unity from the raw materials gained through our twin modes of perceiving, and that how we have fashioned that unity is as something relevant to our purposes. We recognize that how we take our environment has consequences for our happiness and well-being. If we take the sudden motion as a dangerous sign, we may be able to avoid a falling object or an onrushing opponent. If we take the motion as a positive sign, however, we might manage to catch the ball or embrace a lover. If we interpret the kind words as a facade masking deep animosity, we can respond in ways that will not lead us into an embarrassing trap. Yet if we take those words as meaning what they say, we might gain a new friend or improve a business opportunity.

Therefore, educational experiences that are romantic should be ones that have consequences. Not serious consequences, having to do with our very survival, but ones consequential enough to satisfy the interest that led us to those experiences in the first place. The great virtue of playing soccer or any other competitive game is that it creates a world sheltered from the serious world, sets conditions that are interesting both with respect to goals sought and the means for their pursuit, and then offers rewards for success and punishments for failure that are modest and transient. The high school soccer match is exciting and the victory worth celebrating, but those who were defeated will live to try again another day, and both the winners and the losers will soon return from their play to the serious tasks of studying for tomorrow's exam or practicing the piano or cleaning their room.

Similarly, imaginative literature is a kind of game we are invited to play. The world through which a novel leads us may be one in which heroes are lauded and villains punished, or we may be led across a dark landscape into some dreadful valley of death and despair. When the story ends we are still very much alive, however, neither a hero nor a villain but the better for having pretended to be them both or to champion one or the other's cause. The primary point of learning how to give the text a close reading should not be to deconstruct its usual meaning or validate some critical theory but to acquire the ability to enter the author's world fully and responsibly. Thereby, we can better appreciate who the heroes really are and why even a hero's landscape is sometimes so dark, why Arthur whose sin sowed the seed that led to Camelot's destruction is Britain's culture hero rather than noble Lancelot or pious Galahad. And we can thereby better recognize how these insights about such fictional worlds are relevant to the lives we live in our own very real world where Camelot was shattered by a single bullet from beyond a grassy knoll.

In a romantic classroom, teachers should widen and deepen our sense of the serious consequences of our choices, but in a manner that incites us to undertake new and bolder adventures—to do so prudently and with eyes wide open, but to do so eager to rise to fresh challenges, not shrink from them. In romance, all things should still seem possible, teaching us that the worlds in which we dwell are ones we have made, and are therefore ours to engage as we see fit, to confirm or reform or transform them, and through that engagement to find our fulfillment.

In short, the stage of romance is that recurrent period in a person's education when appreciative engagement should be dominant. I have argued that by noting the parallels between romantic appreciation and perceptive experience we can gain an appreciation of appreciation as an active mode of learning. Romance is a process of imaginative engagement—playing with the patterns and contents of those interpretations by which our world is taken to have meaning, exploring ways by which these interpretations locate us effectively in that world or might better do so, always being aware of the values we create or enhance or diminish.

No wonder, then, that Whitehead argues that "without the adventure of romance, at the best you get inert knowledge without initiative, and at the worst you get contempt of ideas—without knowledge" ("Rhythmic Claims" 33). For without an educational moment in which our capacity for imaginative engagement is promoted, there will be little sense of the way what is taken as fact is haunted by importances that might have been and might yet be, and so there will be insufficient interest in how what is good can be transformed into what is better.

Analysis

If we take the stage of precision as akin to what Whitehead calls "conceptual analysis," we can gain some fresh insight into why precision is the obvious and appropriate next educational step after romance. It has to do with the sense of limit inherent in romance, the way in which error is an inescapable feature of interpretation, and how this enlarges our understanding of the pragmatic dimension of symbolic reference.

Romance, understood as embracing the two modes of perception and their integration through symbolic reference, entails a sense of limit easy for us to overlook in our quest for new and fascinating experiences. Romance discloses, but its practitioners tend not to appreciate, that our interpretations and actions are necessarily partial. After all, we are taking the highly abstracted sense-data of presentational immediacy as characterizing the complexly felt concrete realities of causal efficacy, and so obviously that characterization must be inadequate. That's why it is so difficult to express our feelings verbally. "I love you" is a pale reflection of my many-splendored love; words fail me, but a kiss won't.

Despite the inherent inadequacy, the correlation of presentational immediacy with casual efficacy is natural, something we do constantly, routinely, unthinkingly. We "trust" it to continue being effective because it always has been. We experience vague lurking presences and we experience vivid colors, shapes, and sounds; we conclude that the presences are objects here in front of us with those particular visual and auditory features. Yet the presences are too vague to guarantee the legitimacy of their being so characterized, and these characterizations are too abstract and fleeting for us to be certain about assigning them to any particular region of our environment. The only possible justification is a "pragmatic appeal to the future" (*Symbolism* 31). These ways of taking the specifics of presentational immediacy as signs for the location and meaning of the deliverances of causal efficacy have worked. We rely on them and it pays off. The world these linkages effect is one in which we are able to live and to aspire to live better. They work, and that is truth enough.

Why they work is because, as we have seen, the two modes of perceptive experience have "structural elements in common" (30). They are two ways of taking the same concrete reality, alternative interpretations of the same situation. What is given for experience is what Whitehead calls a "natural potentiality." He derives this term from Aristotle's notion of matter as "pure potentiality awaiting the incoming of form in order to become actual" (36). The "settled past" is that actuality. We experience it not as simply settled, however, but as rife with potentialities from which we can wrest our present actuality. "All components which are *given* for experience are to be found in the analysis of natural potentiality. Thus the immediate present has to conform to what the past is for it" (36).

This is a striking claim. The past is settled, a brute facticity. We have no choice but to conform to its demands, to make what we can of a situation not of our own making. We don't conform to the past as it was, however, but as it is for us. We experience it; we don't become it. Because the past is a natural potentiality, the outflowing of vibrantly actual events, we are not steamrollered by its onrush, suffering it as passive victims. Instead, we rise up to engage it with tools its potency provides. We sense it as providing constraints with which we must come to terms but also as providing the resources for doing so. The sense-data we use as the symbols by which to disclose the meaning—the intelligibility and significance—of what we feel pressing on us are abstractions from the same reality as are those feelings. Our correlation of the two perceptive modes by which we experience a world of meaningful things is not arbitrary, because the two modes are versions of the same reality: incomplete versions, to be sure, but versions.

Indeed, the two modes and their correlation arose through aeons of biological evolution as capacities by which certain organisms enhanced their reproductive success. As Whitehead puts it: "The symbols do not create their meaning: the meaning, in the form of actual effective beings reacting upon us, exists for us in its own right. But the symbols discover this meaning for us. They discover it because, in the long course of adaptation of living organisms to their environment, nature taught their use" (57). Symbolic reference works because in a Darwinian world where there are more organisms striving to secure their lives and those of their offspring than there are resources sufficient for those ends, the ones that have been successful are our own ancestors. We are attracted by the finch's song and shrink away from the massif's growl, appreciate the heft of a baseball-sized rock and are suspicious of placid ponds with murky depths. We trust these habits of symbolic reference because they successfully provided our predecessors with "the determination of the positions of bodies controlling the course of nature" (56), which enabled them to avoid dangers, secure needed resources, and find suitable mates for creating and nurturing the progeny we are. If it was good enough for them, it's good enough for us.

These habits do not always work, however. We may hope that what our habits of symbolic reference ignore is unimportant, redundant, superfluous. But it may not be. Error occurs when the symbolic reference is inadequate to the needs of the moment, when it overlooks what should have been taken as crucial resources or avoided as a threat, when it hides what we might have enjoyed or distracts us from what might secure our success. Or error occurs when symbolic reference mischaracterizes that to which it refers, leading us along false pathways away from the available pleasures and opportunities we had hoped to find. Any organism that possesses sufficient consciousness to perceive things presentationally as well as causally, and so to require some modicum of symbolic reference in order to unify its experience, is vulnerable to error. Whitehead mentions "Aesop's fable of the dog who dropped a piece of meat to grasp at its reflection in the water" (19). It mistakenly took the presented image as evidence of the looming threat of a canine challenger's causal efficacy.

Organisms are more likely to survive if they, or at least a sufficient number of their kind, can learn from their mistakes. Such organisms, including human beings but not necessarily limited to them, have evolved the capacity to treat symbolic referencing as a datum, not only to engage in it but to take it as an object of interest, as a fact relevant to how the correlation of sense-data and felt environment might be differently effected. We are engaging in conceptual analysis when we take this reflective stance toward symbolic reference. It is a process whereby the coherence and adequacy of our interpretive symbols are explicitly questioned, the meanings they express adjusted, certain of the data degraded as "delusive appearances" and other data treated as clues leading to newfound truths. In such ways, we "revise our conceptual scheme so as to preserve the general trust in the symbolic reference" (54).

The stage of precision thus has two specific functions. It is where we learn the skills needed to recognize both error and the potential for error. It is also where we learn how to frame alternative conceptual schemes, alternative systems of symbolic reference, designed to remedy those actual or possible mistakes. Romance provides our reason for wanting to do so: to prevent the loss of what we have found to be significant. Precision is where we equip ourselves with the tools by which actually to accomplish the ends for which romance hungers.

Conceptual analysis is a method for ferreting out a problem our enthusiasm for an idea or course of action has led us to overlook. We become aware of the rising tide as more than a routine seaside phenomenon, but as also an intimation that our sand castle will soon be undermined, turned into a replica of the crumbled ruins from which it had arisen as a restored replica of the original castle. The bird's initially unnoticed black bill and white wing bars threaten to undermine our identification of it as a Cassin's Finch.

We could become flustered by these impediments to our purposes, resigning ourselves to the fate that destroys all castles built on sand, bemoaning a complexity of bird differentiation beyond our ability to master, eventually abandoning both projects for other seemingly easier ones. Or we could ignore the problems, denying that there is any threat to our creative engineering or birding prowess, or redefining our purposes after the fact, claiming that our aim all along was to build a sand castle in order to enjoy how the ocean destroys it, that the important thing is not identifying birds but being out in the woods enjoying nature.

Alternatively, we can recognize our mistakes and learn from them. Learning in this context means remaking our world, reformulating the framework of relationships that organizes the context in which we find ourselves so that alternatives are recognized that might remedy our mistakes. Conceptual analysis puts our problematic enthusiasms into a more fruitful context, showing us how what we know is related spatially and temporally, hierarchically and causally, to those things on which it is dependent or that depend on it, and to those things that are incompatible with it or can best thrive at its expense. Grasping this richer context, which had previously gone unnoticed or had been misconstrued, we recognize why we have a problem and how it can be resolved. We consult local tide charts for the likely extent of the ebb and flow along this shore this time of year, then we rebuild our sand castle above the high tide line. We return to our Kaufman guide and discover that the Pine Grosbeak is a better fit for our observations than either the Cassin's or the Purple Finch.

This disclosure of limitation, of the inadequacy of what we take to be the way things are, leads us to appreciate that we are vulnerable to making mistakes. It also leads us to appreciate constraint as good. We are limited in what we can do by previous fashionings, by the ways in which the physical universe, our planetary biosphere, our organismal lineage, and our cultural histories have developed. Some things we cannot do because we are insufficiently enduring or not massive enough. Other things are beyond our ability to carry out because we lack the mathematical sophistication to understand how they function or the concepts by which even to imagine them. We cannot evade the boundary conditions set by our genetic destiny or our linguistic heritage.

And yet, recognizing that these limitations are artifacts, we realize that what we take as possible is not all that could be possible, that by disciplined thought, by careful analysis of what has as yet not been analyzed and by novel but carefully systemized reformulations, we might find our way toward possibilities once not merely unimagined but unimaginable. Castles built on sand with pilings that reach down into the bedrock underneath need have no fear of tides, and those built with seismic dampers, dissipaters, and isolators can survive even an earthquake's destabilizing of the bedrock. Without the biologist's careful categorization of organisms into a taxonomic hierarchy of kinds—individuals into races, races into species, species into genera, and so on up the abstraction ladder to domains—Kaufman would not have been able to insert a handy one-page index at the back of his field guide. In looking up "Finches" within this index, I am taken to a page where I will discover, near the Purple and Cassin's Finch information with which I am familiar, information new to me about their genetic neighbor the Pine Grosbeak.

The discipline of precision comes from the recognition that without subjecting our thoughts and actions, and our memories and expectations, to careful analysis and systematic organization, we will never learn from our failures and often may not even recognize that we have failed. And if this is so, we will never develop intellectually and morally, and so in the long run will be unable to sustain our involvement with what romance has shown us to be the most important things in life. Thus romance needs precision, but so likewise does precision need romance. Precision by itself is boring. Students forced to learn it as a deadly parade of "inert knowledge" will suffer "dulled minds" ("Rhythmic Claims" 31), says Whitehead, and the schools will produce as they so often do "a plentiful array of dunces" (34), "a disheartened crowd of young folk, inoculated against any outbreak of intellectual zeal" (38). If precision blooms as a fruit of romance, however, if it functions as its champion, then the discipline it requires of us can become self-discipline, because we will recognize that, although precision may lack much in the way of its own intrinsic importance, its instrumental importance is fundamental.

The grammar of the natural sciences is where we usually turn for a paradigm of precise knowledge, but unfortunately science education far too often also offers itself as a paradigm of inert knowledge. Teaching the results of prior scientific inquiry as a self-contained system is to divorce those results from the romantic interests that systematic inquiry was devised to clarify, protect, and further. The system in all its splendid details needs to be taught, of course. However, our science teachers should not plunk us down in lecture halls right off, where what we are taught is from first to last a well-ordered array of theories and formulae along with the facts they correctly predict. Instead, we should be in laboratories from the very first, engaged in inquiries that are initially romantic and that become precise only as it becomes apparent precision is called for. We should discover conceptual analysis as a welcome lifeboat when the sea of our romantic adventuring becomes too much of a good thing and we begin to drown in its tidal wave of unrelenting importances.

In the beginning, apart from any measuring instruments and laws of nature, is the unsolved problem—into the presence of which our teachers should lure but not lead us. We need to realize by our own floundering that this problem calls for a Cartesian treatment: will need to be specified more clearly, analyzed into smaller more easily grasped problems, distinguished from all sorts of pseudo-problems and irrelevancies, and some suggestions made for how to set about resolving the little problems and through them the bigger one. Only then, with the issues sized up and the likely lines of inquiry suggested, is it time to take measurements, to begin refining the problem by quantifying it, formulating the hypotheses in ways that are testable, setting up protocols and control groups and other useful assurances of objectivity. As these systematic methods are instituted, and again as preliminary results suggest refinements or even major reformulations, literature searches will be appropriate, and consideration of the established theories and formulae that are likely to be relevant. Science so taught, hands-on, problem-oriented, collaborative, is an example of how to keep precision married to romance, to have its resulting knowledge lively rather than inert.

Precision in the humanities should be similarly construed. There are other ways to be precise than by acts of quantification. The grammar of language has its appropriate precisions, and so our humanities teachers should be always fashioning ways by which we can learn to speak a language competently, to express an idea within the framework of a particular genre's expectations, to think through a complex qualitative issue critically, to express ourselves clearly and gracefully, to argue a case cogently, to reason systematically around a hermeneutical circle. Here too there is a right way and a wrong way, appropriate and inappropriate methods and styles and stances, and the only way to success is through discipline, a discipline at first discovered as necessary by the primrose paths and foolish pronouncements into which blind enthusiasms lead, a discipline then taught to us by a mentoring teacher or a more advanced student, but eventually a discipline become self discipline.

Whitehead at times seems to associate the humanities with romance, the sciences with precision, locating them at different places in his calendar of how the stages of education should mount up from preschool to completion of a university degree. In doing so, however, he speaks carelessly. His stages of learning apply in all three levels to any field of inquiry. Precision belongs to both humanistic and scientific modes of learning. All knowledge must begin with curiosity and imaginative exploration, and then lead on to conceptual analysis with its self-correcting systematization. If learning is to be genuinely developmental, it must in all its instances begin with a stage of imaginative freedom that matures into a stage of well-honed discipline.

Freedom

Both these stages of education, however, ought then to find their completion in a new stage of freedom, which Whitehead calls generalization. A facet of generalization that we have not yet developed is the relational sense of self-fulfillment it implies, the cultivation of those personal and social habits that express, indeed that comprise, who we at our best can be. We are what we make of ourselves but this fundamentally involves what we make of the communities we share with other selves. When this facet of generalization is emphasized, it finds its epistemological parallel in *Symbolism*'s discussion of the art of a free society.

Whitehead says that the "art of life" is the "guidance" of "an adventure of existence," aiming at "the most complete achievement of varied activity expressing the potentialities" of an entity "in the fact of its actual environment" ("Rhythmic Claims" 39). In saying this, however, he is not taking the adventure as involving merely the fulfillment of self-interest, for life has a fundamentally communal dimension. The family into which we are born, the neighborhood in which we live, the nation of which we are citizens, collaborate in both nurturing the emergence of our individuality and permitting it to spread and flourish. The selves we fashion are selves deeply interrelated with other selves, so the task of the art of life is to balance in some viable way both individual freedom and group solidarity.

The solidarity predates us; our freedom as an individual is the task at hand. Life is "a bid for freedom on the part of organisms, a bid for a certain independence of individuality with self-interests and activities not to be construed purely in terms of environmental obligations" (*Symbolism* 65). Our freedom arises because our environmental obligations are cultural as well as biological, just as much a matter of nurture as of nature. As organisms capable of symbolic reference, we live by symbols, by the ways in which we take the sense-data of presentational immediacy as signs for interpreting the impinging importances that we feel in the mode of causal efficacy. As we develop the skills of conceptual analysis, we are able to gain a modicum of critical distance from our genetic dispositions and our unreflective cultural practices.

Whitehead calls these distancing moves "symbolically conditioned actions." They are what "enables an organism to conform its actions to long-ranged analysis of the particular circumstances of its environment" (80). Our actions are disciplined by judgments we make about their likely relevance to tomorrow's or next year's or our grandchildren's interests. We attend not only to the immediate satisfactions an action offers, or merely to the consequences we think are likely to flow from that action. We attend as well to their positive or negative contribution to the realization of our fundamental life-defining purposes. We choose how we wish to live our lives, who we are and hope to be, channeling or diverting or suppressing our natural reactions, shaping those proclivities as best we can to suit our purposes. We not only critique our interpretations of experience, we do so habitually, such that our actions are not happenstantial but are consistently conditioned by our critiques. We thereby develop a style of our own, a way of responding to the world that individualizes us. What we do and think is not just a consequence of our biology and our history but also of our chosen aims. Symbolically conditioned action is the tool by which an organism's bid for freedom results in a unique self, a free person with certain characteristic habits regarding the exercise of that freedom.

Symbols are how genetically derived instincts are transformed into culturally invented emotions. The feelings derived from causal efficacy are vague. Entering the cathedral, I am enveloped by a compelling sense of importances the origin or nature or consequence of which I cannot quite identify. They are too diffuse to grasp; they lack meaning. When certain sense-data derived from my perceptions of arching space, stained-glass light, and choral sound present themselves as referring to those feelings, when these wonderfully definite and highly manipulatable sense-data function as symbols for my feelings, they interpret them as having a specifiable meaning. I do not simply have feelings; I have feelings of mystery and awe, of transcendence.

As symbolic referencing enlarges and clarifies my awareness, I may take this feeling of transcendence as a sense of God's presence in the cathedral, and my response will be to seek out a pew where I can kneel, cross myself, and pray. Or I may take the transcendence as absence, as a belief once vital but now dried up and blown away, the cathedral abandoned to the money-changers and the tourists on whom they thrive. Later, I may find my experience echoed and intensified by recalling lines from a long-familiar poem freshly recalled as suddenly, surprisingly relevant. Perhaps, in the first case, e. e. cummings's

> I thank You God for most this amazing
> day: for the leaping greenly spirits of trees
> and a blue true dream of sky; and for everything
> which is natural which is infinite which is yes. ("I thank You God")

Or in the second case, Philip Larkin's chilling concern that

> Power of some sort or other will go on
> In games, in riddles, seemingly at random;
> But superstition, like belief, must die,
> And what remains when disbelief has gone? ("Church Going")

The symbols enhance the feelings they interpret by lifting them into the meaningful world within which we dwell, but reciprocally the symbols are in turn enhanced by the feelings, which endow them with an importance they otherwise lack. *Anger* and *love* are just words, but when taken as words that signify my feelings those words are filled with the affective power of what they name. A vaguely felt unease becomes my anger at a friend's slight. An ill-focused attraction becomes my love of a dancer's graceful movements. The words gain a connotation, and so in speaking them we bring our conduct into harmony with the emotive power they evince. We speak the words "I hate you" angrily, the words "Let me kiss you" lovingly. We believe, and rightly so, that there is something profoundly inappropriate about hostile words said lovingly or words of endearment said angrily. "The object of symbolism is the enhancement of the importance of what is symbolized," but it also charges the symbols with "emotional efficacy" (63).

Thus for Whitehead an important function of symbolic expression is that it "preserves society by adding emotion to instinct" (70). It does so because symbols that have taken on the intensity of the feelings they symbolize are powerful tools for social cohesion. They evoke an emotional response in a person who sees, hears, or enacts them, and if they are presented to a number of people they are likely to provoke similar responses in each of them. "The self-organization of society depends on commonly diffused symbols evoking commonly diffused ideas, and at the same time indicating commonly understood actions" (76). The flag flying over the battlefield at Gettysburg stirs our sense of identity both with the nation for which it stands and with the others in the crowd who salute it, hand over heart, as the national anthem is sung—even when the field is not a national cemetery but a soccer pitch and what is to follow not a Memorial Day service but the MLS championship. One nation indivisible, but affirmed by each of us as a free expression of our own understanding of who we are, and what our nation means for who we are, and what we mean for what it is. We students need to go to Memorial Day services and soccer matches, pray in cathedrals and dig bones from the Montana shale, not just sit in classrooms, if we are to learn the art of life as free citizens in a free society.

Because symbols can be transported easily from place to place and adapted to varying contexts and purposes, they tend to outlast their initial purpose. So they begin to accumulate connotations that reach back generations. "A word gathers emotional signification from its emotional history in the past; and this is transferred symbolically to its meaning in present use" (84). We have already encountered this notion in the previous chapter, in the guise of an "*It*," a symbol that serves as a portmanteau for innumerable specific images and emotions, stories and ideas that it has come over time to mean.

Whatever the obscure origins of the word *freedom* and its cognates, its primary meaning has been political. It has became vested with the aspirations of slaves and peasants, the conquered, the dispossessed, the marginalized—everyone whose choices about the sort of individual they would make of themselves were subjugated to another's will. Freedom has been the battle cry in ethnic, religious, and regional wars, in struggles for the political, economic, and sexual liberation of women, for the rights of workers to organize unions, for children to be safe from exploitation, for gays and lesbians to marry, for all sorts of differences to be appreciated rather than repressed.

The accretions of meaning are not always positive, however. No one is against freedom any more, although many are content to define their privileged place in society as an expression of freedom while downplaying the plight of the underprivileged, blaming their condition on their unwise exercise of freedom. And many others are quick to twist the meaning of freedom to serve purposes that in fact deny it, as the Nazis posted the slogan "Arbeit macht frei" ("Work Sets You Free") over the gates of their concentration camps, and as many another regime before and after has used Orwellian doublespeak to assure those over whom it rules that their servitude is what frees them from enemies foreign and domestic, that their freedom from a former master is to be found in the chains with which their new master shackles them.

Today, in telling friends over a cup of coffee that "I prize my freedom," my words thus do more than describe a wish to be left alone. They also conjure up flickering images of brave Athenians at Marathon or embattled GIs on Omaha Beach, pictures of a bare-breasted Liberty at the Parisian barricades or Frodo struggling with himself and Gollum in an attempt to cast the One Ring into Mount Doom, memories of suffragettes marching on Washington or Martin Luther King Jr. making his "I have a dream" speech.

These images and countless more haunt my words, investing them with an intensity quite out of proportion to the reality of the situation in which they were uttered. I was, after all, only saying I couldn't be bothered to accept a particular obligation with which others were hoping to saddle me. Yet anyone who wants to gainsay my wish must do battle with all the heroes whose defense of freedom has made my trivial appeal to its value possible. Were I to say merely that I prize my selfishness, that resistance would vanish. For the notion of selfishness conjures narrow virtues and a host of important vices, whereas the notion of freedom is home to virtues that are among the widest, deepest, most profound of our culture's goods, and in thinking of it we rarely think of any associated vices at all. We define ourselves, and protect ourselves against how others might define us, by the symbols to which we pledge allegiance.

The power of historically freighted symbols like the word *freedom* lies both in their massive connotational significance and in their ability to bring people together whose understandings of that significance are not as congruent as they might think they are. "The symbol evokes loyalties to vaguely conceived notions, fundamental for our spiritual natures" (74). These notions remain vague enough that they can encompass a considerable range of actual difference, while yet being precise enough to be lifted from instinct to emotion, to become something consciously embraced by those who feel their importance. For one person, the predominant feature of freedom might be economic, for another religious, for a third sexual. Yet they stand side by side at the barricades, their rifles aimed at the approaching enemies of freedom, believing in their mutual equality and finding comradeship in their common purpose. Their shout of "freedom" is a portmanteau ample enough to hold them all.

The "efficacy of symbols," says Whitehead, is that they are "at once preservative of the commonweal and of the individual standpoint" (66). They both bind us together and, by also individuating us, free us from that self-imposed bondage. Both the binding and the freeing are crucial. Totalitarians forget the importance of the freeing; anarchists, the importance of the binding. If the first function of symbols is to preserve society, their second is to afford "a foothold for reason by its delineation of the particular instinct which it expresses" (70). Symbols afford that foothold by sustaining multiple individual interpretations within the binding unity they create. "Language binds a nation together by the common emotions which it elicits, and is yet the instrument whereby freedom of thought and of individual criticism finds its expression" (68).

We are now in a position to understand why, according to Whitehead, the educational stage of generalization is a return to the freedom that marked the stage of romance, but a helical return, a return that transforms the character both of that initial romantic freedom and of the disciplined precision to which it gives rise. The work of precision has been to hone the skills of conceptual analysis, so that we are adept at clarifying and systematizing our sense-data. With generalization, we take precision a step further by applying its skills to a transformation of the established ways in which our sense-data have been interpreted. Conceptual analysis is not enough. It improves on traditional forms of symbolic reference by correcting mistaken interpretations and enhancing the emotional and pragmatic relevance of successful ones. But it needs to mature, to become symbolically coordinated action, if we are to have any chance of making the transition from mere living to living better or living well. For this upgrade to occur, our critiques must be made in conscious awareness of the wider environment of meanings they inhabit, most importantly the deeply rooted cultural meanings that are the basis for both our community and our individuality.

Generalization thus occurs when reason is put to work in the transformative criticism of our socially accepted symbols and engaging in these critiques becomes our standard practice. The revision is an expression of individuality: it requires the freedom of interpretation made possible by selves who have developed their critical skills in individuating ways, and it results in a furthering of those skills and hence that individuality. But what are revised are the symbols of societal solidarity, those we and our fellow citizens hold in common, our shared heritage. The revision strengthens those symbols and hence those common goods. It binds us closer together even as it sharpens our individuality.

The waterfowl populations are declining because the wetlands in our county where they nest are drying up, the water diverted elsewhere for agricultural irrigation or housing developments. Farmers need to make a living and an expanding population needs more homes in which to live. These changes are not the work of selfish people interested only in their own enrichment; they are foreseeable consequences of an expanding economy. Those who favor these changes may see them as signs of progress, argue that supporting them is to support the common good of this county and its citizens, and marshal corporate money and the clout of establishment politicians in support of a mainstream candidate at the next election. Environmentalists may rail against the developers for their disdain of egrets and pelicans, preach the gospel of deep ecology, stage protest marches at the county courthouse, and campaign for a green candidate. If so, the resulting polarization will force us all to choose between conservation and jobs, between goody-two-shoes elitism and Joe-six-pack populism. Either the established ways will be reaffirmed, reinforced to the point of recalcitrance by the growing resentment of the shrill protesters. Or the protesters will somehow succeed in halting the process, but because they have alienated the now recalcitrant majority it will not be long before a way is found around the restrictions on development. Whatever the outcome, neither development nor conservation will be well served, and the county's sense of community will have been damaged.

The common ground shared by these factions is the common good to which all sides have from the very first appealed: the value of actions that improve the quality of life for county residents. The obvious but difficult strategy for resolving the dispute is therefore to bring that sense of common good from background to foreground, and to articulate its meaning in a way that suggests the possibility of nondivisive courses of public and private action. The palette of such possibilities is a familiar one by now. Hunters need wetlands to draw the migrating mallards and teals they love to shoot. Parklands and greenways associated with wildlife sanctuaries make an area more attractive to tourists and prospective residents, and to employers attempting to attract them both. Home values are protected by well-crafted land-use plans and zoning laws. Farmers find legal arrangements attractive that allow them to trade lower taxes for a permanent commitment of their land to agricultural purposes or for its sale when they retire to a conservancy. And let it not be forgotten that green enterprises create new kinds of jobs.

The reasons that lead citizens to cooperate are as diverse as the citizens, but they mature as individuals each with a distinctive moral character as they find their interests are more alike than they had thought. A win-win, nonzero option begins to emerge, and when it does it usually carries the day. Things often go wrong, of course, as narrow interests persist and are fed by the emotions on which they rest, but the solidarity of the citizenry once rekindled, or perhaps kindled for the first time, is a powerful force. It's not good fences that make good neighbors, it's good symbolically conditioned actions.

As Whitehead puts it, "the symbolic expression of instinctive forces drags them out into the open; it differentiates them and delineates them. There is then opportunity for reason to effect, with comparative speed, what otherwise must be left to the slow operation of the centuries amid ruin and reconstruction" (69). The symbols in need of transformative revision are matters of social ritual and command, acceptable practices and explicit rules, established conventions and legislative acts, systems of value and faith commitments. "Codes, rules of behavior, canons of art, are attempts to impose systematic action which on the whole will promote favourable symbolic interactions. As a community changes, all such rules and canons require revision in the light of reason" (87–88).

Generalization is thus the practice of symbol revision, the way by which frays and tears in the social fabric are constantly repaired, by which a society's dwindling inventory of innovative potential is restocked. It is the way by which the rules of our common life are kept attuned to "the ultimate purposes for which the society exists" (88), attuned to the system of meanings that constitutes the cultural worldview by which our social interactions are nurtured and therefore by which our lives, our distinctively individuated selves, are fulfilled. "Free men obey the rules which they themselves have made" (88). The practice of generalization make us free because by thinking and acting as generalists we make a social order that depends on the freedom of its citizens and by doing so enhances their freedom.

We are free only if we act freely. Unless we are habitually critiquing our established symbols in order to restore their effectiveness as sources of both solidarity and individuality, our freedom will be lost. Insofar as we accept uncritically the standard ways of thinking and acting, we slip into a new kind of instinctive way of living that Whitehead calls "reflex action." We have transformed our instincts into emotions and then shaped those emotions to express our individuality, all by acts of conceptual analysis that are in turn shaped by symbolically conditioned actions. If we don't sustain the transforming critique of symbols central to this process, however, the important beliefs and values by which we live will become blind routines, the emotions they express will fall out of conscious awareness, and we will come to behave in ways no different than we did when our ideas and actions were governed primarily by our natural instincts. We will have reverted to a preromantic stage educationally, to a precivilized stage culturally. "Reflex action is a relapse towards a more complex type of instinct on the part of organisms which enjoy, or have enjoyed, symbolically conditioned action" (79). The acts of jingoistic patriotism to which we so often succumb in times of war are reflex actions, as are our routine acts of conformity in which public opinion becomes unthinkingly our own opinion and the current fads a substitute for our own preferences.

This rebarbarization process is our destiny unless we endlessly labor to prevent it. The endless laboring is the default setting for effective social order because that order is always a fragile achievement, always needing to be regained in order to be sustained. Our communal achievements, the fruit of critique, will wilt or rot in the absence of further critique. Just as education should not be, in Whitehead's vivid image, like "packing articles in a trunk" ("Rhythmic Claims" 33), as though what we know is a box of items that once acquired can be kept safely in a closet until we have need for them, so also with regard to civilized order. Our educational development and the viability of our communal arrangements are like food, needing to be fresh and suitable if they are to nurture us. Symbolically conditioned action, the soul of generalization, is the source of the seed and soil, and also of the plow and hoe, by means of which fresh concepts and practices are able to sprout from established ones, and can eventually be harvested for the continued sustenance of the civilization they express.

Revolutions are not a solution to the problem of reflex action, since their full-bore attack on the social order can quickly become excessive, leading to its collapse rather than purification and renovation. Whitehead notes that the English Revolution "barely escaped a disruption of its social system," and the French Revolution "did for a time experience this collapse," whereas the much more moderate American Revolution "was never in any such danger" (70). The cause of revolution is typically the intransigence of those in power, sustained by the reflex actions of the populace in its blind loyalty to familiar tradition-hallowed ways. For the advocates of change to break through this barrier, they need to build a countervailing force more emotionally intense than the one resisting them, and when this force breaches that barrier it tends like any explosion to eradicate everything around it. Those who have demanded liberty for all soon outrun their initial aim, instituting a reign of terror that in order to destroy the enemies of liberty destroys the liberty that had been achieved. Society collapses into anarchy or staves it off by a restoration of the old authority or the creation of a new authority that is its twin.

The function of education, not as embodied in just a nation's schools and universities but in all its institutions that nurture the practices of citizenship, is to help young people develop the habits of conceptual analysis—typically called "critical thinking" in the current pedagogic literature—that lead to the symbolically conditioned actions—the "creative engagement"—by which the reflex actions of extremist radicals and reactionaries can be avoided and goods at once common and individual continually fostered.

Generalization is the stage of education where students learn the art of life, the practice of which is the art required of a free society. It is a form of wisdom, an "active wisdom" relentlessly "battling with the immediate experiences of life," seeking to "qualify each immediate moment with relevant ideas and appropriate actions" ("Rhythmic Claims" 37). The "final mark" of such wisdom is adaptive power: "the successful adaptation of old symbols to changes of social structure" (*Symbolism* 61). It is also transformational power: "that knowledge which adds greatness to character is knowledge so handled as to transform every phase of immediate experience" ("Rhythmic Claims" 32). Active involvement not passive withdrawal, but for the sake of transformation not replacement, of adaptation not rejection.

And so Whitehead ends *Symbolism* thus:

> The art of free society consists first in the maintenance of the symbolic code; and secondly in fearlessness of revision, to secure that the code serves those purposes which satisfy an enlightened reason. Those societies which cannot combine reverence to their symbols with freedom of revision, must ultimately decay either from anarchy, or from the slow atrophy of a life stifled by useless shadows. (88)

CHAPTER FOUR

Learning to Reason

King Solomon dreams that he asks the Lord for an understanding mind, one able to distinguish good from evil, so that he might be able to govern his people wisely. The Lord grants the king's wish but then also gives him, unasked, riches and honor and long life. Or so the story goes that the priests have spun for us in I Kings 3:5–15.

In this chapter, I will explore the hypothesis that there are striking parallels between Whitehead's notions of romance, precision, and generalization and his notions in *The Function of Reason* of speculative reason, practical reason, and the logic of discovery. By explicating these parallels, I will be in a position to argue that the aim of education should be to prepare us, children and adults alike, to live out the promise of Solomon's dream—to live meaningfully by reasoning effectively, in accord with the truth of the world, and thereby to contribute in some way to its salvation.

The Function of Reason is a metaphysical exploration of the fundamental features of our world—of this universe in which we find ourselves. Whitehead says that if we look at what we know about the history of the world, the way it works, the changes that have taken places over the billions of years it has existed, we can discern "two main tendencies in the course of events. One tendency is exemplified in the slow decay of physical nature. . . . The other tendency is exemplified by the yearly renewal of nature in the spring, and by the upward course of biological evolution" ("Introductory Summary"). These are cosmological concerns, ideas having to do with tendencies in the whole of the natural order. Whitehead describes them as kinds of reason, the speculative sort and the practical sort. So reason is not simply a human faculty but is generalized so that it is key to all natural processes, both constructive and destructive ones. It is also the source of the capacity in nature for reconciling these two warring tendencies.

Thus, we will be carried in this chapter from the aesthetic emphases of chapter 2 and the epistemological explorations of chapter 3 to a focus on natural philosophy. As our horizon broadens, however, those earlier concerns will not be discarded. Rather, they will be expanded. The arts of the enchanter and of a free society are among the ways in which humans reason about their interests, and are key to an understanding of how human history has unfolded and the cosmos has evolved. The need constantly to reconcile Appearance and Truth, causal efficacy and presentational immediacy, expresses both the power and the limits of our rational capacity to fashion through symbolically conditioned action open systems of interpretation, systems the character of which is also found in biological and geological evolution and in the nature of a universe in which all things, including that universe itself, are irremediably transient.

Precisely Ulysses

Consider first the notion of practical reason and its similarities to precision. Whitehead associates this function of reason with the wily hero of the *Odyssey*, the one who devised the Trojan Horse and who after twenty years of adventures on the wine-dark sea made it back to Ithaca in the nick of time to save his kingdom from those who would usurp it. Practical reason, like Ulysses, is "entirely pragmatic, with a short range of forecast" (*Function* 17), concentrating on how best to serve "our immediate interests" (11). It is engaged in "the piecemeal discovery and clarification of methodologies" (37). It is "the discipline of shrewdness" (66), subjecting our urge toward some desired end to a well-ordered strategy for attaining it, but also criticizing the effectiveness of that method by lifting into "conscious experience the detailed operations possible within [its] limits" (37). Ulysses and his ilk take satisfaction in the success of their clever methods, and so reuse and refine them until they become ingrained habits, some of which, "arising out of an immemorial heredity," produce the "primitive deep-seated satisfaction" comprising our common sense (17). Thereby, our spontaneous urges and ephemeral dreams, our emotional outbursts and fitful efforts, are "canalized between the banks of custom" (40).

In the light of this description, we can see more clearly what our education should include during the stage of precision. Precision is where we should learn what the shrewd method-makers have made for us, what our wily elders have wrought so that we, after them, might lead fulfilling lives. Reading, writing, and 'rithmetic are the basic methods, the well-honed time-tested instruments by which we are most likely to achieve our ends. They are what works, the building blocks on which all else depends—the trivium undergirding whatever comprises today's quadrivium. To be proficient in the uses of practical reason, we must acquire certain specific methodological skills. There are right ways and wrong ways to swing a hammer or design a building, to manage a business or build a political consensus, and we need to learn what those differences are.

Such knowledge is not abstract and theoretical. It is practical hands-on knowing that is only interested in an idea if it provides access to an effective method for getting something done. To know is to know how. We learn how a method works by practicing it. We don't learn how to swim by reading books. We get in the water to learn how to swim, and we learn how to swim well by practicing appropriate swimming strokes. We learn how to read by reading books, and we learn how to read well by reading good books. We become leaders by leading.

We learn by doing, but the learning process is not a matter of trial and error. It is a process of acquiring access to a set of precise skills for manipulating a complexly ordered sequence or pattern of steps that if used properly will lead us from an initially unsatisfying situation to one that satisfies us. The system is what counts, the rules by which to proceed, the map indicating the route by which to arrive at our destination. Ulysses didn't just sail randomly west from Troy, hoping for the best. He was wily not only because he could improvise a way out of an unexpected danger but also because he had an end in view and a toolbox of techniques for achieving it. Indeed, his clear-eyed sense of his ultimate and proximate goals, in combination with his set of familiar oft-used tools, is why he was so good at improvising.

So cleverness is not a matter of chutzpah but of sound training in the best ways to get things done. The methods of precision are the recipes by which to make a delicious pie, the blueprints by which to construct a functional house, the tactics by which to win a decisive battle, the laws by which to govern a people well. They are predictions that work, game plans that bring victory, compromises that reconcile differences, aesthetic techniques that turn raw materials into works of beauty.

When we return to the school laboratory with a piece of the weeping rock we found, our teacher suggests that we use a well-established protocol for determining its chemical makeup. Following it, we dissolve scrapings from the rock in water and then mix in some diluted hydrochloric acid.

There being no precipitate, we then add hydrogen sulphide, and when there is still no precipitate we next add baking soda or a similar base to increase the pH of the solution. Still no precipitate, so we take a fourth step and add ammonium carbonate, which results at last in a precipitate that when held to a flame burns orange-red. These steps lead us down a road with many forks, until we come at the end of the road to an answer to our question: the rock is made of some kind of calcium compound.

This protocol is a version of the method of division used by Plato in defining a sophist and a statesman in the two dialogues named after them: divide your unknown into two subgroups and decide to which one it belongs, then divide that subgroup in two and decide to which one the unknown belongs, and continue in this manner until you find out what it is. Chemists today use the direct method of atomic absorption spectroscopy to determine what elements are present in a sample, but the method of division remains the best inexpensive option, especially when fine detail is not needed. It is the method we used in deciding that the bird we had seen was a Pine Grosbeak rather than a Purple or a Cassin's Finch.

The problem with a satisfactory method is that it becomes self-satisfied. It works, and that is sufficient. "There is no interest beyond the scope of the method," indeed there is an "active interest restraining curiosity within the scope of the method" (17). Whitehead argues that this "inertial resistance" to change, to whatever lies outside a successful method, is an "obscurantism" from which we all suffer, a tendency inherent in "human nature," the "refusal to speculate freely on the limitations of traditional methods" (43). Success, in other words, breeds "fatigue," an inclination "excluding the impulse toward novelty," a "baffling of opportunity," a willingness to accept the "mere repetition" of what is familiar as sufficient (23).

Familiarity breeds closure. Undergraduate courses in Modern Western Philosophy are almost always taught by beginning with Descartes and ending with Kant, and textbooks and collections of primary sources are organized that way, as are the secondary sources and handy commercial summaries. It would be difficult in the extreme to beat against that current and design a course that reorganizes the syllabus around two strands, a scientific one rooted in Descartes and a humanistic-historical one rooted in Vico, that meet not in Kant but in Hegel. Or to offer a course that begins with Kant and works backward to Descartes, or one that meets nine to twelve hours a week in seminar format, students and professor engaged in line-by-line analyses of only Descartes's *Discourse on Method,*

Locke's *An Essay Concerning Human Understanding*, and Kant's *Foundations of the Metaphysics of Morals*.

Such ventures would be thought idiosyncratic at best, and showboating at worst. Courses of this sort would soon disappear, along with their authors, and the natural way of teaching Modern Philosophy would reappear, to everyone's relief. This recalcitrance to change should be no surprise, however, even in an academic environment that officially honors innovation and is composed primarily of young people who supposedly disdain tradition. After all, in each course for which we students enroll, we sit each subsequent day in the same seat where we chose to sit the first day, and our teachers at their department and faculty meetings are equally unimaginative.

The need for closure, Whitehead argues, finds ready expression as an "anti-empirical dogmatism," a refusal to accept evidence lying "outside the scope" of our accepted methodologies (15). This dogmatism was once the bane of the medieval scholastics; it now mars the work of their successors, especially those at the apex of our current academic pecking order, the natural scientists. Once these children of Galileo and Newton led the attack against scholastic ways of thinking, which they said used theological concepts and deductive reasoning in a field of study for which they were unsuited. These advocates of scientific method trumpeted first-hand empirical investigation and inductive reasoning as the better way to study nature, and the proof that they were right was the success of their method at materially improving our lives. But a few centuries of success have bred a contentment among scientists as dogmatic as that of the scholastics. Cardinal Bellarmine couldn't be bothered to look for the moons of Jupiter through Galileo's telescope because he knew for sure there could be none. Today we can't be bothered to look because we know for sure there are some.

Uninterested in what lies outside their method and unaware of their own basic assumptions, modern scientists and we who are their loyal followers have a tendency to push scientific theories beyond the "proper scope" of their use, confident that they will work wherever they are applied. Yet when applied thus in situations for which they were not designed, "definite error results" (75). Quantification, for instance, is an important trick by which to organize our experiences. Although the scientific method is not a single way of doing things but rather a wide range of procedures for explaining empirically derived information, what these procedures all have in common is that they fit their information into a system of relationships expressible in mathematical or logical symbols, by means of which further empirical information can be predicted and verified. That we think of this cluster of approaches as the paradigm for precision, however, as the only trick for system building worth our while, is because it is the method that dominates our era. Indeed, it is so dominant that approaches to knowledge for which other methods are better suited often try valiantly to model themselves on the natural sciences, or at least to call themselves sciences as well.

Economics makes valuable use of quantification in devising models of dynamic processes within a market, although the presence of "externalities" and the impact of choices made in awareness of those models makes it notoriously difficult for the models to have the predictive power needed for economics to call itself a legitimate science. Political science is a discipline ill suited to concocting nontrivial covering laws that have precise predictive power, although many of its practitioners claim to be doing so or at least to have that goal as a realistic aspiration. Even historians have flirted with the idea of making their discipline a science, but they come closest to succeeding only when writing narrowly focused monographs.

Literature professors write essays in which their intuitions are dressed up as precise hermeneutical hypotheses, and are easily spoofed by books such as Frederick Crews's classic, *The Pooh Perplex*, and its sequel, *Postmodern Pooh*, in each of which a dozen different literary theories are exposed for their pretentious claims to respectability. Analytic philosophers love to translate their protocol sentences into symbols, number them with primed and double-primed variants, and then manipulate these symbols as though they are the well-formed formulas of a predicate calculus in which syntactic precision is matched by semantic precision.

Valorizing scientific method in this way is an indication of its status as the reigning dogma. The problem is not the method, of course, but the dogma—the confidence that it has worked successfully in some areas and that therefore there is no limit to where it will work if appropriately applied. Any method accepted as legitimate, even one not involving quantification or lacking predictive power, will be a source of obscurantism if it is taught as a dogmatic finality. The success of one kind of method can lead us to be so blinded by that success that we treat other methods as also sources of finality as long as they are validated as genuine methods.

Much of our world today is marked by a titanic struggle for dominance between the dogma of a scientific approach to things and the dogma of a religious approach. The religious dogmas are predominantly Islamic and Christian, the scientific dogmas secular and atheistic. This clash of obscurantisms bodes ill for the civilizations they hold hostage, because all the parties to the conflict suffer a fatigue the consequence of which can only be decay and collapse. "Some of the major disasters of mankind have been produced by the narrowness of men with a good methodology." Ulysses disdained what was not pragmatically workable, "and the bones of his companions are strewn on many a reef and many an isle" (12). From this widespread hubris there can be no escape short of a critique that comes from outside of any dogma, a critique that lies not only beyond the familiar methods but also beyond all method. Educationally, this escape can come only by rejecting the practice of centering the learning process on the stage of precision.

Platonic Romance

For Whitehead, as we know, the stage of romance should precede that of precision. My hypothesis paralleling these stages to the modes of reason suggests that investigating the nature of speculative reason will give us insight into the character of romantic learning.

Speculation is the sort of reasoning Whitehead identifies with Plato: "enthroned above the practical tasks of the world" (*Function* 37), seeking "with disinterested curiosity an understanding of the world" (38). Speculation has the "power of going for the penetrating idea, even if it has not yet been worked into any methodology" (45). "Transcending all method," it is a "flight after the unattainable" (65) that manages, if it is lucky, to "clutch" something attainable, "some refreshing novelty" (23).

The ancient notion of genius identifies this transcending power as divine, and sprinkles the world with minor deities who account for wondrous features of nature and the extraordinary abilities of some humans. Socrates has his *daemon*, who warns him about an impending poor choice or tendency toward false consciousness. Merlin is able to foresee what others cannot and so in mysterious enigmatic ways is able to protect Arthur from his enemies and from all but the most costly instance of his own foolishness, guiding him from a distance toward his destiny. Hegel conceives of the spirit of an age as its genius, its exceptional manner of historical being, a spirit that fills a world-historical hero with its alluring possibility and through whose actions it is thereby actualized.

Except for the lingering notion of guardian angels, our secular age no longer imagines the source of genius to be divine, but it remains a power transcending the ordinary, breaking free of the chains of normal methods, soaring beyond the expected, able to see not so much into the future as into the heart of things. We are disconcerted, often annoyed, when a genius enrolls in one of our classes—the math student who always "intuits" the correct answer and so has no work to show how it was arrived at; the art history student who "sees" effortlessly not only the meaning the painted surface expresses but also the meaning of that meaning; the political science student who "senses" with unerring accuracy the shift in voter attitudes before the polls have provided any confirming data. Arthur Schopenhauer is credited with putting it succinctly: "Talent hits a target no one else can hit; Genius hits a target no one else can see" (e.g., Bergman 137).

This "disturbing element" in human nature has a dark side, however, for it has "goaded races onward, sometimes to their destruction" (65). It has been expressed historically "in the guise of sporadic inspirations" by "seers, prophets, men with a new secret," offering "fire, or salvation, or release, or moral insight" (66). Unfortunately, for the most part these seers have been "presumptuous, ignorant, incompetent, unbalanced," a bunch of deceitful "false prophets" (67), their inspirations "aberrations of the mere undisciplined imagination," mere "airy generalizations" that were "tenuous, unpractical, and a waste of time" (76). We are surrounded by a thousand such prophets, who predict the end of the free market, the end of history, the end of the world, the victory of the proletariat, the birth of a new age, an opportunity for making money that can't be missed, a rainstorm that will end the drought. The probability that their speculations might prove worthwhile are so slim, says Whitehead, that "perhaps it is safer to stone them, in some merciful way" (67).

The stoning is wiser than it might at first seem, since speculation can be a destructive force, its appetition anarchic, achieving quickly "the descent toward nothingness" that obscurantism slowly brings about (34). The geniuses prophesying an imminent end of the old ways and emergence of a new way come bearing gifts we should hesitate to accept: passionate first love promising lifelong commitment, upfront money leading to a guaranteed Ponzi payoff, a Kool-Aid ticket to Paradise, a Reign of Terror preparing the way for an earthly Utopia. It would seem that the bleached bones of the followers of Plato are also, like those of Ulysses, strewn over the world's reefs and isles—even if with more panache.

The problem with speculation, from the perspective of practical reason, is its fancy "apparatus of vague notions" (58). Its governing principles are not "clear, distinct, and certain" (49), and so it cannot attain the method that practical reason makes central to its activity. Whitehead, however, thinks this insistence on precision in fundamental matters a "pathetic desire" we should resist (51). We should not only tolerate the vague, blurry, uncertain products of speculation, we should actively seek them out. It is the aspiration of romance that we will come to love and cherish these impracticalities lurking everywhere across the landscape of our seemingly everyday world, ready to surprise and delight us if we are inquisitive enough to glimpse their presence.

Notice how my proposed analogy confounds what one might at first expect, for Plato's mode of reasoning is abstract and theoretical whereas romance is aesthetic and concrete in its concerns. Why not associate Plato with the stage of precision and Ulysses with the romantic stage? The answer is that speculative reason is not about abstraction. It is about disinterested curiosity, being exuberantly inquisitive about things, wondering about anything whatsoever, whether concrete or abstract, and curious about them for their own sake, apart from any practical interests they might serve. Plato's reason is about unbounded exploration, an adventurous poking and prying not walled in by some abstract system and its defining methodology. Speculating about what might be under a rock is not to spin a theory but to turn it over.

Practicality means being oriented toward an end, having some outcome in mind the attaining of which will be in some sense satisfying—fulfilling a desire, keeping a promise, reaching a goal, realizing a good. Hence its tendency to dogmatic closure, because excluding what is irrelevant to the task at hand is crucial for success. Single-mindedness is a practical virtue. But romance and speculative reason are impractical because they are not interested in outcomes, in goals and goods. They offer us journeys unconstrained by established pathways—undisciplined meanders, flights of fancy, off-road imaginings, unbelievably strange adventures.

Romantic pedagogy is difficult because applying it in a classroom situation means teachers cannot predetermine the structure within which we students will be expected to operate. A standard lesson plan is a method for accomplishing a particular educative end: acquiring a body of information or learning a procedure for acquiring such information. The lesson plan is appropriately evaluated by determining whether that end was indeed accomplished, whether we learned what the class session was designed to teach us. A standardized objective test is a device appropriate to precision learning, a method for measuring the effectiveness of a student's grasp of a methodologically defined subject matter. It is irrelevant as a device for assessing romantic learning, since romance has no defining subject matter or methodology, and so there is no way to measure success in acquiring and utilizing it.

In a classroom operating at the stage of romance, outcomes are incidental if not simply beside the point. Teachers need to provide not a structure to be followed but a structure that encourages sidestepping such structures, that gives our curiosity free reign, letting us forge ahead willy-nilly. A romantic learning environment is one in which we make foolish mistakes, head off down blind alleys, uncouthly barge in where angels fear to tread. It is not chaotic, however. The structure is there, but it is one relevant to processes rather than to outcomes. Teachers should provide occasions for inquiry, for stirring our imaginations, and then encourage us to continue whatever we end up tentatively initiating, to follow up on our vague notions or even to hop around randomly from one thing to another as it catches our fancy. The skills to be honed are those involved in noticing an opportunity for exploration, sniffing out the hidden possibilities, cantilevering an idea out onto the landscape of our understanding toward its ever-receding horizon.

We are most likely to learn these skills of romance when put in curiosity-kindling situations and encouraged to see what we can see. Our professor divides us into groups and gives each group a rigid metal plate with a heavy pillar of wood attached at each end, a handful of wood strips of various lengths and thicknesses but all of them decidedly shorter than the metal plate, a ball of string, scissors, and thumbtacks. Our task is to construct a bridge with the strips that reaches from one pillar to the other and can support a full soup can placed at its midpoint. We are not engineers; we bring only our general common sense and creative energy to the task. There is no right way to go about this task and no single correct solution to the problem: any bridge that can hold the soup can is a correct solution and any way that gets the group to such a solution is the right way. There will be lots of trial and error, lots of promising starts that collapse when the nth strip is attached or that make it from pillar to pillar only to collapse as soon as the soup can is added. Leaders will emerge and be replaced, some groups may give up, others persist, and anywhere from all of them to none of them will finally succeed.

The point of the exercise, however, is not for us to succeed, whether by dumb luck or by having reinvented some of the relevant laws of physics, but to learn something about how to go about doing things collaboratively, how to handle problematic situations for which we and our group have no solution ready at hand to apply, how to attain the poise with which to start over when the obvious solution goes awry and the clever alternative proves even less effective. What is at stake in these explorations is not facts or protocols or theories previously learned and now to be regurgitated, but practice in deciding what can be done with what is already known, imagining alternatives, learning from failures and partial successes to be even more inventive and persistent.

By what predetermined standards are such things measured and students and instructors held accountable? Is the professor to be praised because some of her students were clever enough or lucky enough to have built a successful bridge, and her school rated a failed institution if they didn't? Of course not; indeed, it is rather silly to imagine that learning or teaching effectiveness might be judged in that way. The reason for praising the teacher is that she devised this task, created a classroom environment within which her students could learn how to think more effectively, whether they did or did not in fact learn how. The reason for praising the school is that it encouraged this kind of pedagogical imagination. Nothing here is among the 5,000 items on E. D. Hirsh's cultural literacy list, and a school curriculum able successfully to teach students about all of those items would have done nothing to further their capacity for uninhibited speculation.

The burden of my argument is *Rethinking College Education* is that the essence of education has nothing to do with purposes and outcomes. Its primary function is to create a context within which students are able to learn the general conditions governing their pursuit of whatever purposes they might have. To begin with the practical is to be ignorant of these constraints that condition our choices of ends and means. They comprise, to use Michael Oakeshott's terminology in *On Human Conduct*, the "moral practices" of "civil association" that set the conditions within which the particular "prudential practices" of our various "enterprise associations" can flourish. These moral practices comprise, in Whitehead's language, the conditions for "civilized existence."

Because the stage of romance pays no attention to our practical purposes, because it focuses on a process defined by skills that open out an unbounded landscape of fresh possibilities for practical pursuit rather than focusing on the skills needed to achieve some particular purpose or set of purposes, it allows the general character of these undertakings to surface. It asks us to set aside our practical concerns for a moment, to bracket our Ulysses-like interest in this or that end, and to focus instead on the how of coming up with worthwhile ends and ends-justified methods. It asks us to focus on the adverbial how of our actions rather than either the nominative what and for-what or the verbal when and whereby.

Romantics come to appreciate these governing adverbs, these moral constraints to civilized behavior, because their noses are not being rubbed constantly in issues of practicality. They become alert to the ways by which an end can be judged good or a means right because they do not have to choose just now to commit themselves to the pursuit of some particular end by means of some particular method. They can play with the possible alternatives because at the moment there is no work needing to be done that calls for settling on a single course of action. This playfulness thus has a double virtue. It expands the repertoire of our experiences, exposing us to variations on familiar themes and to a widening variety of novel themes, such that in aspiration if not in actual achievement "naught that happens is alien to it" (38). Simultaneously, we rehearse again and again, as a constant amid these particular differences, the respect we owe the general conditions under which it is appropriate for those explorations to proceed.

In soccer, we engage a hundred different opposing teams in athletic contests, winning some and losing some, but in all hundred games we learn how to conform our efforts to the rules that define us, and therefore govern us as contestants. Rules for a sports contest, however, are not like rules for making a pasta sauce. The rules of a game are accepted not followed, understood as constraints on what we are permitted to do not steps we must take to reach a certain destination. Everyone who follows Julia Child's recipe for making a pasta sauce has the same goal in mind: to produce a tasty sauce as part of a meal plan. And although the end for which the meal is planned can vary tremendously—perhaps the goal is dietary or political or erotic, perhaps to honor its author or show off one's skill as a chef—the end for which the recipe is followed is the sauce.

My soccer teammates and I want to win our game, a goal the polar opposite to our opponents' goal, and our way of pursuing it follows no recipe but involves for each of us, in ways unique to our differing roles, constant innovation and split-second insight into available opportunities. The soccer rules set the conditions within which we seek our goal, and the same conditions apply to the opposing team. For the soccer game to be played, for us to achieve our goal or for them to do so at our expense, both teams must respect the same rules, must find the shared conditional requirements for play more important than the contrasting goals. We hard-nosed pragmatists cheer the winners, and the more soft-headed idealists among us cheer those who played the game well, but rarely do we cheer the referees who incarnate the rules without which a game cannot be well played or a victory attained.

In reading fantasy or science fiction stories, we enter a hundred different universes alternative to our own, and even in a wild flight of fancy imagine some of them existing simultaneously and interacting. In doing so, we also learn the limits to which even the most wildly invented universe must conform for us to find it intelligible and therefore morally interesting, worth our inventing and exploring. The Arthur myth attracts fantasy writers because it lends itself to what-if speculations about Arthur's origins, and Merlin's, about their powers and purposes, and the meaning of Avalon, about who the Lady of the Lake really was and what happened to the Knights of the Round Table after Arthur was gone.

Suppose the Lady of the Lake were a princess who survived the destruction of Atlantis, as Stephen Lawhead would have it, or suppose she were a high priestess of the Earth Goddess at Avalon, as Marion Zimmer Bradley says. Suppose Merlin learned his magical arts from the ancient Galapas in a crystal cave, as Mary Stewart tells us, or suppose he had no magic at all but simply the skills of a blacksmith and a Roman soldier, as Jack Whyte recounts it. From the great medieval poetic speculations found in the alliterations of *Sir Gawain and the Green Knight* and the octosyllabic couplets of Chrétien de Troyes's romances, to the prose of the contemporary novelists just mentioned, the attraction is in experiencing a familiar tale told from an unfamiliar perspective.

What fun it is to have our eyes skinned, our minds blown, by these speculative novelties. Not any speculation will do, however, for what makes them work is the logic of an unexpected premise or a slight departure from the taken-for-granted constants that all the familiar tellings have in common. The new world makes sense, not merely allows our suspension of disbelief but encourages it because of its plausibility once we accept the new premise or the slight departure. The stories that don't work as well are those unable to sustain the coherence of their innovation or, even more importantly, are unable to weave it in a manner consistent with the constraining basics of the original myth. Like the best soccer players, the best

Arthurian writers are wildly wonderfully innovative, but only within a set of preconditions normative to any assessment of the success of their endeavor or, more accurately, to any assessment of whether the endeavor is of a kind eligible for such assessment. It might be a good novel, but one has to play by the Arthurian rules of the game for it to be a good Arthurian novel.

I help build a hundred wood-strip bridges, including those that function as drawbridges across moats to my sand castles, before I realize that elegance in the manner of construction and parsimony in the choice of materials utilized are aesthetic considerations that I might wish to take into account, that there is more to bridge-building excellence than engineering. When aesthetic criteria are added to the governing constraints on bridge design, the result is not a further limitation on engineers but the formulation of a different notion of design. The game itself has been changed, in a way that doesn't fetter speculation but instead redirects it.

It was easy enough to bridge the moat by accumulating enough wood strips and gluing them together until they were long enough and solid enough to stretch between pillars placed on each side. But now I wonder if I could pull off this bridging by using only a few strips somehow arched across the span and therefore requiring not pillars but only anchors at each end. My imagination is stirred by the newly added aesthetic conditions, not constrained. Physical principles come into play that were previously irrelevant, that perhaps were only discovered by me in the process of exploring this novel thought. Alternative uses for string begin to tease the corners of my mind, and examples of spanning that don't have to do with bridges become of interest, like how a saddle-backed roof shape can span two widely separated walls that normal pitched roofs can only do with supporting center posts. The engineering issues remain crucial, of course, but their focus has been shifted. It's just like how the focus on efficient movement shifts when a skater abandons speed skating for figure skating, or when an aging baseball pitcher abandons a focus on wins and strikeouts in order to become an effective middle-distance reliever.

By associating speculative reason with romance, we can see that romance is about more than the pokings and pryings of random curiosity at the edges of the familiar. It also has to do with a more holistic kind of curiosity, with the conditions that make novel standpoints and perspectives possible. Seeing things afresh, imagining afresh what cannot or cannot yet be seen, appreciating novelties for what they are, simply for their being there: these are aesthetic proclivities that romance nurtures. Speculative reason expands the range and interdependence of what stirs our curiosity, thickening our experiences of the things that are and might be, by imagining novel conditions for what we think perceivable or perceive as cognizable. Speculative romance stretches the character of aesthetic experience from earth to sky, from right here to the farthest edge of the imaginable, by exploring new kinds of principles by which our lives and all their particular aims and interests and desires might be governed. We learn amid our aesthetic play the conditions of civilized existence, the constraints that when acknowledged, respected, internalized, and then finally loved, mark our emergence as responsible productive adults.

Educational practices such as those mandated by the federal "No Child Left Behind" laws are profoundly inadequate because they in fact leave every child behind by skipping over, or downgrading the importance of, the stage of learning without which the testable stage of learning has no point. The aim of education is not to train us to be architects, ornithologists, baseball pitchers, or poets who are functional barbarians. And we have had enough, surely, of programs claiming to prepare us to be governmental and business leaders that prepare us, as it turns out, to be leaders whose managerial skills are well honed but whose moral compass has rusted from disuse. Too long we have been taught facts and methods and theories but remain unable to imagine that there might be more worthwhile things that those things presuppose.

Scheming Greeks

What we have seen so far might suggest that Whitehead is describing a dyadic relation between romance and precision, between practical and speculative reason. As Plato saves Ulysses from dogmatism, so Ulysses saves Plato from dreaming irrelevance. Without romantic curiosity we become trapped inside the narrow confines of our familiar views and values. But unless our flights of fancy beyond those narrow confines are subjected to the discipline of some kind of systemic precision, their value will be dissipated by their incoherence and irrelevance, and they will simply vanish into the thin air of inanity. As we have seen, many people therefore interpret generalization as a return to romance in a new context, one where precision has ordered the world in some pragmatically beneficial way and now needs to be reminded of its limits. True enough, but there is more to generalization than this, and what that more is we can glimpse by returning to the analogy I've been proposing.

If generalization is a third stage of learning, one that carries us beyond a dyadic back and forth between the other stages, then what in *The Function of Reason* gets us beyond endlessly yo-yoing between the practical and speculative modes of reason? The new factor, argues Whitehead, is "the logic of discovery" (67), a mode of reasoning that, after hundreds of millions of years of animal life and millions of years of human life, emerged less than three thousand years ago. The "discovery of mathematics and of logic introduced method into speculation" (40). It showed that "the speculative Reason was itself subject to orderly method" (66), that it is possible "to be bounded by method even in its transcendence" (67).

The Greeks, who were the first to develop this mode of reasoning, "robbed it of its anarchic character without destroying its function of reaching beyond set bounds" (66). Speculation was transformed so that it "produced systems instead of inspirations" (41), "schemes of thought" (70) instead of intuitions. A scheme is an abstract relational network, an "interwoven group of categoreal notions" designed to "allow of derivative extension" that carries one from the scheme toward experience, by means of "a correlate practical methodology of experiment," until it yields "observable contacts with fact" (71).

Whitehead's explanation comes close to explaining the obscure by the more obscure, but what he means is familiar. He is referring to what philosophers of science call the hypothetico-deductive method. We arrive at a validated theory not by induction from particular observations or by deduction from self-evident principles, but rather by formulating a hypothesis that purports to explain observed facts and to predict additional ones. If the explanations and predictions are accurate, our hypothesis is confirmed, and when they continue to be confirmed the hypothesis is given the status of a theory, a scheme of thought with explanatory and predictive power sufficient to warrant calling it true.

The features of the logic of discovery thus echo Whitehead's four criteria for a valid metaphysical theory stated at the beginning of *Process and Reality*, which we discussed briefly in chapter 2. In *The Function of Reason*, Whitehead reiterates these criteria in slightly different language (67–70). Consistency and coherence are expressed as the requirements that "the content of a belief" should possess external and internal "logical consistency," and that the "propositional content" be clear. Applicability is expressed as the requirement that this content should conform to "intuitive experience"; adequacy, that it be marked by "widespread conformity to" and "no discordance with" experience, and that it have "methodological consequences."

A hypothesis that meets these criteria is not merely an accurate insight or fruitful intuition. It has become a scheme of thought, a potential theory. Whitehead insists that "the development of abstract theory precedes the understanding of fact" (75). What we perceive, and therefore what we take as fact, is guided by the framework of interpretation we bring to our experiences. When we spot a bird flitting in the trees we open Kaufman's guide because our initial interest in birds is to determine their location within a taxonomic scheme. Were birds messengers from the gods or gods themselves, our interest would be in how to propitiate them appropriately, or how to capture them so that their entrails might be read prophetically. We can't count unless we have an idea of number, or count beyond the number of our fingers (or maybe our fingers and toes) unless we have a number system that can generate new numbers from old. A mother merganser, losing one of her brood of ducklings to a hawk, hurries the rest to safety without knowing that their number has shrunk, or maybe knowing her loss but not its extent.

Astronomers discover a new planet around a distant star by looking for a momentary decrease in the light coming from the star, which they interpret as being caused by a planet coming between it and their telescope. They confirm their find by looking for the wobble in the star's orbit that would result from a planet's gravitational pull. No one would build a telescope powerful enough to secure such information, much less spend time calculating likely places in the universe toward which to aim it and then painstakingly analyzing the data it collects, unless they already had in mind a theory about planet formation that has generalized what we know about the formation of the planets in our own solar system and the character of their interactions with the sun. "From a million observations of fact beyond the routine of human life it rarely happens that one useful development issues," for "if there be no scheme to fit [an observation] into, its significance is lost" (72).

This need for such schemes is why disparaging the fruits of speculation is "treason to the future" (76). Schemes of thought that have not been validated are a "capital of ideas which each age holds in trust for its successors," a "reserve of potential development by which [civilization] has profited" (72). These seemingly useless speculative schemes await some possible future validation when old understandings are in decay and a new approach is being sought. "Millions had seen apples fall from trees, but Newton had in his mind the mathematical scheme of dynamic relations[;] . . . millions had seen animals preying on each other, . . . but Charles Darwin had in his mind the Malthusian scheme" (73).

The logic of discovery is thus an engine of progress. It is the reason why Western civilization has outpaced all other cultures in its improvement of the material conditions for human life. "Apart from the capital of abstract ideas which had accumulated slowly during two thousand years," the scientific revolution and its technological transformations would not have occurred. Without a repertoire of available schemes of thought, in this case mainly mathematical ones, modern science would not have developed, and without modern science "modern life would have been impossible" (74). Whitehead's claim, it should be added parenthetically, is made in full awareness of the destructive uses to which science can be put. He was prepared to argue, however, that the gains have outweighed the losses.

When we carry these notions about subjecting speculation to orderly method back into a consideration of the educational stage of generalization, we see that the recovery of romance in this third stage is our recovery of the repertoire of interesting schemes that we had uncovered or fashioned in our romantic phase, schemes in which we had taken delight but which the critiques of precision had led us to discard as irrelevant or ill-founded, as unverified or unverifiable. Recovering this repertoire, furthermore, means recovering the facts neglected by the reigning scheme of thought we mastered in the stage of precision. As generalization returns us to the resources we had to set aside in order to develop the skills requisite for methodological competence, its wider vaguer viewpoint throws a new light on our familiar world, a world with which we have become familiar through having mastered one or more of the effective methods that define it. Now we see that world afresh, see it indeed as a new world. Our eyes are opened to its wondrous but until now unnoticed or unappreciated features. We see the familiar as though for the first time.

Our high school science class goes on a field trip in the nearby Appalachian Mountains. We stop to chip a few pieces of rock from a limestone outcropping and discover that the pieces contain fossils of creatures with a helmet-like head and with a body composed of an array of sections that look like ribs. Our field guide leads us to identify the creatures as trilobites, an arthropod that flourished from the early Cambrian to late Permian era, 540 to 250 million years ago. Growing curious, we take a closer look at the intricacies of the exoskeleton, and begin competing for who can find the most complete specimen.

What we learn is quite interesting, but it's still safely within the familiar world of what we already know about organisms and their fossil remains. Until we remember what we had learned back in grade school: that limestone is a sedimentary rock composed mainly of calcium carbonate derived from skeletal fragments of tiny marine organisms. So these trilobites must have been part of a similar environment—creatures that when they died sunk to the bottom of a body of water. Which means this mountain we are climbing was once an ocean bed! Our view of the way things are is suddenly reoriented: these mountainous heights were once below sea level, and someday might be again. The solid ground is not so solid after all. But solid nonetheless, so it must have taken a long time for things that were once below sea level to slowly push up until they are a couple thousand feet above sea level. No more than 240 million years, however. That's a long time, though, a stupendously long time, considering that members of the genus *Homo* have been around maybe one thousandth that long and our nation one thousandth of that.

It was precisely this information about fossils of sea creatures found high in the mountains that led first James Hutton and then Charles Lyell to imagine the past as unimaginably vast, vast enough to allow a seabed to be pushed up into a mountaintop by processes that have always worked as slowly and steadily as they do now. Without this conception of "deep time," Darwin would have been unable to imagine that species of organisms also could change gradually, that very small alternations in an organism's form could eventually lead by natural selection to significant differences (see Gould's *Time's Arrow, Time's Cycle*; and, in delightful fiction, Chevalier's *Remarkable Creatures*).

Darwin was not the only biologist to notice that these differences are not eternal, that the kinds of creatures have changed over time. Indeed, he turned to contemporary animal breeding for some of his best examples of genetic alteration. But in order to translate the purposefully controlled selection procedures used by the breeders into a natural selection process, one not guided by purposes, he needed a temporal duration thought impossibly long until Hutton and Lyell provided a framework of interpretation for the empirical evidence that justified claiming it to be true. Darwin read Lyell's *Principles of Geology* while on his trip to the Galapagos, and his eyes were skinned. And seeing the world thus anew,

Darwin was able to write the most eye-skinning work of science since Newton's *Principia*.

We should expand our understanding of the romantic phase of education to include not only our own discoveries, the novelties our curiosity unearths or makes up. Romance should also include our appreciation of others' discoveries and inventions. Romance should involve an appropriation of the heritage that encompasses our own cultural past but also the past achievements of other cultures and of other creatures. What makes this heritage important is not the factual particulars but those facts as organized by an interpretive framework, as comprising a standpoint, a theoretical perspective, a worldview. In the romantic stage, these schemes and their contents should be taught not as settled systems but as stories of discovery and invention, stories about their imaginative creation, their successes and failures, trials and tribulations, growth and decay. These stories in all the glory of their romance should come to be as familiar to us as the practical understandings that precision at the next stage of learning will insist we thoroughly know and utilize.

For example, it is insufficient that we learn science only in the stage of precision, where what we learn is a well-ordered system of postulates and theories, principles and methods, along with the facts they explain and by which they are justified. We should first have learned that science as a story, as a history of scientists and their discoveries, including those discoveries we have come to recognize as inadequate or as simply false. So we should know about the achievements of Ptolemy and Copernicus as well as those of Kepler and Galileo, the physical theories of Aristotle and Newton as well as those of Einstein and Schrödinger, the biological theories of Cuvier and Lamarck as well as those of Darwin and Mayr. The history of science is in a sense the history of theories that have been shown to fail one or more of Whitehead's criteria for validity: Aristotle's theory proved to be inconsistent; Ptolemy's, incoherent; Newton's, inadequate; Lamarck's, inapplicable. They have all been superseded by better theories, theories that will most likely be superseded someday themselves. Yet by knowing these mistaken theories, by loving them for what they accomplished, we come to appreciate how they made their successors possible and how they might harbor, with suitable transformation, novel theories suited to the needs of a new day.

An invaluable approach to teaching a science course would be for the instructor to allow us to be led by the facts we garner to a theory that, although seemingly adequate to those facts and once widely accepted, has been superseded by a better theory. By shooting billiard balls on felt tables or rolling them down inclined planes, we will probably end up devising a theory of motion that is some version of Aristotle's theory that moving objects come eventually to rest unless acted on by an external force. That this is not so for objects moving in a vacuum comes therefore as a shocking surprise, a repudiation of common sense, of experiences verified in our own experience again and again. This surprise helps us appreciate the importance of Newton's theory that friction is an external constraint, in the absence of which balls in motion will continue in motion, and why it is the better theory even though so seemingly unlikely.

Even when we are college physics majors who have been taught Newton from a textbook and can apply his formulae for motion with supreme effectiveness, we often give an Aristotelian reply to a general question about motion. Asked to name the forces working on a ball that has been tossed into the air, we describe a struggle between the upward force imparted by the throw and the ultimately triumphant downward force of gravity—forgetting in a fit of common sense that only the force of gravity is working on the ball once tossed. We are so adept at manipulating the up-to-date theories we have been taught that we do not realize we are still looking at the world with eyes 2,000 years out of date. We know the current theories but we do not live within the worldview they provide. Deep down, we are Aristotelians, still needing to learn how to think in a Newtonian manner, so that we might be ready someday to repudiate it for an Einsteinian manner, and then be able to begin wondering about things as unimaginable as quantum gravitation or string theory.

Generalization is learning a method for transcending method, for developing and appreciating hypotheses that go beyond existing explanations, that offer a promising alternative to those explanations as they begin to show their limits, that reveal how they are inadequate or incoherent, how they have lost their adaptive effectiveness and are being used more to impede thought than to empower it. In Whitehead's third stage of learning, the resources we uncovered in romance are used to rescue our precision from its stultifying and so eventually "downward" tendency, setting us back on an "upward" path, enabling us "boldly to exercise our creative energies" ("Rhythmic Claims" 59) and so "enter upon the adventure of living better" (*Function* 19).

Solomon's Dream

The rhythm of education, cycling in helical fashion through the three stages of learning we have been exploring, echoes what Whitehead, speaking cosmologically, identifies as "three ways in which stabilization is secured" in a dynamic universe (*Function* 20).

The Way of Blindness suffers from an excess of practical reason. The instability threatening a system by the intrusion of "vivid novelty" is overcome by excluding "novelties and their reasoned emphasis" (21). Stability is regained and its protective boundary conditions strengthened, but because this is accomplished by ignoring important changes in the way surrounding realities are and how they work, the resulting system functions at a "lower level of operations" than previously. "There is stabilization," but at the cost of "progressive relapse" (21). The object or organism or society hunkers down, attempting to protect its quality of achievement, but it produces a rigidity that cannot cope with change. Its adaptations are defensive retreats. Fatigue sets in, routines are uncritically repeated despite their increasing ineffectiveness, resulting in a steady decline, a series of setbacks and withdrawals that will only cease with the entity's complete dissolution.

We are familiar with the pedagogical versions of this approach in which each of our classroom lessons is presented as a building block on which other blocks are built, carrying us step by step from fundamentals to derivatives. The rigidity of the blocks and their relationships assures that what needs to be covered gets covered, and our teachers need pay little attention to whether we might find the lesson uninteresting or irrelevant. This approach has its value, of course, where the subject matter is well established, as when we are taught the multiplication tables, the chronology of the kings of England, or other educational catechisms. Since the learning is rote, however, it is not easily adapted to an influx of new information or a seismic shift in its theoretical underpinnings. Recall the sad cliché of the professor lecturing year after year from the same yellowed notes, teaching theories to current students that are as outdated now as they were when their parents were taught them.

The Way of Transience is the opposite alternative, which suffers from an excess of speculative reason. It involves substituting "short-lived individuals" as a strategy for "protecting the species from the fatigue of the individual" (21). Instead of being excluded, novelty is embraced, but in the form of generating fresh iterations of the old to replace the ones that have decayed. This strategy is not effective, however, for novelty as mere repetition of a particular accomplishment is only blindness in a more complex form. "It procures novel individuals to face blindly the old round of experience" (21).

The educational version of the Way of Transience erases our fixed classroom structures and demolishes the prefabricated blocks of learning, inviting us to proceed through a course of study in whatever way it pleases us or our teacher. We flit from flower to flower like Siamese monarchs, never pausing long enough to become bored, dabbling in topics without exploring what might be made of them. Such an unremitting need to stimulate interest afresh is eventually uninteresting, however; it is as boring to be always stepping across the threshold as to never step across it. This approach also has its value, of course, for it opens doors to new ideas. It helps us overcome our distrust of what is unfamiliar, our fear of the unknown. In the absence of distribution requirements, it may be the only sensible way to lure us into courses that have no commonly agreed-on relevance to our major or our career aspirations. However, the lure is often not the content of the course but the sweet honey of its catalog description or the rumor that the grades are easy and the teacher a knockout. An interest rooted in such superficialities lacks sufficient heft to keep us interested much less to make a difference in our lives.

The Ways of Blindness and Transience, says Whitehead, are the "two main tendencies in the course of events" disclosed by our firsthand experience and by our knowledge of history and nature: that of "slow decay" and that of "renewal" ("Introductory Summary"). Some things are all the time wasting away and other new things all the time emerging. However, the originative element, dominating the Way of Transience, is anarchic, and so its energy of renewal is fundamentally unsustainable, substituting rapid for slow decay.

Both Blindness and Transience are therefore entropic, and so if they were all there was, there would be no cosmos. Reason, however, is also "the self-discipline of the originative element" ("Introductory Summary")—not Plato's reason, not the reason of Ulysses, but both of them working in tandem. Together they create a rhythm in which the pragmatic adaptive wile of Ulysses functions to preserve a wider speculative Platonic system, and the speculative novelties that Plato imaginatively evokes offer insights that enable Ulysses to invent the new tricks he needs for the new day's surprises. Working together, the two otherwise entropic modes construct and then sustain an integrative negentropic harmony of constantly varying contrasting differences. This third way, the Way of Rhythm, is the key to how our cosmos functions and how it came to include organisms able to develop cosmological interpretations of its character. It is how our educational schemes should be constructed so that young human organisms will learn how to engage their learning creatively, open-endedly.

The Way of Rhythm, which is the secret of evolution, "pervades all life, and indeed all physical existence" (21). It involves repetition of a process rather than a content, the "preservation of the fundamental abstract structure of the cycle," combined with "the variation of the concrete details of succeeding cycles" (22). Each cycle is "self-repairing": variants of the old details are generated that are adjusted sufficiently to preserve the viability of the established structure through the instabilities of changing circumstance (see my development of this point in *The Patterns of the Present*, especially chapter 5.1, "Stabilizing Variation"). Fatigue and decay are thereby avoided; renewal has become systematized. "The good life is attained by the enjoyment of [new] contrasts within the scope of the [same] method" (22). Value is sustained in the cosmos by intertwining speculative and practical reason by means of the logic of discovery—by the development of what might be called pragmatic methods of speculation or speculative methods of practical effectiveness, in which the content of a concrete achievement is adjusted in order to preserve the process by which it was made concrete, with these adjustments slowly altering in turn the process. This restless self-repairing dynamic is the way of all enduring things.

The pedagogical versions of the Way of Rhythm are those in which our teachers use novelty to refresh constantly our developing intellectual skills, our ability to create effective procedures for achieving clearly defined goals, and then use those improved skills in helping us learn to assess the relevance and appropriateness of our procedures and goals, prizing creative imagination as the key to both. We can learn the multiplication tables through classroom "Jeopardy" contests as easily as by means of flash cards, and the significance of such tables can be transformed by playing around with number systems on bases other than ten (So what's 4 x 3 in base 7?) and then in the on-off base two of computer logic. When professors teach us the basic building block of chemistry or biology, there is nothing preventing them from linking that information to significant real-world situations, as Primo Levi does in *The Periodic Table* and Matt Ridley in *Genome*. We need to learn the facts but never just the facts;

ideas, but never just ideas. What is most important by far is learning how to relate them effectively.

Whitehead seems contradictory when, after claiming that "the basis of all authority is the supremacy of fact over thought" (80), he goes on immediately to argue that "the study of the ideas" underlying societal institutions and the practical methods they embody "is an appeal to the supreme authority" (81). On the one hand, he says that our thoughts are tethered to cultural facts, speculative reason to practical reason. We are creatures of our culture. Its institutions give shape to our world, locating us within its confines. They teach us how to speak and how to think, they define the kinds of ideals we imagine worth pursuing and the kinds of strategies we think might allow us to actualize them. Ideas that do not fit within this cultural world, ideas that have no practical value, are thought to be trivial, merely speculative. On the other hand, Whitehead argues that the validation of the facts marshaled by practical reason lies not in the cultural institutions embodying those facts but in the speculative ideas underlying them, in "what those institutions stood for in the experience of their contemporaries" (85). For it is by means of its underlying speculative ideas that a society is able to adapt to change, to adjust its institutions to circumstance.

Whitehead is not wavering indecisively between these contrasting claims about what is primary. He resolves the dispute by concluding that "the interplay of thought and practice is the supreme authority" (81). Neither the authority of facts nor the authority of ideas is final; neither practical reason nor speculative reason suffices. Nor does it suffice that both function side by side or sequentially. The supreme authority lies in the systematic interplay of the two, in the stability their unstable relationship makes possible. The supreme authority lies in the recognition that any and every authoritative achievement will eventually need to be transcended.

Thus cosmology, like the cosmos it seeks to understand, is an endeavor: an effort, a task. It is the attempt "to frame a scheme of the general character of the present stage of the universe" (76), "to submit itself to the authority of facts without loss of its mission to transcend the existing analysis of facts" (85), to fit the various specialized schemes of particular disciplines into a general scheme, modifying in the process both the specialized schemes and the general one. "The cosmology and the schemes of the sciences are mutually critics of each other" (77). This practice, this sustained interplay of metaphysical generalization and disciplinary focus, is the logic of discovery the Greeks invented, a way of reasoning that has produced over the course of the two and a half millennia of its existence "all the great religions, . . . the great rational philosophies, . . . the great sciences" (41), and, in the last two centuries, an "enormous advance" in technology (42). Constantly falling short of its goal, constantly needing to transcend what it has achieved, reason functioning as the integration of its practical and speculative modes has converted "the decay of one order into the birth of its successor" (90).

In his dream, Solomon asked for a wise and understanding mind so that he might attain the moral virtue by which to rule his people well, and he was told that by means of such qualities he could also achieve riches, honor, and long life. Our systematized understanding of things, when it is an open-ended endeavor, a quest for adequacy and completeness that recognizes its shortcomings and so also recognizes the need always for a fresh endeavor, can have positive results. "The antithesis between the two functions of Reason is not quite so sharp as it seems at first sight" (39). The practical and the speculative need each other, need to be woven together by means of the logic of discovery into an instrument for the creation of a viable societal order and a viable understanding of that order. "A satisfactory cosmology"—and therefore the satisfactory civilization for which it provides the underlying ideas that give it viability—"must explain"—and in its institutional structures must exemplify—"the interweaving of efficient and of final causation"—the weaving together of Plato's encompassing account of truth and Ulysses's translation of it into the civilized practices of a successful societal order (28).

The good life is a life lived in community with others, and it is possible only when a practical scheme of attitudes, customs, and laws has been worked out historically, a practical scheme nested within a scheme of thought that gives that historical achievement both its present meaning and the resources for its constant renewal, gives worth to the story of how it came to be what it now is and gives worth also to its aspirations for what it might yet become.

We must remember that Solomon's dream was only a dream. His understanding was far too limited, his wisdom problematic, in matters other than identifying a baby's proper mother. His material riches were stupendous but always threatened by enemy armies from without and pretenders to his throne from within, the length of his life did not exceed what was typical for his times, and his honor was transmuted into myths having little touch with reality. His kingdom, as happens to every human society without exception, flourished for a while, then stumbled, decayed, and has long since become as one with Nineveh and Tyre.

Solomon's dream was an open-ended ideal. It expressed the hope that he might be able to save his world from its tendency to relapse into chaos. Solomon's dream did not perish, however, because it is our dream as well, a hope that we might in this present age build amid the collapsing of the old order a better and more enduring successor. As educators, accordingly, we should aspire to create the conditions for new Solomons to emerge. Our endeavor should be to prepare today's young people for the responsibilities of adulthood by engaging their creative powers through a helical rhythm of romantic, precise, and generalized learning. Our dream should be that our students, or at least those among them who can rise to the opportunity, will develop an understanding imbued with wisdom and virtue.

The ability required to weave practical and speculative ways of thinking into a satisfactory social fabric is neither a genetic inheritance nor a teachable skill. It is an art, a practice. As Socrates says at the end of *Meno*, "it is through right opinion that statesmen follow the right course for their cities. As regards knowledge, they are no different from soothsayers and prophets. They too say many true things when inspired, but they have no knowledge of what they are saying" (99c). What the Greeks discovered is how to be effective amid inadequacy, how to fashion interpretive theories and courses of action adequate for the occasion while being ready and able both to call them into question and to attempt altered versions for altered occasions.

An education that brings us to the point where we can contribute positively to the efforts needed to adapt our established ways, our civilized habits and assurances, to a changing world is as difficult as it is necessary. It is a call to thought and action demanding our full allegiance but impossible for any of us, alone or in collaboration with others, to fulfill more than partially and for a time. The statues of Daedalus can never be tethered, but they can be momentarily corralled. And redesigned statues—reformulated hypotheses, revamped attempts at getting opinion right—can constantly be commissioned. As Socrates says earlier in *Meno*, "I do not insist that my argument is right in all other respects, but I would contend at all costs both in word and deed as far as I could that we will be better men, braver and less idle, if we believe that one must search for the things one does not know" (86b–c).

Solomon's dream is a dream too difficult ever to translate into the realities of our wakeful life, but it is a dream without which we and our civilized ways are doomed. "Our aim is upwards" (*Function* 82), says Whitehead, but our efforts, however valiant they may be, row upriver against a persistent downstream current, against our yearning for closure, for a quiet shelter from the raging storm, for an end that is attainable. Our aim is upward, toward the better, the more adequate. But the actual course of our lives—and the course of history, and of the cosmos—is often not upward, and certainly is not cumulatively upward, not upward and onward to some utopian culmination. The relentless current is all the time undoing our best efforts, but we should be content that often we can make some headway against it, even if only for a time. And no matter how much the day's loss, our aim should always be for a measure of headway on the morrow.

Solomon's dream tells us that our task as educators and leaders, as students and citizens, is gloriously Sisyphean. It means struggling endlessly to save the old world by redeeming it, by renovating its past accomplishments so that they can still prove useful in a world that would otherwise have passed them by, only to find that what we have wrought is soon once more in need of renovation. "The stable universe is slipping away from under us" (82), says Whitehead, and our task is to restabilize it by fashioning a new universe—a new world, a new civilized order, a new sense of self and purpose—which, of course, in the very apotheosis of our success we will experience as also slipping away from under us.

"There is in nature some tendency upwards, in a contrary direction to the aspect of physical decay" (89). We are aware of both these tendencies, and our task is to join with the upward one, to contribute as best we can to the "discrimination of appetitions according to a rule of fitness" (90). In accepting this task as our task we instantiate the "reign of Reason," which is "vacillating, vague, and dim." It is a reign promising no triumphant victory, offering no clarion call to the barricades, barely discernable amid the rubble of the endless failures of the past. "But it is there" (90).

CHAPTER FIVE

Learning to Create the Future

We come now to the last of Whitehead's metaphysical writings, *Modes of Thought*. Although the three previous books that we have considered are also metaphysical, their attention is directed to limited domains. This book is concerned with metaphysics itself. It is not a metaphysical reflection on the nature and function of art or sense experience or reason, but a metaphysical reflection on the nature and function of metaphysical ultimates.

My aim in this chapter is to explore similarities between Whitehead's stages of education and the two "ultimate notions" *Modes of Thought* interprets. I hope this exploration will shed light on what Whitehead means when he opens the book's "Epilogue" by saying: "The task of a university is the creation of the future, so far as rational thought, and civilized modes of appreciation, can affect the issue" (171).

Two Ultimate Notions

Whitehead identifies "ultimate notions" as those "general characterizations of our experience" which "occur naturally in daily life" (*Modes* 1). They are presupposed in our social structures, our cultural expressions, and our scientific understandings. We take them for granted; they go without saying. There is nothing more "far-reaching" than our ultimate notions, nothing more fundamental in terms of which they can be explained. They are that in terms of which we develop our explanations of all else. Whitehead never offers an inventory of these ultimate notions. Instead, he selects a single one, "importance," as the ultimate notion on which he will focus, and immediately contrasts it with another ultimate notion, "matter-of-fact." They are "antithetical," he says, but they "require" each other (4).

A matter-of-fact is a particular thing: a this-here-now, as distinct from all the other things that are but which are not here or not now, which are at another place or another time. There are a lot of thises and thats, an inexhaustible multiplicity of them, each one uniquely itself. I hold this pebble in my hand, not that one or any of the myriad others scattered along the beach. Its graceful shape and striking color distinguish it from the other pebbles, but it also differs from them by being the only pebble in my hand.

In contrast to a matter-of-fact, importance is a value—a generalization or idea or feeling—that gives matters-of-fact some kind of unity. It brings them together meaningfully, disclosing a whole of which they are components. My pebble is composed of the same kind of rock as all the other pebbles on this beach, all of them calved off from larger rocks and worn smooth by wind and wave. They are significant aspects of the beach ecology because they offer shelter to various organisms that in turn are food sources for other organisms, and because they protect the beach against precipitous erosion and other ecology-destroying instabilities by dispersing the force of the ocean as it crashes ashore.

The paradigm of conscious experience, claims Whitehead, is the linking of these two ultimate notions, the "fusion of a larger generality with an insistent particularity" in a judgment that "This is important" (4). The particular matter-of-fact is not taken as a bare indifferent thing but as something of value, because of its inherent qualities and because of the wider significance it evokes. When emphasizing the inherent qualities, "the individuality of the details" of a thing's importance, we often speak of its intrinsic "interest" and therefore our interest in it. When emphasizing the wider implications, "the unity of the Universe" this interest intimates, we speak of its "importance" (8). Whitehead treats the two terms as synonymous, as emphasizing different facts of the same paradigmatic judgment that a particular matter-of-fact is significant. I chose this pebble because its sparkle caught my eye and its shape reminded me of a childhood friend who gave me a similar pebble she found as we walked together at sunset on a similar beach, long ago when our futures still sparkled with promise. I will bring it home, this pebble of mine, and set it on the fireplace mantle as a reminder of my resolve to be for others the friend I can no longer be for my childhood companion.

For Whitehead, judgments about the importance of facts come in a variety of "emphases" (6) or "species" (11) or "senses" (26). His lists vary, but in each case the kind of judgment correlates to a fundamental kind of human endeavor. Judgments that "this is right" correlate with morality; that "this is sacred," with religion; that "this is beautiful," with the arts; that "this is valid," with logic; that "this is true," with practical activity and, when combined with logic, the sciences. All of these senses of importance are part of the heritage of modern Western civilization, but Whitehead notes that the first two, religion and morality, were emphasized in the ancient world by the Semites, logic and aesthetics by the Greeks, and practical observation by the Egyptians. It is our task now, he argues, "to conceive of importance and matter-of-fact in some disengagement from the mentalities of the ancient world" (6). We need to re-express these species of judgment in versions appropriate to our own times, to the contemporary world.

The implications of Whitehead's comments for education are immediate and unsettling. Judgments involving importance and matters-of-fact are cultural artifacts. Our ancestors experienced their world in ways that led to the development of habits of thinking and doing that presumed ultimate notions of reality—a reality understood as fundamentally governed by, and humanly governable by reference to, publically accessible judgments of objectivity and worth. As inheritors of these ancestral presumptions, we have a sacred trust to pass on what was passed on to us, to be sure our successors in each new generation acquire these same habits. Included among them is a belief that living by means of such habits as best we can, and teaching them to our successors, is a fundamental aspect of who we are.

Our world is increasingly global, however, our ancestral heritage pluralistic, a legacy no longer only from the ancient Mediterranean but now also from India and China, western Africa and pre-Colombian America. We must see to it that our children learn as we did to think and act in terms of the goodness, the truth, and the beauty of things, but these values are no longer to be found solely on a Grecian urn or in stories of the wanderings of Odysseus, Abraham, and Muhammad. The new wine of our planetary cosmopolis requires cosmopolitan wineskins, a revamping of the ultimate presuppositions of our humanity and, indeed, of our creatureliness. That this daunting task is a sacred trust and not merely a prudential admonition is itself a manifestation of the ultimacy of these notions.

The *daemon* who spoke to Socrates said he should be guided always by the attempt to know himself. We too should hunger for the self-knowledge that comes only in drawing constant nourishment from the assumptions by which alone we can live as civilized human beings. Whitehead calls our attention to two of those assumptions, matters-of-fact and importance, but self-knowledge comes not from the assumptions as such but from their interplay. A proper education is not a matter of learning our basic cultural repertoire of useful facts, or a matter of teachers filling our heads with our culture's most widely accepted repertoire of pious platitudes, not even when this repertoire is made global in scope. Rather, becoming properly educated means learning to make for ourselves sound judgments about the importance of matters-of-fact and the factual basis of importances.

If ultimate notions are pervasive features of civilized experience, then they should be a fundamental facet of educational experiences, a presupposition of teaching and learning. It should be possible, therefore, to associate the notions of importance and matter-of-fact with Whitehead's stages of education. To that task I will now turn.

Assemblage

Romance and importance are a close fit: "Our enjoyment of actuality," says Whitehead, "is a realization of worth, good or bad. It is a value experience. Its basic expression is—Have a care, here is something that matters!" (*Modes* 116). This caring sensibility is easily associated with romance: appreciating the things of the world for what they are. Each of the matters-of-fact we experience—perceive, imagine, feel, think—is a wondrous reality in which to delight, without attention to moral judgments or practical considerations. We do not arrive at a judgment concerning the worth of an object or person or idea belatedly, only after having first become familiar with it. We do not assess its value by comparing it to a standard, judging it as conforming to some ethical rule or hedonistic calculus, as adhering to some logical or systemic formation conditions, as meeting some criterion of artistic or pragmatic excellence. Our initial discovery of a matter-of-fact involves a spontaneous judgment of its worth, of it mattering. Factual, rational, aesthetic, moral, and sacral judgments will come later. Our first response is to heed its presence, to take it into account, to have a care for it as this actuality now present in our experience. We are thrilled by this bold new idea about the origin of life, intrigued by that beautifully shaped pebble, distressed by a pelican entangled in fishing line.

Romance is a feature of our education whenever we appreciate something in this immediate way. In earlier chapters, we have associated romance with restless curiosity, being open to what is novel, to strange facts and unfamiliar ideas, to brave new worlds and their unexplored possibilities. *Modes of Thought* emphasizes our immediate sense of the inherent worth of these things. The fact of a thing's existence is not prior to and distinct from its attractive or repulsive qualities. The thing *is* its mattering. The spontaneity of our curiosity, our wanting to toy with a risqué thought, pick up a sparkly object, or help an injured animal, is because we experience them as mattering. And because we care about them, we take the time to figure out what they are and what we should do with them or for them or because of them.

This link between what things matter and how they matter highlights a further aspect of romance. The "primary glimmering of consciousness" that reveals for us "something that matters" is a more complex experience than appreciating its worth.

> "Totality," "Externality," and "Internality" are the primary characterizations of "that which matters." . . . They are presuppositions in the sense of expressing the sort of obviousness which experience exhibits. There is the totality of actual fact; there is the externality of many facts; there is the internality of this experiencing which lies within the totality. (116)

A few sentences later, Whitehead restates his point in slightly different language: "the dim meaning of fact—or actuality—is intrinsic importance for itself, for the others, and for the whole" (117). And earlier he says that

> the primitive stage of discrimination is not primarily qualitative. It is a vague grasp of reality, dissecting it into a threefold scheme, namely, "The Whole," "That Other," and "This-My-Self." . . . We are, each of us, one among others; and all of us are embraced in the unity of the whole. (110)

Immediate experience is threefold: myself who is experiencing, this thing other than myself that I am experiencing, and the totality of all such experiences and things experienced.

Whitehead is able to find so much in something seemingly so simple because the appreciation of a thing as mattering is a discrimination of it, lifting it into prominence, into presence for us, and so setting it against a background of what has been left out. This pebble I am cushioning carefully in my hand is something I am aware of having picked up recently while strolling back there along this beach. I have only a vague sense of the pebbles I set aside or ignored because they had less sparkle or because their shapes were uninteresting or because I simply overlooked them in my focus on the one I selected. Yet even if my sense of the character of these other pebbles is vague, it is nonetheless real. In cherishing the one pebble as more valuable than the others, I recognize that the others have value as well, and that I and my precious pebble and all the pebbles I forsook are intertwined. Without the other pebbles, my pebble would lose its special significance as the one that is different from the others because it is similar to the pebble that evoked those bittersweet memories of a lost love and a resolve to cherish all the more my present loves.

The one vivid example Whitehead provides of this complexity of the world given in immediate experience is when he asks us to consider "the subtle beauty of a flower in some isolated glade of a primeval forest" (120). No human is experiencing its beauty; no other kind of creature has a sufficiently complex consciousness to do so; the cells of which the flower is composed are unaware of the beauty to which they are contributing. "And yet this beauty is a grand fact in the universe" (120). Our experience of the world around us, of the things that we take as mattering, leads to the thought of such an unknown flower, which I picture in my mind's eye as a daffodil. It is an example of the innumerable components of our world, so vastly many of them not ever experienced by us, not mattering to anyone or anything, and yet each exhibiting an achievement that matters intrinsically, that matters whether or not it matters to anyone, whether or not it has any specific influence or endures for more than a moment. "Then our sense of the value of the details for the totality dawns upon our consciousness" (120), which is simultaneously also a sense of "the value, for its own sake, of the totality of historic fact in respect to its essential unity" (119), what Whitehead calls the "sense of sacredness," an "intuition of holiness" (120). This bright yellow daffodil, the contrasting green blades of grass surrounding it, and the totality of all those things great and small that encompass it, the glade and the forest, the rainfall and the sunshine, the swiftly moving planet and the cosmic order—all of these swirl around our experiencing, at Whitehead's behest, the subtle beauty of an unimportant, indeed a merely imagined, forest flower.

The "primary stage" of philosophy, says Whitehead, reveling as it does in the rich complexity of direct appreciation, should be an occasion for "assemblage" (2), for a process of inclusion, of attempting to leave nothing out of consideration, not even discarded pebbles and fanciful flowers, ignoring for the moment questions of truth or falsity, sanctity or utility, priority or relevance. What holds for philosophizing holds also for learning: the romantic phase of education should be one of assemblage. We with our teachers should be doing exciting things, meeting interesting people, exploring entrancing ideas and intriguing places. Our motive should be wonder, with nothing ruled out in advance as unworthy of our caring about it.

So-called teaching moments are romance occasions. Something unexpected happens, arresting the routine flow of the day's lesson plan, catching our attention. "Stop what you're doing," our teacher exclaims. "Come over here and take a look at this—what do you suppose it is?" With the teacher's encouragement, what we have come across is taken not as an intruder to be chased off but as a gift to be welcomed in, an opportunity for expanding or deepening everyone's experience. Life happens, and to welcome its surprises as moments of serendipity is to embrace assemblage as the proper method of romance. The class's pet goldfish is found floating belly-up in its bowl, the students wonder what can be done to bring it back to life, and the teacher encourages discussion about why living things die. A scuffle in the hallway over whose soccer team is the best leads to the class organizing a formal debate between the disputants before a jury of their peers. When a student is bewildered at being called an Uncle Tom, the class heads for the library and computer room in a search for the origin of the term and its pejorative significance.

The intrinsic importance of these moments should not be treasured as isolated bits of exciting information, however, for what matters in and of itself adumbrates the presence of other things that matter and of the whole universe of such things. What we assemble is not just additive, a pile of this and that and the other thing. It's a collection, the sum of all those things but as meaningfully albeit vaguely arranged. Each this implies other thises and then the whole of which they are aspects. Goldfish swim in a world where even the innocent die. Communities can tolerate, even encourage, disagreements among their members by transmuting the hard rock of brute force into the malleable gold of persuasive argument. We stand on the shoulders of giants, beholden to predecessors as far back as our protohuman ancestors on the African savanna, even when in our narrowest and shallowest moments we sneer at a neighbor for not being just like us.

For good Darwinian reasons, animals generally and humans especially have a propensity to emphasize "the superficial aspects of their connexity with nature," and by focusing on these "trivialities" have "obtained a manageable grip upon the world" (30). We smell the foul odor and avoid it; we see the fruit and reach for it; we detect the pattern in the occurrences and so are able to anticipate what will happen next. Yet in doing so, we neglect the "underlying necessities of nature" (30), the vague environment of things that encompass these saliencies and make them possible. This neglect is dangerous because it allows us to take the manageable superficialities of our experience as fundamental realities and therefore to ignore that "direct insight," which although "vague as to detail" is nonetheless "the basis of all rationality" (31).

Whitehead makes an interesting observation in this regard about the importance of verbal communication. Language is a repertoire of readily identifiable items and rules for their combination that we use as signs by which to direct attention to other more complex things. The signs are simple to make: a fluid two-handed downward gesture tracing symmetrical curves, a breathy rounded sound followed by a plosive with a tongued closure, five standardized alphabetic marks in the sequence *w-o-m-a-n*. These signs all attempt in their differing ways to refer those who see or hear them to a particular human being or to a general idea of the female human. Of the three kinds of sign systems, the one composed of sounds probably was the first developed. Whitehead wonders why this is so, and answers that it is because we make sounds with our lungs, throat, and mouth. We use what is at the center of our organic being to utter the signs by which we express our understandings of the world, and in doing so convey as well a "sense of the vague intimacies of organic existence" (32). We make simple sounds but their creation involves our central bodily organs. The organic resonance of the words we utter suggests that the realities to which our words refer are not as simple as are those words themselves.

This is why, for instance, self-instructional texts, filmed or televised lectures, and computer-based distance learning turn out after an initial period of excitement to be poor substitutes for direct student-teacher interactions. These technologies use signs that have no organic resonance, and so convey a sense that the realities thereby signified are no less simple than the signs. Discourse of this flattened sort has its place, of course, but not during a romance phase of learning, not when the point is to convey the importance of things.

Hamlet famously admonishes Horatio that "there are more things in heaven and earth . . . than are dreamt of in our philosophy" (*Hamlet*

1.5.168–9). Without words spoken and heard, without face-to-face conversations among students and teachers in which unfamiliar aspects of familiar things are discovered and explored together, our students will never bump against the limits of their inherited philosophies. They will grasp the external highlights and their internal relevance but miss the greater but elusive totality. They will think the world as they find it is all the heaven and earth they need.

Assemblage is the gathering of things that matter, enjoying them for their uniqueness, respecting their intrinsic worth and relevance over against our claims on them, and appreciating the awesome sanctity of the whole to which both they and we belong. Disconnected and passive appreciation is insufficient. Romance is not a form of tourism, a perfunctory visit to a museum or zoo, in which students glance at this painting and then walk quickly around that sculpture, clap first at a performing monkey and then laugh at the polar bear's antics. The romantic phase of education is fundamentally learning to appreciate things as having relevantly meaningful contexts, the painting as expressing truths that go far beyond what it depicts, the antelope as wonderfully adapted for life on a grassy plain. It is having experiences that convey a sense of themselves as more than they seem, more than they are.

The value of a story is that it is all about meaningful wholes, which it evokes not by imposing relationships on otherwise self-standing elements but by showing how those elements are inherently relational and developmental, unfolding an initial organic unity into its complex possibilities or pulling a multitude of divergent contributions into one integrated complex. Elementary school teachers who ask students to report on how they spent their summer, to draw a picture of the most interesting thing they saw on a recent walk in the park, or to write a story about their grandparents' lives, are taking seriously the fundamentally relational character of romance. As are high school teachers and college professors who use journal writing as a classroom tool for increasing their students' actively personal involvement in what they are studying.

Even better at developing a student's awareness of holistic complexes, however, are those courses in which students tell their stories to their classmates or open their journal reflections to the comments of fellow students. For in these cases, the stories are shared among the storytellers, who learn from one another's stories how better to fashion their own. I'm reminded of Frank McCourt's account in *Teacher Man* of how his high school English class came to give public readings of cookbook recipes set to music, exploring thereby what can only be called the most unlikely of connections, and in doing so acquiring to their surprise an appreciation for poetic expression. The recipes and the music are at first items of their own choosing but eventually of their own creation. From an appreciation of food they develop an appreciation of how to make it, then an appreciation of the form in which the instructions for making it are typically couched, and a sense of the way such a form is like other kinds of form, such as that on which music depends. McCourt's students end up writing recipes in various poetic forms and composing music able to accentuate those forms and their affective resonances. There was more of heaven and earth in their recipes than they had ever dreamed.

The hubris of romance's engagement with the modalities of importance—its celebration of the worth of aesthetic, religious, ethical, logical, scientific, and practical matters-of-fact—is the temptation to take one of the modes as exhaustive, to think that the values that mode expresses are always and everywhere applicable. Having affirmed the importance found in a work of art, for instance, it is easy to begin insisting that aesthetic importance is the only criterion by which adequately to judge the worth of anything, to claim that what's important about a statement is not whether it is true but whether it is well said. Or, to take another example, the story of civilization is replete with princes or priests who have insisted that we accept our leader's incontestably authoritative determination of the moral worth of each one of our public and even private actions, that we accede to the leader's infallible understanding of the divine will and the concordant sacred mission of our community.

No modality of importance is absolute, and in some contexts many modalities are not even important. Whitehead points out that although Bizet's opera *Carmen* is about a bunch of outlaws and a woman "carefree as to niceties of behaviour," while the performers are "singing their parts and dancing on the stage, morals vanish and beauty remains" (13). Ethical or religious values are often quite relevant to theater, but not to *Carmen.* Similarly, although logical consistency is of immense value in scientific reasoning, Emerson is correct to insist that in other contexts it can be "foolish," and that those who under any circumstances insist on it are in thrall to "the hobgoblin of little minds," a hobgoblin with which "a great soul has simply nothing to do" ("Self Reliance" 138).

Importance is not a universal. It is necessarily a function of a mode of thought, a judgment of worth limited to the perspective that mode imposes, and to the historical and cultural context interpreting it. What the Hellenic Greeks or Tang Dynasty Chinese took to be the conditions for an object's beauty are not ours. We cannot understand those ancient cultures without taking seriously the distinctive ways in which they gave life to the various modes of importance and how they weighed their relative significance. And we cannot understand ourselves without appreciating our own unique cultural interpretations and weightings, and how they are different and how similar to Hellenic and Tang realizations of importance. It is important for us, whether or not it was for either or both of them, to respect these differences, even as we also respect the historical or potential relevance to their judgments of worth to our current ones. Whitehead is not affirming subjectivism or relativism, but rather insisting on the finitude of human judgment, the importance of recognizing the limits of any judgment of importance.

Dogmatic certainty about the unambiguous meaning and absolute authority of any claim that "this is important" is a distortion, presuming clarity and imposing closure on what is unavoidably open-textured because invincibly vague. Nothing of importance is ever finally settled. Questions need constantly to be asked, such as whether moral judgments can apply to reasons of state or the death of goldfish, whether a sunset or a pebble can be beautiful since it is not a work of art, whether a religious belief can ever trump a scientific theory or influence the outcome of a soccer game. Education should all the time be involving students and teachers in discussions and activities that explore the limits of the various answers proposed to such questions, and that uncover or invent fresh answers or better questions. Romance is the occasion for taking questions seriously, and therefore playing with their resonances, their historical vintage and their likely fruitfulness.

The educational importance of asking questions of importance is for students to experience them as real questions, as life-orienting modalities that for those who ask them open avenues of exploration into a sense of oneself, of others, and of the totality of things. Only as we discover the worth of these questions of worth, their existential bite, their exhaustless relevance, their fathomless mystery, are we ready to move from romance to precision, to pass from assemblage to system building.

Systematization

Precision typically emerges in response to the problem of the vacuity of romance and its vague assertions about how much things matter. Precision is a return to an emphasis on matters-of-fact, the details, the multiplicity of particulars, seeking greater clarity and specificity concerning the "this" that romance has been indiscriminately praising. Attention shifts to the facts apart from their worth, since by doing so it is easier to specify their features and the forms of their relatedness. "Systematization," says Whitehead, "is the criticism of generality by methods derived from the specialism of science" (*Modes* 3).

The key to scientific method, and hence the key to how the stage of precision differs from romance, is the pursuit of a specified end, the deployment of a well-formulated aim around which the facts are then organized. Whitehead defines the notion of an aim functionally: it is "the exclusion of the boundless wealth of alternative potentiality, and the inclusion of that definite factor of novelty which constitutes the selected way of entertaining" those facts and potentialities of fact that bear on that "process of unification" (152).

The enjoyment of boundless possibilities is the vocation of romance. As I'm warming up for the soccer match, it is fun to imagine my header slipping past the keeper for our go-ahead goal, our victory a step along a pathway to the championship, although I may also imagine with dismay my missing a crucial goal kick or our team losing on a penalty kick in overtime. When the whistle blows and the game begins, however, this wealth of idle speculations is replaced by a focused aim at playing my position well, contributing as specifically and appropriately as I can to a team victory. I may daydream in my leisure moments of bending it like Beckham or being another Pelé, but with the game underway my concern is with more functionally immediate possibilities: whether to continue dribbling downfield or to pass the ball to a teammate cutting toward the box, whether to try a slide tackle on an opponent who has outmaneuvered me or to alter my angle of approach in order to intercept him further downfield.

This constriction of possibilities and facts to those judged relevant to an identified aim is a familiar feature of our experience. We have things to do and promises to keep, so we pay attention to what will help us realize these aims and neglect the rest. We organize the data of experience around our goals. Our aim, however, is not merely to transform a possibility into a fact, an aspiration into a datum, but to experience that fact as a possibility now realized, the datum as a dream come true. "The aim," says Whitehead far too abstractly, "is at that complex of feeling which is the enjoyment of those data in that way" (152). I want us to win the soccer match and in doing so to celebrate our victory, drinking beer and basking in the cheers of our fans. I want not merely to win the game but to do so by successfully engaging the opposition in a manner worthy of a celebrative conclusion. An aim is the attempt to carry through a unifying achievement in a way enjoyed by the achieving agent.

The work of precision is to introduce a specific aim into the aimless enthusiasms of romance and thereby to create a boundary to boundless possibility, a structure canalizing enthusiasm into a trajectory leading to the realization of that aim. Whitehead says this method of boundary formation is derived from the scientific mode of thought, and certainly science is its paradigm. For instance, an aim in scientific inquiry might take the form of a hypothesis attempting to explain why certain well-established facts aren't making sense.

Observations of the planet Uranus are diverging from where Newton's theory predicts the planet should be. Inexplicably, its orbit is suffering perturbations in its elliptical trajectory. These facts can be enjoyed for what they are: this bright point of light at an unexpected location in a crowded field of starlight, that dark in the field where this bright point of light should have been. But there is no further use that can be made of them. They are confusing, inconsistent, problematic anomalies, facts that diverge from the theory that explains them at too many points and in too great an extent to be explained in the usual way, as errors in observation, defects in the telescopes, or mistakes in recording the data.

A scientific hypothesis is then devised, proposing that these facts be interpreted as illustrating a different pattern, perhaps a version of a familiar one or one not previously noticed or one until then not even dreamed of. By means of this new pattern the facts can be taken, despite appearances to the contrary, as comprising a system. The proposal is that this system extends beyond its organization of these known facts, and that appropriate observations will identify other previously unknown facts it also organizes.

The gravitational pull of a heretofore unobserved planet in an orbit farther out than Uranus's would account for its orbital perturbations. The hypothesis is verified if the facts it predicts will be observed actually are observed. The previously unknown planet Neptune is observed at the places it would have to be in order to influence Uranus's orbit in the ways that had seemed so anomalous. Now located within this new verified relational pattern, the facts once again make sense and so can once more be utilized in the pursuit of our ends. Predictions of planetary motion based on Newton's laws are reaffirmed as accurate, and therefore effective uses of these predictions by professional and amateur astronomers are once more legitimated.

This method is also a feature of other modes of thought, even though Whitehead occasionally seems to imply otherwise. The systematization of matters-of-fact around an aim, the identification or invention of an ordered relationship among facts for the sake of some end, is a technique fundamental to all modes of thought. Art is the obvious example, where disparate materials and their qualities are unified in the making of any aesthetic work, whether a painting or performance, a building or tapestry. A life well lived, a virtuous act, an offering of homage to one's lord or god, a validated logical proof, are in their quite differing ways also processes centering around an organizing aim that issues in a concretely unified whole. The worth of the process is determined by how well it functions in achieving its end, as well as in the scope and complexity of what is involved, and the integrative intensity of the outcome. Any "this" may be intrinsically important, but it is excellent only when it functions as it should with respect to the end it serves, or when it is a component of an effective system.

System-making is necessarily a narrowing process. "We always think within limitations" (15), and always act within them. We cannot be fully adequate to experience if we are to make sense of it. Some things will need to be emphasized, foregrounded, valorized, while others are ignored, diminished, denied. Procrustes is the mentor of intelligibility and effectiveness, forcing Proteus's boundless bounty into a finite bounded whole—bending, stuffing, distorting, lopping off as needed in order to make things fit properly.

The reason why hands-on active learning is educationally crucial is that proposing and then achieving a specific viable result from a confusing welter of possibly relevant elements is an art and not just a technique. It's a matter of style. We learn to do things in an effective way by practicing how they are done, by getting good at doing those sorts of things. By attempting to come up with an answer to the question of why Uranus is behaving strangely, how life originated, or why goldfish die, we learn how better to go about solving other scientific problems. By doing the best we can to make an accurate pencil drawing of a gracefully shaped pebble on an ornate mantelpiece, we learn how to respond in a more creative way and with greater aesthetic insight to our next artistic challenge. By trying to bring to a peaceable conclusion a heated exchange over which soccer team is best, we become more adept at finding workable solutions to divisive political issues.

Watching others do these things or studying theories about how such things should be done can be helpful, of course. A good role model or an explanatory theory is no substitute, however, for firsthand experience. Studying French grammar and vocabulary, listening to native French speakers, watching French TV, and reading French novels can contribute immensely to our learning French. We have to speak it, however, making mistakes and being corrected, talking with different Francophone people in differing contexts, before our sentences begin to come naturally, our foreign accent begins to fade, and we are able to communicate our thoughts in that language effectively.

There is nothing mysterious about why system-making requires practice: becoming good at doing something is fundamentally a process of learning how to form effective boundaries to conditions that are ill-bounded or unbounded. The vague delight of being outdoors on a bright clear day pricks my companion's curiosity. She asks me, her eyes bright with wonder, why the sky is such a glorious blue. I answer her question by identifying for her the relevant causal influences in the physical environment, excluding all else no matter what its intrinsic importance. By focusing her attention on light from the sun, she will understand my account of how when it interacts with oxygen molecules in a cloudless sky the oxygen absorbs all but the blue portion of the light spectrum, which will appear to her observing eye and mine as though it were a transmission of information about a distant blue canopy. That the day is warm, my companion attractive, and my reputation as a top physics student at stake, are irrelevant—irrelevant, that is, to the truth of my answer, even if those other matters may be far more relevant to how I feel about the questioner and about myself, and about how she might feel about me.

For the purpose of answering a question, of solving a problem, some aspects of the situation must be devalued and the worth of other aspects enhanced and then organized in a systematic manner, one that provides the requested answer as unambiguously as possible. There is no automatic procedure for deciding what to take as relevant in order to identify a relational pattern that can effectively direct attention to a plausible solution to a problem. A repertoire of general rules and a stock of attested previous successes are available resources from which we can draw, but the choices we make need to be sensitive to the specifics of the situation. And once made, our choices need constantly to be reassessed and modified in the light of how effective the answers are that they propose. Only by making systems we think will do the job can we learn to make better ones and make them more efficiently.

We should be contributing members of our community, and in a complex society this means becoming an expert in something that has a useful social function. The importance of communal life rests on the division of labor it both requires and makes possible. Some of us make shoes while others grow vegetables, and within a properly functioning system of exchange we will both end up well shod and well fed. Expertise necessitates specialization, however, limiting our labor to an activity that calls for only a few skills and a limited range of relevant information. Experts pay a price for their expertise, having to narrow their field of endeavor, having to work within the closed system of abstractions it presupposes. In exchange, they gain clarity and extendability, a precise grasp of what is needed and the ability to build on previous achievements.

By focusing solely on the quantitative features of the pebble I plucked from the beach, I can extend what I know to other pebbles since most of the features of my pebble are replicated in all the others on the beach. This expanded knowledge allows me to ask why the beach is full of pebbles rather than bigger rocks or simply sand, and in searching for an answer I will be led to a consideration of how littorals are formed and of the conditions under which they develop flourishing complex ecologies and those under which such environments degrade. It is then a short step to understanding why goldfish die so easily in bowls, and only a step or two further to understanding why even the most successful republics eventually decline and fall.

There are certain skills and ideas and information we all need, and so the learning that takes place in primary education and in the general education portions of secondary and higher education requires no expertise. We recognize the need for specialization, however, and so students are sorted into tracks based on whether it is thought they have the ability to go on to college, and in college are sorted by majors and often are even able to satisfy their general education requirements by taking major-oriented versions of a general subject—physics for poets, chemistry for nurses, economics for business majors.

A danger in simplifying a situation, in clarifying its vague features and resolving its incoherence, is oversimplifying it. Too much may be omitted, the focusing orientation may distort aspects beyond recognition, or a structure may be imposed arbitrarily on the facts rather than discovered as a neglected relational feature. Whitehead notes that these oversimplifications are sometimes "fortunate errors." Aristotle's ordering of biological organisms into categories of sharply distinguishable natural kinds was a significant advance over Plato's much vaguer method of division. The genus/species mode of analysis "was one of the happiest ideas possible, and it has clarified thinking ever since" (15), even though Plato's approach was more sensitive to the dynamic complexities of organic life and hence a better anticipation of the Darwinian approach to the classification of organisms.

The hubris of precision is taking a successful system of our devising and extending it beyond the limited domain in which it was a success. We forget that the system is a simplification, a strategy of abstraction valuable for the way in which it helps us achieve certain of our aims. We take the "purely formal relations" as "the final reality" (18). The ancient Greeks were "dazzled" by the "static attainment" of geometric form, says Whitehead, by how "motionless, impervious, and self-sufficient" it was. They thought it offered a "glimpse of eternity," and so they "conceived ultimate reality in the guise of static existences with timeless interrelations" (81), as "complete in itself" and therefore "self-sustaining," the realm of the "completely real" (68).

We moderns, entranced by quantitative measurement, make a similar mistake. Scientific methods, by limiting themselves to the quantitative aspects of things, yield a profound understanding of the regularities of nature and their relevance to our material needs and desires. It is easy to begin thinking that these quantities are the only objective features of things, in contrast to their unmeasurable qualities which are merely subjective. Thus in the halls of academe these days an objective examination is one with multiple-choice answers that can be graded by machine, whereas an examination involving judgments about the literary merit of a novel, the wisdom of a diplomatic initiative, or the relevance of a theory to anomalous data are said to call for subjective responses that can only be graded subjectively.

The key to the success of those who make systems is that they limit their concern to some finite and therefore manageable arena. They set boundaries to their subject matter—and take the matters-of-fact comprising that subject matter as each similarly bounded. When they cease to respect those limits, they treat the bounded content as all there is. They presume that facts always come in finite units organized into finite systems. Since it is possible, at least in principle, to know completely any finite fact or system of finite facts, those who have achieved such knowledge tend to be certain about it. And if they think what they know is all that can be known, they tend to be absolutely certain. Their knowledge knows no bounds. They are like the one-time Master of Cambridge's Trinity College who Whitehead reports was said to claim, as the debunking rhyme would have it, that "I am Master of this College; / And what I know not, / Is not knowledge" (43).

"A single fact in isolation is the primary myth required for finite thought, that is to say, for thought unable to embrace totality" (9). Whitehead is highly critical of the system-makers who have bought into this myth. He bemoans "the triviality of quick-witted people" (39), whose work "degenerates into a dull accumulation of minor feats of coordination" (57) and whose self-satisfied certainty "sterilizes imaginative thought, and thereby blocks progress" (43). He rails against the "deadening closure" resulting from "the certainty of completed knowledge," angrily calling it "the antichrist of learning" (58), a celebration of "the supremacy of the desert" that "bestows on learning a fugitive, and a cloistered virtue" (19).

Precision, for all its pragmatic value and civilizing functionality, is, when taken as sufficient, as deadly as is romance when taken as sufficient.

Further Assemblage

Although Whitehead's key modes of thought, importance and matter-of-fact, have provided fresh insights into the nature of the romance and precision stages of education, we are confounded by the tension between them, their polar opposition. The strength of each is the other's weakness, so in recognizing the weakness in one we are led to embrace the other for its strengths—only to discover eventually its weaknesses and so to reach out once more for the other. The uncritical embrace of whatever comes to the attention of our romantic curiosity leaves us unsatisfied, and so we seek the clarity and orderliness precision provides. The narrowing of thought and action endemic to an insistence on a systemic approach eventually becomes stifling, however, increasing our susceptibility to the open vistas romance promises.

Generalization offers a way out of this endless back and forth between romance and precision. In order to explicate how this is so, I shall begin as Whitehead recommends, by assemblage, identifying five ideas in *Modes of Thought* that suggest how this impasse can be resolved.

1. *Self-evidence.* Understanding, says Whitehead, is "a process of penetration" leading to a sense of "completion" (43). This sense of completion "arises from the self-evidence in our understanding"—indeed, "self-evidence is understanding" (47). When we develop an argument in support of what we understand to be the case, when we offer a proof of our claims, we are utilizing "a feeble second-rate procedure . . . unless proof has produced self-evidence and thereby rendered itself unnecessary" (48). Yet any intuition of self-evidence "is limited, and it flickers" (50).

An experience of a matter-of-fact is not self-evident, neither is a feeling of importance. They simply are what they are. However, when we combine them in a judgment that "this fact is important," when we interpret the experienced fact as meaningful, we understand them. They are self-evident not in themselves but as related in a judgment that understands both the matter-of-fact and the importance as constituting a significant fact.

The data our teacher asks us to gather in the course of conducting a laboratory experiment on the correlation between temperature and pressure are just numbers and Boyle's Law is just a formula that can be satisfied by assigning those numbers to its variables. Our teacher hopes, however, that as we conduct the experiment we will come to see the data as revealing a dynamic interaction that can be graphed by means of a line, a line with which the data points are correlated although they do not exactly conform to it. We will see the pattern in the facts while recognizing that the pattern is general not specific, that it is not a fact but a value that renders the facts meaningful. We will realize that Boyle's Law is a value found in the facts not imposed on them, and that the line it defines is objective not subjective. If by running the experiment we come to understand what Boyle's Law is and what it is not, we will have learned something important about how nature works and how theories are models rather than descriptions.

Some of us will fudge our experimental results so that the data points all fall exactly on the line. Others of us will argue that the absence of a perfect fit disproves the theory. Most of us will be content simply to gather the data, plug the numbers into the theory, graph the results, and turn in our work without worrying about such niggling matters. If we are among those who carry out the experiment in this manner—the fudgers, the contrarians, and the docile alike—we will not have understood what we were doing. We will only understand when we take it as self-evident that the facts we have observed are more complicated than any systematic account of how they work, but that these orderings are nonetheless true to those facts, and that they are therefore powerful tools for anticipating how subsequent facts are likely to work, for discovering how they once worked, and for reworking their conditions here and now for the better realization of our ends.

If we find it difficult to understand how our knowledge is an idealization of what it is knowledge about, it will be even harder for us to understand that this understanding is fragile. After all, when something is self-evident it no longer needs defending. The proofs and arguments have had their day; now at last we've got it right. Confidence and self-evidence go hand in hand. Yet, as Whitehead insists, understanding flickers: like a Fourth of July flare, it bursts into sight, burns brightly for a time, and then fizzles out. We need to be taught not only the current brightly burning theories but also those that have fizzled, that have been disproved or simply fallen out of fashion. We need to appreciate these failed theories not as quaint relics from an ignorant past era but as understandings we would have found self-evident had we known only what was known when they were thought to be unassailable truths.

Common sense lags a generation or two, sometimes a century or two, behind the reigning theories, so an effective pedagogical strategy for understanding the limits of understanding is for our teachers to confront us with a problem they ask us to solve without our knowing the currently accepted solution, and then to expose the commonsensical self-evidence of our answers as relying on a discarded theory, an out-of-date understanding. The history of science should be taught as an integral part of any science's curriculum, so that the ontogeny of our learning recapitulates the discipline's phylogeny. Self-evident truths are progeny that have descended with modification from long-dead ancestral truths.

2. *Perspective*. A matter-of-fact, a particular thing, "essentially involves its own connection with the universe of other things." This connection is "the perspective of the universe for that entity" with respect both to "accomplishment" and "potentiality" (66). A multitude of possible connections, of "alternative potentialities," is reduced "by elimination of alternatives" to the single connection that is that perspective (67). Whitehead's notion of an "actual occasion," developed in *Process and Reality*, is a model of this understanding of a fact: that it emerges from the diverse realities of its past by integrating them into a unique fully determinate new unity, a concretely complex spatiotemporal event. The swirl of cosmic dust

becomes a planet; the dying marine organisms become bedrock limestone; the fertilized egg becomes a fledgling finch; the milling crowd of angry farmers becomes a rebel army.

And yet "the very character of concrete realization . . . is suffused with the potentialities which it excludes with varying types of relevance" (83–84): characteristics of the past "partly reproduced and partly excluded," characteristics of the present "partly shared in and partly excluded," and possibilities for the future "partly prepared for and partly excluded" (84). A matter-of-fact is important because it integrates past and future into its present perspectival achievement. It is a microcosm of the macrocosm, in its own special way. "In the absence of perspective there is triviality" (84): as is, for example, the reality of the self-contained billiard-ball atoms of a mechanical universe, the reality of each determined independently of the contexts in which it is pushed about by other atoms that are indistinguishable from it except for location and causal role.

A theory is also a perspective on the experienced world, a view of it from a specific standpoint, and so it is necessarily partial. It leaves things out in order to make sense of what remains, but it doing so it always includes intimations of what it has omitted. We can acquire a sense of this incompleteness by discovering that a given theory is not the only way the previously collected and currently observed data could be organized, and that there are other ways than the theory's to extrapolate from that organization in making predictions of what will happen henceforth.

Valid proofs in logic are one of the ways to disclose such intimations, to make explicit aspects of a theory that are not immediately obvious. A logical proof moves from premises to conclusion along a series of transformations to the premises governed by rules for doing so, transformations that under a truth-functional interpretation preserve whatever truth it has been determined or presumed the premises have. However, there is typically more than one valid proof for a conclusion in a logical system, more than one series of truth-preserving steps that will lead to the same conclusion. Some proofs make use of only some of the available premises while others use different ones, some use rules others ignore, some may meander excessively or complicate their trajectory unnecessarily, but they all arrive at the same conclusion. A theory intimates conclusions that a proof makes self-evident, but that proof intimates alternative proofs equally able to disclose that self-evidence. We prefer the most elegant proofs, however, the beautiful ones, those with the fewest steps and the greatest transparency, and we privilege a system with a minimum of premises and rules, the apotheosis of which is a system with one axiom and one derivation rule. Our preference is justified, however, not for logical but for aesthetic reasons.

We would better understand what we are learning if our teachers would spend less time showering us with the facts illustrating a theory and more time encouraging us to play with alternatives that are or might be as adequate. Assessing the comparative worth of Ptolemaic, Newtonian, and Einsteinian theories of planetary motion when all three seem to account equally well for the relevant astronomical data, puzzling over two contrasting predictions regarding the economic consequences of a proposed governmental policy when both predictions have utilized the same macroeconomic theory—these are obvious examples of how we can learn that theories are perspectives rife with hints of their limitations, and that these limitations are often as important as their strengths because they suggest the possibility of alternative and perhaps more fruitful perspectives.

We ourselves are perspectives as well, says Whitehead, each in our own special way a microcosm of the macrocosm. When Hamlet (3.1.58–90) wonders whether it is better "to be or not to be," he imagines how pleasant it would be to die and thereby avoid the "slings and arrows" of living, its endless "heartache" and "natural shocks." But he then worries about what might happen to him after death, what greater ills he might suffer in that "undiscover'd country from whose bourn no traveler returns." Hamlet takes one stance toward life and then another, imagines himself embracing death and then fleeing it. His actual perspective, of course, is one of vacillation; how he truly comports himself is indecisively. The "native hue" of the resolution to which he aspires is "sicklied o'er with the pale cast" of his irresolution. Hamlet *is* his indecisive view of things, his inability to chart a course of action through a "sea of troubles." The boundless possibilities Hamlet's youthful philosophy until then had not contained threaten to undo him.

This indecisive perspective, however, carries hints of its eventual transformation into a perspective that will lead Hamlet resolutely on to avenge his father's death, to murder, poison, the rapier—and silence. Shakespeare convinces us that the indecisive Hamlet can be father of the decisive Hamlet by showing us the intimations of the latter in the former and then telling a story that makes self-evident a character potential that was initially obscured. Hamlet is a perspective of the world who over the course of the play is transformed into an alternative perspective, which from the first was implicit in that original perspective—not necessitated by it, but understandable as a way for it to have developed.

Perspectives when they are human are redolent with their manifold limitations and potentialities. The Great Books that are supposed to comprise the core of any first-rate liberal arts curriculum should be those that show us people, actual or fictitious, as perspectives of this sort: more than just reflections of their culture, more than just their various matter-of-fact accomplishments or their various aims and hopes, more just than the lessons their examples teach, more always than what we can fully comprehend.

3. *Greatness.* "The generic aim of process is the attainment of importance" (12). Morality, as one of the specialized forms within which importance is sought, is therefore not fundamentally about moral codes, not about striving for excellence, nor about calculating optimal satisfaction, nor about conforming to a categorical imperative. Rather, argues Whitehead, "morality consists in the control of process so as to maximize importance" (13–14). Its aim is at "greatness of experience," at a "union of harmony, intensity, and vividness which involves the perfection of importance for that occasion" (14). The primary task of human moral action is not to prevent the death of a person or to ensure the survival of a society, neither is it to help in the progression of one or more lives from mere living to living better and from living better to living well. "Whether we destroy, or whether we preserve, our action is moral if we have thereby safeguarded the importance of experience so far as it depends on that concrete instance in the world's history" (15).

No achievement is simply good or bad, no way of behaving simply right or wrong, because our actions always involve incompatible values. For instance, Bentham's utilitarianism seems straightforward: seek pleasure avoid pain. But the hedonistic calculus by which to adjudicate among alternative possible pursuits is fearsomely complicated: add up a quantitative measure of the pleasures associated with a possible action, taking account in measuring each pleasure of its intensity, duration, certainty, propinquity, fecundity, and purity. Then subtract a similar summary of pains. Do this for every person likely to be affected by the action, do the same for alternative courses of action, including taking no action, and then undertake the action that your calculation indicates will afford the greatest happiness for the greatest number. Such a calculation would be a gargantuan undertaking, and the more concretely detailed the calculation becomes the more problematic the judgment assigning a specific quantitative value to each of its relevant factors.

Imagine assigning students in an ethics course, or more appropriately in a course on management or public policy, the task of making a Benthamite calculation, with regard to some specific case-study situation, of what constitutes the best of the available policy choices. The pleasure and pain quantities will be hard to discern, especially the predictions of duration and fecundity. The relevance of many of the so-called externalities will be controversial, as will any decision to quantify, much less include, hopes, fantasies, and other imaginings. The supposed clarity will dissolve in a maze of ambiguities. A blur of gray on gray will replace the sharply distinguished blacks and whites the calculus promises. And the students still will not have faced up to the embarrassing question of whether the happiness of not just a majority but of almost everyone would be justified were it at the involuntary expense of even one person's happiness.

Rule-based ethical theories generate similar paradoxes and complications that threaten to engulf their supposed clarity. Indeed, what makes an ethics course interesting is when these questions are discovered by the students themselves as they attempt to penetrate to the meaning of a moral theory, to get past the verbiage, the rules and the formulae, to an understanding of what the philosopher is proposing. There is no better reason than this for avoiding an ethics course that uses a textbook that explains lucidly and in a well-ordered manner primary material we are not asked to read ourselves, or uses a collection of brief snippets from that material. The focus on conclusions leaves no room for the ambiguities, complications, and inconsistencies found in the philosophers' unabridged presentations—which are the resources by which serious readers will be able to find their way to deeper and often unexpected meanings.

Whitehead's admonition to safeguard above all else the importance of experience, indeed to enhance its importance, forces us to face up to the haze of moral complication. Ethical theories are not irrelevant to our task, but they can never be more than orienting suggestions, maps that can help guide our choices but can never determine them. We simply don't have time to make all the necessary hedonistic calculations, the accepted moral standards do not seem applicable to the situation at hand, all the facts we need are not currently available, and yet we must make a decision right now. In the *Bhagavad-Gita*, Arjuna is able to choose how to act because he believes his choices make no difference, that his actions are insignificant shadows flickering across the surface of a timeless underlying

Reality: "Strike, stay your hand—no matter / Therefore, strike" (11.32). The question for us, however, is whether we will have enough courage and insight to make a good choice when, although we believe that our choice will make a difference and much of value will be gained, we recognize nonetheless that much of value will be lost because of what we do and that the difference between the lost and the gained will be too complex to grasp adequately, too bottomless to understand.

The greatness of experience that according to Whitehead should be our ultimate aim is to be found in our attempt to harmonize the cacophony that is disrupting our situation without eliminating the diversity that has created that cacophony, realizing that it is impossible to do so—but not impossible to try. Moral development comes through creative failure. That this is so is an understanding that, although it cannot be taught, should be the ultimate aim of our educational institutions to foster.

4. *Completion.* "In proportion as we penetrate towards concrete apprehension, inconsistency rules," whereas "consistency grows with abstraction from the concrete" (59). Whitehead argues that logic and aesthetics, the two great methods for creating composite unities, are rooted in inconsistency.

The satisfaction we find in discovering a logical complex, and the "enjoyment of that complex when discovered," is due to the rigorous consistency it has achieved by abstracting from the concreteness of the elements out of which it is composed, understanding "the abstracted details as permitting that abstract unity" (61). Similarly, although aesthetics begins with the whole, with "a totality disclosing its component parts" that "force themselves upon us as the reasons for the totality of the effect" (62), the dependence of the whole on its parts is fundamental. In both cases, however, something of the intrinsic importance of the details is lost in the compromise involved in harmonizing them, in transforming them into components of a whole. The unity of a complex whole, whether logical or aesthetic, is dependent on negating in some manner and to some degree the individual unities of the elements unified.

In a logical system, the primitive form of all the key operators involves negation. The definition of material implication, for instance, is that "if *p* then *q*," which by substituting *p* for *q* yields the tautology "if *p* then *p*," which is truth-functionally equivalent to the law of excluded middle—"either *not-p* or *p*"—and the law of noncontradiction—"not both *p* and *not-p*." Finitude is "that which excludes other things comparable to itself" (52), and so logic, which rests on the exclusion of *not-p* from *p* is necessarily finite. We typically teach symbolic logic as a finite closed system that encompasses all true propositions and excludes all not-true ones, and that has an unambiguous decision procedure for distinguishing between them. Unfortunately, Gödel's incompleteness theorem is usually studied only in advanced logic courses, so most students never have to come to terms with logic's fundamental limitation, the fact that a logical system can be made complete, containing all true propositions, only by being made inconsistent, allowing at least one not-true proposition, and therefore that no system can be both complete and consistent.

A work of art is a finite system that although open nonetheless also pays a price for the unity it achieves. It can be complete aesthetically, integrating its components into an affectively and intellectually intense harmony, only by compromising the integrity of each of those components. In *Adventures of Ideas*, as we have seen, Whitehead extols the facade of the cathedral at Chartres because it incorporates a number of distinctive sculptures of individual saints and heroes into its encompassing unity. However, their uniqueness is unavoidably sacrificed, for the value of each individual sculpture is transformed by its cathedral location, becoming a function of how it contrasts with the other individual sculptures and of how those contrasts differ from each other. They were made as the unique individuals they are in order to be components in a complex facade of a great cathedral. The whole of which the sculptures are a part alters each sculpture's isolated individuality so that it might enhance the whole.

A vast congeries of negation thus haunts the great aesthetic achievement of the Chartres cathedral. Excluded from the cathedral that was built at that location are those that were not built there, possible cathedrals in which its sculptures would be otherwise enhanced or ones that would have no sculptures at all on their facade. The free-standing sculptures that might have been carved as self-sufficient works of art are not the ones that were carved. Those on the facade are not the works of art they would be were they removed from the cathedral and displayed in a museum as are the Elgin marbles, or set on pedestals along the Appian Way, or photographed and displayed on a projector screen after turning the cathedral background into a pale blue emptiness. Possible intrinsic importances are lost when something is created, so that a different intrinsic importance might be achieved.

An interesting educational assignment in our art class would be for the teacher to have us find an example of a work of art that maximizes the distinctiveness of its components without losing a sense of the whole, and to compare it to a work of art in which the intensity of the whole is maximized without losing an appreciation for the distinctiveness of its components. A Matisse, for example, as compared to a Brancusi. Then after discovering the merits of these opposing strategies, we might be asked to create artworks of our own that express our best judgment on how to resolve this incorrigible dilemma of how to do justice both to the whole and to its individual components—an impossible assignment, designed to teach us the hard truth that beauty is always a compromise, that justice can never be done in aesthetic creation.

5. *Solemnity*. Our sense of wholeness, our intuition of self-evidence, is unavoidably "incomplete and partial," says Whitehead, "presupposing relation to some given undefined environment, imposing a perspective and awaiting exploration" (43). Because "any knowledge of the finite always involves a reference to infinitude" (44), a sense of completion also involves sensing "dimly the unexplored relationships with things beyond" (48). Matter-of-fact finitude is achieved by exclusion, but "the full solemnity of the world arises from the sense of positive achievement within the finite, combined with the sense of modes of infinitude stretching beyond each finite fact" (78).

Hence, although "system is essential for rational thought," nonetheless "the closed system is the death of living understanding" (83). Whitehead mentions Plato and Hume as examples of philosophers who developed important ideas that have come to be transformed by others into closed systems, into "neat little ways of thought," but whose thinking provided insights "hard to reconcile" with those systems (82). For example, try reconciling what Plato says in the *Phaedo*—that when a person dies the body, "the mortal part," perishes but the "deathless part," the soul, "goes away safe and indestructible" (106e)—with what he says in the *Symposium*—that "reproduction and birth in beauty" is what we "mortals have in place of immortality" (206e). The challenge for our teachers is to teach Plato, or Hume, or any of the other great system-makers, as thinkers aware of the limits of what they have achieved, authors who give us a sense of intellectual completion but one that involves a sense of further unexplored relationships with what lies beyond their system.

The inexhaustibility of the perspective we are invited to share kindles, as our understanding deepens, awareness of the world's solemnity. We grasp this solemnity, or rather are grasped by it, when we realize both the grandeur of the author's perspective and its inadequacy. We stand in awe before the scope and subtlety of the interpretive system a finite mind has fashioned, brilliant in the meanings it invokes, in the way it orients our purposes. Yet simultaneously we are overawed by the numberless possible perspectives that have escaped its viewpoint, the actual and possible perspectives of other authors, other moral agents, other things, and other kinds of things. And this awe continues to expand, toward the infinitude of a totality stretching endlessly beyond even that unimaginable vastness.

Textbooks and CliffsNotes provide the neat little ways of thought to which Whitehead objects, and yet a disproportionate amount of how we are taught involves such condensations. Our teachers argue that the original work is too complex, its ideas too subtle and its language too sophisticated or too technical, for schoolchildren or even college undergraduates to understand, too esoteric for the uninitiated or the unbelieving to grasp. Or they say that the original work is out of date and needs to be replaced by something more current and hence more accessible, although the substitute for the original is almost always not so much modernized and simplified as bowdlerized and rendered simplistic. A good teacher can help us find our way in a great text, but if the text is mediocre, a closed perspective masquerading as a living one, not even a great teacher can bring it to life. If in our classroom experiences, in the hours we spend in laboratories and libraries, field trips and discussion groups, we are not invited to experience the solemnity of the world, it should not be surprising that so many of us fail to take our education seriously, that we think of it only in terms of its usefulness in securing a job.

Matters-of-fact are inherently interesting, and knowing a lot of them firsthand can be immensely satisfying. Learning theories that organize matters-of-fact into closed systems give us an equally satisfying grasp of the importance of perspectives, their capacity to make sense of things, to order matters-of-fact in meaningful, predictable, useful ways. Appreciating the beauty of a fact or a system of facts, a sunset or an explanation of sunsets, can be an exquisite experience, sometimes even a sublime one. Yet only when a system is appreciated as both an achievement and a failure, as a bright light revealing something about the world but revealing as well its penumbra of shadows and the dark umbra beyond the shadows, only then does the world's solemnity dawn on us. Only then does our education become an endless adventure essential to who we are, an adventure we receive as a priceless inheritance, pursue for a brief moment, and then bequeath to our successors.

Rationalization

And so I have completed an assemblage of five particular fragments from *Modes of Thought*, all of which express the same important dilemma in different ways. First, the goal of understanding is self-evidence, but self-evidence is flickering and fleeting. Second, each factual reality is a perspective implying its particular past and big with its particular future, but since each is limited there can be no single all-encompassing reality. Third, the good is about maximizing importance, which means creating, sustaining, and enhancing achieved value, but in doing so values every bit as important are destroyed. Fourth, logic and art are based on a fundamental inconsistency, which in their differing ways they seek to overcome, but they cannot do so without compromising the unique value intrinsic to the various specific elements of which a consistent integrative whole must be constituted. Fifth, the creation of finite systems—interpretive theories, social institutions, works of art, personal character—are the greatest of human achievements, but they are great only if able to reveal their inescapable inadequacy.

These five expressions of the dilemma of how importance and matter-of-fact can be reconciled echo Whitehead's modes of thought: science, practicality, morality, the arts and logic, and religion. These dilemmas are also echoed educationally in the oscillation between romance and precision. Just as generalization is the way this educational oscillation can be overcome, its polarities reconciled, their differences transformed into developmental stages of growth, so likewise in the ontology of *Modes of Thought* the polarities of matter-of-fact and importance are reconciled by the exercise of what Whitehead calls "rationality."

We seek perfection, but it comes in two flavors. The ideal of a complete unification of things, the amalgamation of everything whatsoever into a perfect harmony, is one mode of perfecting the world as we find it. But the ideal of a unique fully self-sufficient individual, independent of anything extraneous, not needing anything else in order to be complete, is equally a mode of perfection we extol. These two sorts of perfection are unreachable, however: no individual is absolutely unique, no totality absolutely encompassing. For every matter-of-fact there are other matters-of-fact that are similar to it in some way and to some extent, compromising its uniqueness. For every totalizing system there are others that have a similar form or genetic structure or function, compromising its universality.

A sonnet is obviously not a sonata, but we may notice and then exploit some ways in which they have interestingly similar formal structures. For instance, a standard English sonnet is divided into three quatrains, each with its own *abab* rhyme scheme, followed by a closing rhymed couplet. A standard sonata is likewise composed of three sections—an exposition of one or more themes, a development of the thematic material, and a recapitulation—often followed by a coda. We might imagine a sonnet in which the three quatrains traced, in sonata-like fashion, a theme-exposition-recapitulation pattern, with its closing couplet functioning as a calming coda-like conclusion. Or a sonata might be written in which its coda does not simply conclude the piece but, as is typical for sonnets, takes a fresh look at the themes that have been previously explored.

Square dances are similar to both sonnets and sonatas, but more tenuously so, for although they also can be divided into sections that can be repeated in standard ways, their structure is far more flexible because far more modular. Similarities such as these may seem trivial, and making much of them may strike us as a violation of common sense. But not necessarily. After all, the quantitative relation among lengths of a lute string and the qualitative harmonies produced when those strings are plucked is as surprising to common sense as it is important to understanding music.

Forms come in versions: subtle variations that often develop into distinctive varieties. Both Milton and Shakespeare write fourteen-line sonnets, each line composed of ten syllables. Shakespeare follows, indeed is the paradigm for, the English version of the sonnet form described earlier. Milton uses the so-called Petrarchan version, however, in which the first eight lines, in two quatrains each in *abba* form, state a problem that the last six lines, in two tercets each in *cde* form, resolve. Some of Gerald Manley Hopkins's sonnets are three-fourths of a Petrarchan sonnet: ten and a half lines instead of fourteen, composed of two tercets rather than two quatrains, followed by a quatrain rather than two tercets, and then a half-line ending. These "curtal" sonnets, as well as the ones Hopkins wrote using the standard number of lines, also use a "sprung rhythm," counting only stressed syllables, five for each line, plus any number of unstressed syllables. Hopkins's sonnets are versions of the Petrarchan form so radical as to constitute a whole new species of sonnet.

Standard forms, versions of forms, variations of versions: the parsing of identities into differences, sameness into similarity, has no end. Two sonnets written in the same version, even when further narrowed as in the Shakespearean variety of the English version where each line is in iambic pentameter, are still two different distinctively unique sonnets. Having read a few of Shakespeare's sonnets, we do not shrug off the rest on the grounds that having read some we've read them all. The uniqueness of one sonnet is not undermined by it having the same form as another, because it individuates that form through its specific theme, its choice of rhymes, the mood it creates, the point it makes. Each sonnet has its own special form, inseparable from its content and aim, and yet in being this sonnet rather than that it discloses something about the sonnet form—and about poetry, and about form as such—that no other sonnet does.

Metaphors and analogies are how we rationalize the polarities that result from literal thinking: by marking the partial identitics to be found amid the diversity of things and the partial diversities to be found amid their identity. My love is like a red, red rose; when the child of morning, rosy-fingered Dawn, appeared; the dawn comes up like thunder; the night has a thousand eyes, and the day but one. "The procedure of rationalism," says Whitehead, "is the discussion of analogy" (*Modes* 98). To understand is to seek out common features among a multiplicity of divergent particulars. In doing so, "we necessarily introduce the notion of potentiality" (99): the potentiality of many facts fitting into one form, the potentiality of a single form giving shape to many particulars.

Such forms are not static, however. They are what Whitehead calls "forms of process" or "serial forms" (99). The "fundamental intuition which lies at the basis of all thought" is fourfold: that there is an "essential passage from experience of individual fact to the conception of character [form]," that this form is stable "amidst the succession of facts," that it provides those facts with a character, a "partial identity" along "a given route of succession," and that there is thus a "potentiality of the facts for maintaining such partial identity amid such succession" (99). The organizing patterns never fit perfectly; they provide the multiplicity of particulars with a stabilizing but not permanent character. They are approximate forms, useful in the context for which they are fashioned but not necessarily in a different context. They are temporary scaffolds not timeless templates.

The smooth wash of dull red over its head, upper body, and rump, and the absence of dark stripes on its sides, leads me to identify a bird as a male Purple Finch. My identification is strengthened when I notice that other nearby birds of similar size and shape but without any red coloring have the distinctively striped sides and light eyebrow of the female Purple Finch. This identification is good enough for a report to a local birding listserve, but were I to have identified the birds as Cassin's Finches, which are infrequent visitors to our region, my judgment would not survive without securing further verifying specifics.

Similarly, we can gain striking insights into the Arthurian legends by organizing them within a Freudian pattern of interpretation. Seeing Arthur's relation to Merlin as oedipal illuminates both his dependence on the wizard and his efforts to free himself of Merlin's influence. We can then easily expand the oedipal theme to explain Mordred's rejection of his father and attempted usurpation of the throne, and perhaps to permit us reading Arthur's mortal wounding by Mordred on Salisbury Plain as the killing of the primal father that liberates the surviving Britons from their allegiance to a dying past, freeing them to contribute to England's future greatness. This Freudian characterization is exceedingly unstable, however, its value more heuristic than hermeneutic, for it quickly collapses in the face of a more adequate marshaling of the legend's details.

"A fortunate use of abstractions is of the essence of upward evolution" (123). We think rationally—we are conscious in a rational way—when we abstract from the matters-of-fact that fill our concrete experience, taking their insistent vivid particularities as instances of something general: an interpretive pattern, an organizing rule, a guiding orientation. We find an analogy that binds things together: the gigantic planet Jupiter and the much smaller Mars have orbits similar to a mathematical ellipse. Then we explore the possibility that this analogy might apply to other planets as well, such as strangely ringed Saturn or distant Pluto with its distinctively tilted orbit. We can even extend our analogy to planetary moons and the electrons swirling around atoms, to planets orbiting other suns, to the movement of whole galaxies, and, if we are bold enough, to vague unknowns we conjure as maybe somewhere somehow existing beyond our spatial and temporal horizons but as nonetheless also bound by the same pattern or rule or purpose: the federated planets of the Galactic Empire in a galaxy far, far away, or those orbiting suns in alternative universes parallel to our own.

Learning how to formulate a good scientific hypothesis or to invent an illuminating fictional world should be among the most important goals of education: learning how to exercise our powers of rationalization, our capacity to think analogically, in order to further our understanding of things and hence to guide our appropriate use of them. The trick is to do this while preserving a sense of the concrete, of the solid ground from which the abstractive flight into metaphorical connection departed, so that a reversal is possible, a descent from the abstract back to the concrete.

I've read many a student philosophy paper, and many an article by an established scholar, in which theory is spun from prior theory into a vast web of coherent abstract prose unrelieved by any reference to particular matters-of-fact. From Hegel's assertion, for example, that "pure insight . . . knows the pure self of consciousness to be absolute" (*Phenomenology* 561), bereft as it is of the concrete experience from which it presumably arose, there is no way back to the concreteness. It's William Perry's bull without cow, what Benedetto Croce calls a "ballet of ghostly abstractions" (*My Philosophy* 195), or as another translator phrases it: "a foam of abstract phantoms" (*Philosophy, Poetry, History* 513). Of course, I've also read many a student essay composed of fact after fact without any interpretive pattern to give it coherence, essays illustrating the conviction attributed to Henry Ford that history is "just one damn fact after another," a herd of lonely cows with no fructifying bull in sight.

The opportunity for the needed reversal from theories to their tethering facts lies in attending afresh to the metaphors by which we have rationalized our experience. Our hypothesis or storyline is necessarily inadequate in certain ways, a perspective suited for some purposes but not others, functioning well in some contexts but poorly elsewhere. As our way of doing things changes, as we alter our purpose or shift our context, as sharp-edged new facts are discovered that shred the fabric of our theory, we need to reexamine the metaphors on which we have been relying, the scaffold we have been using to construct our perspective. It may be time for a new scaffold, a metaphorical sally better suited to our needs. For new and newly relevant matters-of-fact make old importances uncouth.

The narrow specialist who begins to widen the range of her concerns, and the scholar who searches for a context more complex in scope or subtlety than the one in which he is expert, are both trying to break out of the confines of an interpretive framework, calling in question a taken-for-granted method or paradigm. Her motive may be a healthy curiosity about the implications outside her field for what she has accomplished. The facts have been filtered by an organizing form that has served her well, but her strategy now is to strip away the filter as best she can and to see if there are other ones that will do the job as well or better or simply differently. His motive may be to find some fresh tools for attacking a problem within his speciality. It doesn't work for him just to switch from one generalization to a different one; his trajectory must be from the abstraction back to the concrete and from there toward a fresh abstraction, a new paradigm.

Generalization reconciles romance and precision by rationalizing their absolutist tendencies. Matters-of-fact are intimately related and derive their importance from the enduring character they have in common. But that character is only partial, enduring only for a limited time across a limited space. If we recognize that the commonality is metaphorical not literal, if we are habitually on the lookout for the disanalogies even as we explore the analogies, then our practice will be to set the accomplishments of precision against a background of romance. In searching always for a better fit between facts and theories, we will be ready to abandon our theories, deconstruct our interpretive standpoints, call our stories into question. This seeming negation is actually a recovery, however, an enrichment of our abstractive frameworks by recourse to the concrete resources from which they were constructed. Romance is the fertile soil, precision the fertile plant, and generalization the cultivator's art by which living forms sprout and grow from an environment rich in nutrients, mature and flourish, wither and are harvested, and in dying make way for new forms for which their growing and their dying have supplied the seed and nutrient.

Every academic discipline, every course of instruction, and every teaching moment should involve the rhythmic back and forth between romance and precision, which under the rationalizing guidance of generalization is not an oscillation but a helical development. Learning should always involve a transformation of generous appreciation into well-ordered knowledge, leading to a deeper and wider appreciation and therefore to a more suitably ordered knowledge. Should, not must, of course, because the appreciation is never sufficiently generous and the ordering is never sufficiently adequate. Deeper and wider, better and more suitable, are rational ideals not necessities. They do not guarantee us understanding, but they point the way and provide the tools by which we can proceed and by which we can constantly reassess their worth. Our endless quest for understanding is a rational activity grounded in a familiarity with serial forms, their intellectual and practical power and their limitations. Hence the keystone to the arch of effective learning is acquiring the ability to fashion and interpret metaphors—to think analogically.

Philosophy and Poetry

Thinking about analogical thinking leads us to the analogy with which Whitehead begins and ends *Modes of Thought*: "philosophy is akin to poetry" (vii, 174; and also 50); or as he puts it midway through the book: "philosophy is analogous to imaginative art" (117). Philosophy and poetry are in some ways the same, for "truth is to be sought in the presuppositions of language rather than in its express statements" (vii), and each "suggests meaning beyond its mere statements" (117), makes "reference to form beyond the direct meaning of words" (174). Because of their ability to take us beyond the confines of the familiar world as we know it, both philosophy and poetry "seek to express that ultimate good sense which we term civilization" (vii, 174).

The assertion that "This is important"—the "fusion of a large generality with an insistent particularity," the marriage of importance with matter-of-fact—is for Whitehead, as we have seen, the paradigmatic expression of "civilized experience" (4). The problem with large generalities, however, is that they are vague. Whitehead mentions Coleridge objecting to a group of tourists who gush about "how pretty" the view is, using an insipid cliché to describe "an awe-inspiring spectacle" (5). The normal function of words is to "indicate useful particularities" (5), to refer to concrete specifics such as the sweet smell of those lilacs, the yellow of that daffodil, this pebble's strikingly beautiful shape, Hamlet's mortal wound. We therefore have trouble finding words to express our sense of the broader and deeper significance of those particularities, the way or ways in which they are important. So we lapse into empty verbiage, glittering generalities, pious platitudes; or tongue-tied, we fall silent.

Great literature and great philosophy are the highest forms of civilized expression, because in the presence of something awe-inspiring they untie our tongues and give content to our verbiage. Both are "mystical," in the sense that they offer "direct insight into depths as yet unspoken" (174). They do so by abusing language, using it in ways for which it was not designed in order to transgress its limits. Their abusive techniques are diametrically opposite, however. Philosophy and poetry, therefore, are analogous rather than identical.

Literature invests words expressing the vividness of particular matters-of-fact with overtones of their inherent general importance. It "fastens upon the accidental precision which inevitably clothes the qualitative generality" of our linguistic assertions, using these precise meanings to convey "our naive general intuitions" of their "fundamental emotional importance" (5). Think of the sacred river described by Coleridge's Kubla Khan, which roared out of a cavern in a mighty fountain, churning up pieces of rock that ". . . vaulted like rebounding hail, / Or chaffy grain beneath the thresher's flail" ("Kubla Khan" lines 21–22). Vividly precise words, used metaphorically to evoke a vaguely felt importance their literal meaning obscures. "It is one function of great literature to evoke a vivid feeling of what lies beyond words" (*Modes* 5).

Philosophy is the inverse of literature. It invests words expressing conventional generalities with overtones of the vivid particularity in which they are rooted. It takes an everyday word that is "capable of more precise use," but that in common discourse only "expresses the obvious" in vague generalities, and uses it in a novel way (5). Philosophy speaks of such things as "formal causes," a "categorical imperative," truth as "what works," but by investing those words with expanded and therefore disconcertingly unfamiliar meanings it gestures toward the precise particulars they encompass. It is able to avoid the tourist's trivialization of language by jarring us out of our taken-for-granted sense of what the vague generalities mean, helping us recognize that "the obvious embodies the permanent importance of variable detail" (5), of details obscured by the vagueness to which we have become accustomed. Expanding the things that work well from John Henry's hammer, and from the jackhammer that worked even better than he did, to scientific and metaphysical truths, we find ourselves thinking about what makes organisms and machines function effectively and what it could possibly mean to say that truths are effective functions.

What this further bit of assemblage makes clear is the importance of language for breaking through the constraints it is so crucial in fashioning. The precision provided by linguistic symbols allows us to describe particular matters-of-fact thoroughly and clearly. Language also articulates the systems governing those facts, formulating abstractions able to capture the relational structures that convey their importance, by which we can understand what is going on and anticipate what is likely to happen next. These systems, however, taken for granted because of their reliable success, turn out to be blinders. The limits they set to our thoughts and feelings are why they are so effective. But they are limits, and so they cut us off from possibilities that in changing circumstances may be crucial to our continued ability to understand and anticipate.

Philosophy and poetry use language to break through the boundaries that language has imposed on our sense of what facts are important and why. They rationalize experience by creating the tools through which we are able to expand the depth and scope of the meaningful world, to repair its inadequacies by disclosing new kinds of fact and fresh ways of interpreting how these new kinds and the familiar kinds are related. Philosophy and poetry offer the tools for developing the habit of thinking rationally, which is to say metaphorically, for rising to the stage of generalization in which the separately inadequate stages of romance and precision are transformed into interactively creative modes of experience.

Poetry is taught in creative writing classes where the emphasis is typically on endeavor and critique. We students write poems and our instructor and fellow students critique those efforts, then we write new poems and these are critiqued, and so on to the end of the course. We learn to be poets by writing poetry, and our poems are judged by their ability to open others' eyes, to unplug their ears, to blow their minds. It is important to read great poems written by poets living and dead of all cultures and climes, to find our eyes and ears and mind led beyond the familiar by their words. It is important to study theories of poetic form and style, to become versed in the technical tools of poetic creation, and to become familiar with the history of the schools and traditions that have grown up around the various poetic tools that have been invented and the ways in which they have been utilized. But the heart of the matter is to embark on our own expressive adventure, trying as best we can to push against some boundary, to probe its limits, to poke a hole in its constraints, to breach the barriers imposed by accepted truth. It's a lonely journey, and yet it is best undertaken in the company of others who in their own lonely journeyings need our criticism and are willing to provide us with plenty of theirs.

All the arts, not just poetry, should be taught this way, although there is an unfortunate tendency in our professors to split classes on the history of an art from classes in which works of art are made. A history of artistic boundary breaking is not likely by itself to break artistic boundaries binding us. And likewise our creative efforts untutored by a knowledge of prior efforts will tend to break against the boundaries rather than breaking through them. Interestingly, some of the most effective education these days that utilizes the creative writing format occurs in our science classes where we learn by making experimental inquiries in laboratories and out in the field. Proposing and testing solutions to scientific problems through collaborative explorations, stopping for lectures on theory or history or method as needed, is a powerfully effective way for us to develop the keen senses, imaginative boldness, and logical acuity required to think and act as good scientists do.

Philosophy, because it is akin to poetry, should be taught as poetry should be taught: in workshops where students are constantly attempting to philosophize, to sunder familiar connections and to find them where none were thought to exist. These oral and written efforts should then be critiqued, followed by fresh attempts and further critiques. A lecture as the primary way of teaching philosophy is a travesty because it substitutes information about the conclusions and methods of important philosophers for learning to wrestle in our own philosophical way with the puzzles that kindle a need for philosophic inquiry. The lectures have their place, but we must philosophize to learn to think as philosophers think. Neither the metaphysical systems philosophers create nor the exacting analytic monographs they write are the primary worth of their philosophizing. It is rather their effort to rationalize the conventional wisdom, to disclose its scope and its limits, and hence to grasp after its unexplained implications. Philosophy is the love, not the science, of wisdom; it is a pursuit, not an attainment.

Whereas "poetry allies itself to metre" in order to embed the general in the particular, philosophy in order to embed the particular in the general allies itself "to mathematical pattern" (174). This difference between meter and pattern as the tool for boundary-shattering rationalization gives philosophy an additional special aim: to transform the individualized intensity of poetic expression into common discourse, in order to make it easier to connect the insights of the poet to other modes of thought. Philosophy, says Whitehead, is "the endeavour to find a conventional phraseology for the vivid suggestiveness of the poet." It attempts to re-express poetic expressions in prose, and thus "to produce a verbal symbolism manageable for use in other connections of thought" (50). Philosophical expression attempts to build a bridge from aesthetic forms of process to moral, religious, scientific, and practical ones. It seeks to rationalize the modes of thought by expressing the great good, deep foundation, general truth, and workable payoff that an artist's expression of profound beauty harbors.

Philosophy is therefore uniquely positioned to fashion generalizations that bridge not only from poetry to the other modes of interpretive thought but from any mode to the other modes. Its task is to articulate how the other modes of interpretive thought are actively present in a scientist's expression of a general truth, in an ethicist's moral judgments, in the foundational beliefs and practices of priests and prophets, and in the practical endeavors of engineers, entrepreneurs, and bureaucrats. The aim of philosophy should be to rationalize experience by linking the modes of thought into a single integrative whole, fashioning an interpretation of the sense in which that whole is an important fact. It does so, however, realizing that any such whole is yet another attempt to make a finite boundary, to clothe the infinity of matter-of-fact in a finite form. Philosophy loves a whole it can never possess:

> If you like to phrase it so, philosophy is mystical. For mysticism is direct insight into depths as yet unspoken. But the purpose of philosophy is to rationalize mysticism: not by explaining it away, but by the introduction of novel verbal characterizations, rationally coordinated. (174)

The "Perfect Dictionary," says Whitehead, is the belief that "mankind has consciously entertained all the fundamental ideas which are applicable to its experience" and that human language "explicitly expresses these ideas" (173). Within a specific context with a fixed scope and unquestioned fundamental notions, this perfection is a legitimate ideal. Scholarship—exemplified by normal science and analytic philosophy—works within these conditions with considerable success. Scholars investigating "human thought and human achievement, armed with a dictionary," are "the main support of civilized thought" because of their "power of delicate accuracy of expression" (173).

The work of the scholar is necessary as well as useful, but it is not sufficient. It operates "within the limits of the dictionary," presuming "a fixed specification of the human mind" for which the dictionary is "the blue print" (173). There is more, however, in heaven and earth, in the unbounded and constantly evolving totality of things, than can be contained by any finite system of understanding. To think otherwise is to commit "the fallacy of the perfect dictionary" (173), to take an abstraction, an interpretive pattern, as a concrete whole. Philosophy, in contrast to scholarship, "appeals to direct insight, and endeavours to indicate its meanings by further appeal to situations which promote such specific insights. It then enlarges the dictionary." It values "adventure" more than "safety" (173).

Without precision's "delicate accuracy of expression" civilized thought is not possible, but without romance's "appeals to direct insight" civilized thought stultifies. Philosophy and poetry, in their differing modes of carrying on the task of generalization, which is to rationalize this polarity, use the precision of linguistic expression metaphorically to create situations that promote boundary-breaking romantic insight, and use those insights to promote new precise boundary-makings.

The Task of Education

And so we come at last to the quote that prefaces this essay: "The task of a university is the creation of the future, so far as rational thought, and civilized modes of appreciation, can affect the issue" (*Modes* 171). We need to rationalize this quote, interpreting the university as a metaphor for education in all its kinds and shapes from day care to postdoctoral study, from formal schooling to informal book groups and conversations over donuts and coffee. They are all analogous, various structures developed by communities to assist their members in learning to think rationally and therefore to contribute meaningfully to the life of those communities and to their own personal fulfillment.

Education at all levels, and higher education as its culmination, should develop in students, in us all, the capacity and motivation to create a viable future for ourselves, our country, our world. Since the future will unavoidably be different from the present, this ability involves being able to anticipate those differences in order to adapt to them and to shape them, differences as salient and fleeting as today's headlined events, as fundamental and overlooked as our culture's ultimate notions. Recognizing and shaping these changes means being able to rationalize the unknown by deploying established or imagined patterns of continuity in new ways, by using language metaphorically to fashion novel pathways into the wilderness beyond the cultivated fields of our familiar understandings.

Whitehead at times contrasts philosophy and poetry with the sciences. He should not, however, because this work of expansion and rationalization applies across all the ways in which the modes of civilized thought are expressed. Metaphors and analogies are obvious features of philosophic prose and poetic literature, but they are fundamental to all disciplines, for it is by their means that a discipline is able to transcend itself, to adapt other perspectives to its special needs, to develop a wider cross-disciplinary perspective that serves those special disciplinary needs by reconceiving them and revaluing their significance.

The skills involved in generalization are manifold: techniques of invention and insight, a sensitivity to the implicit, an eye for unnoticed and opportune pattern. The key to generalization, however, is not a skill but an attitude—a habit of analogical thinking and acting, understanding something as like something else in some interesting way, acting as though things were different than they are in order to sniff out opportunities for remaking them that way. Generalization involves imagining, improvising, experimenting, and accepting the inadequacies, mistakes, and outright failure of those endeavors as occasions for imagining more boldly, improvising more cleverly, experimenting more sophisticatedly.

The task of the university is to nurture the development of rational thinkers—of generalizers. To do so, its faculty will need to abandon the uncritical adulation of carefully bounded expertise that inexorably desiccates their love of scholarly research and of teaching, sapping the combined power of both as a primary engine of creative change. They will need to recover their long-forgotten love for that other primary engine, the imaginative imprecision and adventurous undiscipline of the amateur and the genius. Only then will university faculty be able to reaffirm the intercourse between those two loves, the fostering of which justifies the privileged status of the university as civilization's crowning glory.

The function of education is to equip the rising generations—to equip us all—with an ability to create the future, to think rationally in all the modes of thinking all the time. If we are to do so in a way that affects the issue of civilized endeavor, our thinking must not begin in metaphorical wonder in order to end in literal certainty. It must not begin with open-ended romance and conclude with self-enclosed precision. We must learn instead how to rationalize the wonder so that our beginnings as creative thinkers are alive in our endings and our endings are always occasions for improved beginnings: "Philosophy begins in wonder. And, at the end, when philosophic thought has done its best, the wonder remains" (168).

CHAPTER SIX

Learning to Be Good

Whitehead's rhythm of learning has been portrayed in prior chapters as a cycle moving from romance to precision, these polar opposites then reconciled in generalization. This cycle recurs in every sort of learning situation: in each daily class session, throughout a semester-long course, during the whole of a school year, and at all educational levels. The cycles do not simply repeat themselves, however. They are open not closed, generating a helix in which the content changes with each repetition of the cycle, the new cycle both constrained and enabled by what the old has achieved.

Whitehead says very little about the developmental aspect of education, although he says at one point in "The Rhythm of Education" that "the whole period of growth from infancy to manhood forms one grand cycle" (25). This cycle overarching all the lesser cycles begins with romance that "stretches across the first dozen years of life," from early childhood through primary school learning, moves to the precision that "comprises the whole school period of secondary education," and culminates in the generalization appropriate to university study and postgraduation adult life (25). It is a progressive movement from lesser to greater sophistication in the scope and intensity of the challenges students must master. In "The Rhythmic Claims of Freedom and Discipline," Whitehead parses "the whole period of education" into approximately the same three groupings, but immediately qualifies what he's said by noting that "these are only average characters, tinging the mode of development as a whole," for no one "completes his stages simultaneously in all subjects" (38).

Typically overlooked in considerations of this "grand cycle" is a brief but stimulating account of the developmental aspects of education found in the concluding Part IV of *Adventures of Ideas*, titled "Civilization." My aim in this chapter is to explore that account.

Wanting to Be Good

In the first part of *Adventures of Ideas*, Whitehead tells the story of how an idea about the supreme worth of every human soul came to be concretely actualized in the beliefs and institutional habits of civilized Westerners. This story might suggest that the process of human history is a complex form of linearity, that history is progressive, that the path is upward even if it involves momentary setbacks. It might suggest that our educational journey likewise traverses a continuing spiral of gathering, systematizing, critiquing, gathering more effectively, perfecting the system, deepening the critique. On this interpretation, Whitehead is claiming that the movement both of learning and of history rises slowly but steadily from lesser to higher values, from the good to the better and toward the best.

This is an unjustified interpretation, however. Whitehead is proposing an ideal pattern relevant to understanding history, not a description of the way events actually have been or necessarily will be structured. How an idea of the soul's worth worked itself out historically is the account of an adventure. The idea need never have arisen, nor need it have found the varieties of historical expression it did. But ideas have consequences, and there is a general pattern to these consequences that can be abstracted from them, suggesting a tendency for robust ideas of this sort to reshape slowly, by fits and starts, the character of social institutions.

Similarly, with respect to education, Whitehead proposes his three stages of learning and the developmental trajectory from childhood to educational maturity as an ideal pattern by means of which to discover important features and tendencies in how learning takes place. Individuals learn at differing rates, due to differences in native ability, character, and societal influences. In any given class session, students are scattered across the three stages and along the developmental trajectory in a distribution that challenges a teacher's ingenuity in devising a way to engage all of them at once.

Individuals vary from an educational ideal such as Whitehead's in the same way that those data points on the graph in a physics lab varied from the line that interprets them. The ideal patterns are norms for how we ought to develop educationally, a criterion by which our progress or lack of it can be measured, our work assessed as deficient, average, or exceptional. Abraham Maslow's self-actualization hierarchy (*Motivation and Personality*) and Jean Piaget's theory of cognitive development (Piaget and Inhelder, *The Psychology of the Child*) are well-known examples of such patterns. William Perry, author of that little story we discussed in chapter 1 about bull and cow, also has a schematic hierarchy, one that is concerned specifically with the intellectual and cognitive development of college students (*Forms of Intellectual and Ethical Development in the College Years*).

Many moral theorists think that moral education is simply a matter of learning the appropriate rules. For hedonists, these are instrumental rules, directions for how to get to whatever end is in a person's or community's interest. For deontological approaches, these rules are intrinsic, having to do with ends it is everyone's duty to pursue. The convenience of rules is that they can be taught to us easily, and so are easily transmitted from one generation to the next. Bentham's seven criteria for calculating the greatest good for the greatest number or Kant's three criteria for applying the categorical imperative can be memorized, and then tested for by administering an objective examination—list the criteria, explain them briefly, put them to work in calculating the worth of a particular action.

Whitehead's approach to moral judgment finds two basic problems with rule-based approaches, however. They presuppose the Perfect Dictionary discussed in chapter 5, the belief that we can grasp "all the fundamental ideas" relevant to moral judgment and formulate a set of ethical instructions that "explicitly expresses these ideas" (*Modes* 173). The fallacy is to think that the conditions for good are both precise and fixed, and so can be expressed as timeless laws, as self-evident truths. Furthermore, we can know what we ought to do or what is in our interest to do without doing it. To dissuade us from such moral failures, Bentham evokes various sanctions and Kant appeals to our respect for the moral law as such. But these expedients hardly suffice. Augustine knew quite well that it was wrong to steal pears from his neighbor's orchard, but he did it anyway: "It was foul, and I loved it" (*Confessions* 29).

For Whitehead the conditions of our beliefs and actions are the result of earlier beliefs and actions. Who we manage to be and what we choose to do are emergent, fragile, and transformable achievements. We grow morally not only by improving our understanding of good and its conditions but by altering those conditions. When we achieve our goals, we not only fulfill our desires but also improve the character of what we desire. When we successfully embody a moral rule in our actions, we not only do what is right but also reshape the meaning and import of that rule. As people become better they make a better world, and as the world becomes better it stimulates the emergence of better people. Growth entails decay, however. There is no predetermined ascent from the worst to the better and then onward to the best, no natural law or genetic code or divine promise that guarantees a better outcome. The trajectory of moral improvement is an ideal pattern, never more than a possible pathway, a hope worth working for but one always at risk.

Alistair MacIntyre's distinction in *After Virtue* between "values" and "virtues" is relevant here. Values are qualitative facts assigned to, or discerned in, external objects and events or subjective states of mind. Virtues, in contrast, are qualities of self: matters of character, habits of mind and feeling and action, in particular the disposition to aim at excellence, at doing things well. Value-based approaches to ethics say that I should respect my parents either because an external standard such as the Fifth Commandment identifies it as a primary value, or because respecting them accords with a mental state such as my enlightened self-interest. For a virtue-based approach, in contrast, the respect I have for my parents is the style of my relationship with them, a way of treating them that is an expression of my character. Insofar as I am virtuous, I am the sort of person who is mindful of others and who shows particular concern for those of whom I am an offspring. I am not following a rule, whether duty based or hedonistic. What I am doing is being true to myself, which self includes as one of its essential features a respectful concern for my parents. Whitehead's approach, like that of Confucius and Aristotle, is virtue-based.

In the last part of *Adventures of Ideas*, Whitehead links his reflections on history to his understanding of "those essential qualities, whose joint realization in social life constitutes civilization" (284). He notes that "civilization is one of those general notions that are very difficult to define." It evokes "a certain ideal for life on this earth," but the ideal is ambiguous because it "concerns both the individual human being and also societies" of human beings (273). Civilized existence is a virtue, a developmental ideal regarding a moral possibility of human and societal achievement for which we ought to strive both individually and collectively. It is not just any possibility, however, but the highest one: the ideal of a fulfilling excellence, an actualizing of who we most truly are.

Whitehead finds a pattern to this ideal in the dynamic interrelationships among five civilizing qualities. Three of them are Truth, Beauty, and Art, which we have already considered in chapter 2, where we explored the way in which Art uses Beauty to burst the bounds of established Truth, disclosing the possibility of unrealized Truths worth our pursuing.

A fourth quality, Adventure, is implicit in the interplay of these three. The lure of Beauty, in pulling us away from our comfortable practices, leads us down unfamiliar pathways which, although merely interesting or perhaps a bit tantalizing, become increasingly unsettling, daring, dangerous, even terrifying. We find ourselves on an Adventure into the unknown.

To be sure, the new Truth to which our Adventure leads may not be any better than what it has replaced, and even where it is an improvement the gain will have been at the price of other Truths that were ignored or suppressed. The helical movement of our development as persons, and the movement of cultural development as well, is forward but not necessarily upward. Adventure is not a climb toward some all-encompassing absolute perfection, much less an arrival at such an absolute. It is always a climb, however, and it is always toward a perfection of some sort.

These four essential qualities for civilized existence are therefore sufficient, says Whitehead, to generate the "'life and motion' in which all actualities must partake" (275). But "something is still lacking": a quality without which "the pursuit of 'Truth, Beauty, Adventure, Art' can be ruthless, hard, cruel," and hence, "lacking in some essential quality of civilization" (284). Whitehead, in typical fashion, plays with a number of terms that capture aspects of this fifth civilizing quality, although each misses more than it captures. "Tenderness" and "love" are too narrow; "impersonality" too dead, too static; "anaesthesia" too negative; "hope" too future oriented. He settles on the term "Peace," which he describes as "that Harmony of Harmonies which calms destructive turbulence and completes civilization" (285). Definitions are as faltering as terms, however, and Whitehead quickly offers other descriptive phrases. For example, he says that Peace is "self-control at its widest," in which "interest has been transferred to coordinations wider than personality" (285), a fruit of which is "that passion whose existence Hume denied, the love of mankind as such" (286).

The language here is decisively moral, which should not be surprising since Peace along with its four companions are the qualities we need to be fully participating members of a civilized community—good citizens in a double sense. Good because we are able to do good, to fulfill our social function well, accepting our responsibilities as citizens and carrying them out effectively. Good also because we are able to aim at ends worthy of civilized existence, to perceive and embrace ends able to fulfill our excellence as persons.

Peace is the capstone of Whitehead's five qualities needed for civilized existence, adding the moral dimension the others without it lack. I propose, therefore, that we think of Whitehead as offering us at the end of *Adventures of Ideas* an ideal pattern for becoming good, a developmental pathway that leads from Beauty and Truth by means of Art and Adventure to Peace. It is a developmental ideal, a normative guide by which persons who follow it learn to be good and by which societies can fashion institutions that nurture the development of that goodness in their members.

Becoming Good

Learning to be good in the sense of learning to be virtuous is not something that can be directly taught. Virtue is not a piece of information, like rules are, that can be transferred from one brain to another, spoken by a teacher and inscribed by students in their notebooks. So that we can learn to be virtuous, we need to have experiences that call for moral judgment. We should be put in situations requiring us to assess the relative worth of certain things, to make choices that include or exclude, to weigh alternatives and take other viewpoints into consideration. Having made such judgments with the help of our teacher and other students, we should then be asked to assess those judgments, examining why they were made and to what effect. These judgment-making experiences can be about firsthand right-now issues, or they can be in the form of case studies, simulations, fictional stories, exemplary biographies.

The key is that we engage these issues, that we deal with them in ways that have explicable reasons, and that we then be open to the criticisms of others. So although our teachers can't teach us virtue, under their tutelage we can develop some of the habits of thinking and acting by which we might become better persons than we were. Our teachers can nurture the sprouting of our virtue, stimulate its growth, and weed out interfering distortions, but only we ourselves can become more virtuous.

The increasing adequacy in the scope and depth of a student's moral practices is suggested by the pathway to Peace that Whitehead briefly sketches in his comments on this last and morally critical of the civilized virtues. I will organize this pathway quite a bit more explicitly than Whitehead does, creating six levels to be traversed, six mile-markers on the road leading to Peace, which is the seventh and highest level. I will suggest as we go how these levels might be negotiated in a classroom setting, and I will also mention in passing how the stages of romance, precision, and generalization function at each level. Since I've already referred to the fifth of the Ten Commandments, I will use the virtue of honoring our fathers and mothers as a running example by which to give our question about moral development more specificity.

Level 1: Self-absorption. When we are young, notes Whitehead, our lives are marked by "whole-hearted absorption in personal enjoyments and personal discomforts" (*Adventures* 287). We are typically immersed in the joys and sorrows of the moment, quick to laugh and quick to cry, quick to be concerned about something but just as quickly to be indifferent about it, at one moment extremely generous and at another extremely cruel. Our experiences are relatively disconnected, each for its own short span filling fully the horizon of our concern. We seek vivid novel experiences able to satisfy our immediate desires, but these actions are not selfish so much as short-sighted. We pay little attention to the consequences of our actions, neither anticipating their likelihood as we decide to do one thing rather than another nor wondering later, in the light of what resulted, if what we did was worth it.

This absorption in the moment involves no appeal to moral theory. Not even carpe diem, for Horace's call to seize the day (*Odes* 1.1: 32–33), to take each moment as it comes and wring from it all the satisfaction it has to offer, is a plan of action, whereas our actions at this stage of moral development are not guided by any plan. We do not aim at maximizing pleasure or at following only universalizable courses of action, but not because we have rejected these or any other moral theory. We are simply ignorant of such things, largely because we lack sufficient firsthand experience to feel the need for guidance, for reassurance that what we are doing is what we will be glad later to have done. "Youth is not peaceful in any ordinary sense of that term," says Whitehead. "In youth, despair is overwhelming" because there is "no memory of disasters survived" (287). We seek not happiness but vivacity, and we find not peaceful self-content but disquieting ignorance.

There are few things more frustrating for our parents than trying to break through our self-absorption, getting us to show some respect for others, including doing what our parents ask us to do: sit still, don't hit your brother, say *please* and *thank you*, stop whispering to your sister and go to sleep. Teachers are our surrogate parents, facing similar challenges in getting us to be concerned with more than our momentary preferences. Teachers have some advantages, however: the resources of the school and its traditions, on which they can draw.

For instance, every year our school honors parents by holding a Parents Day, and the kindergarten class prepares for its first one by posting on the wall evidence of what we've been doing. When our parents come that Day, we invite them to sit with us, and our teacher talks about the class's various projects. She wisely uses the fruits of our limited attention span, the pile of disconnected works we created in recent weeks for a variety of different class assignments, as props for a set of experiences that writes itself. The postings on the walls surrounding us plead to be seen, and we respond by asking our parents to inspect them. Shortsightedness is accepted, but directed away from individual concerns. We only spend a moment at each wall posting, mine first, the crayon drawing I did of a stick figure walking stiffly along the top of a bright yellow beach under an orange sun in a pink sky. But then we check out the postings done by those who sit on either side of me, and here's one by that red-haired boy, and look what the sassy girl did. Other students show my posting to their parents, and my parents ask me to point out who did a piece they find especially interesting. Our movements become the Day's main program and the interactions with other students and their parents makes the event a communal one.

Whitehead says of romantic experiences that they stir our feelings, excite our appreciation, and incite our impulses to kindred activities ("Rhythm" 21). They enlarge the compass of what absorbs us. Slowly a vague sense emerges of the day's events being not just for our own enjoyment but primarily as a way of showing our respect for each other's parents. Honoring our parents, we realize, is something everyone should do. It's not just the way our family interacts but also the way other families do, even though their interactions are different from ours in a lot of important ways. It's what teachers also think we should do, and for them its importance seems right up there with learning to read or how to cooperate with one another. Whatever we may already have thought it meant, our sense of the importance of honoring our parents expands and deepens as we find ourselves doing that honoring on a special occasion, alongside our classmates and teacher, in the presence of other parents, and in the context of our school's authorization of the event.

Level 2: Self-Forgetfulness. Whitehead sees the fledgling possibilities for movement to a second level of moral practice implied in youth's craving for vivid experience. When we are young, he argues, we are "peculiarly susceptible to appeals for beauty of conduct," attracted by "motives which presuppose the irrelevance of [our] own person" (*Adventures* 287). We can become enamored of doing some unusual thing just for the joy of doing it—trying out new attire, new speech patterns, new behaviors, or new beliefs for the sake of their novelty, intent on overcoming the always present threat of the boredom that shadows our every moment. We surrender ourselves absolutely—even if only momentarily—to the sheer fact of some enterprise. Insofar as we are caught up in such extravagances, we have a first intimation of "the harmony of the soul's activities with ideal aims that lie beyond any personal satisfaction" (288).

Now that we are in third grade, we decide to organize a different sort of Parents Day, one featuring stories or poems about mothers and fathers that we have written ourselves. With the assembled parents as our audience, we present our texts, reciting the words in various voices, enacting the events, costuming ourselves in illustrative ways. The visitors laugh and applaud, and over punch and cookies congratulate the author-actors on what they have done. Perhaps our texts have been collaboratively produced and performed, perhaps they are solo efforts, but in either case they are caught up into a collective extravaganza, the whole class's common project.

The Day is about parents and for them, yet the focus is on the inventive things we students are doing—the silly doggerel about eating your vegetables recited in a rabbit costume, the sad tale of the lost fauns told in the frantic tones of the doe and buck searching after them, the strange story of the magic pebble I found on the beach that cured my mother of a dread disease, the somewhat vulgar Simpsons routine performed in yellow face. What great fun it is to plan this Day and then to do what we have planned, an exciting possibility successfully pulled off, a vivid moment shared with other students and with our parents. It is an event beyond the ordinary, one in which we have explicitly honored our parents in some genuine ways: inviting them to "their" event, organizing it around a parental theme, creating poems for our parents to hear, performing for them, hoping they will find it all enjoyable. There are elements of the stage of precision in this endeavor, since it involved planning: we had to attend not only to what our program will be but also to the process by which we can end up with one and with an audience ready to receive it. Romance still dominates, however, because our feelings are the heart of the matter, the fun of imagining the clever program we will devise and our excitement as we create the elements that combine to make it a success.

This is a more sophisticated kind of romance than we enjoyed at level 1. It is still appreciative enjoyment, but the enjoyment is not of facts but of ideals, the exploration of new possibilities and new routes to their realization. It is a first glimmering of what we learned in chapter 4 to call Platonic romance, "the conceptual clutch after some refreshing novelty . . . [,] lifting a conceptual flash into an effective appetition, and an effective appetition into a realized fact" (*Function* 23). Whitehead associates such romance with the "vigour of civilized societies" which "harbour a certain extravagance of objectives" so that in the pursuit of those objectives their citizens "wander beyond the safe provision of personal gratifications" (*Adventures* 288). We have fashioned an event that in the process of fashioning it has lured us momentarily beyond ourselves. We have glimpsed the contrast between our own self-perpetuating activities and other kinds of activity. And we have felt that contrast as good.

Level 3: The Desire for Fame. These experiences of self-forgetfulness may eventually modulate into its seeming opposite, says Whitehead: "the egotistic desire for fame" (288). Our aim is once again self-centered as it was at the first level, involving delight in our own powers, but it is now combined with the second level's awareness of the importance of values beyond our own subjective feelings. A concern is emerging that there be some sort of objective evidence of the importance of our achievements. I am still interested in my own personal success, in composing a poem that will be special and in presenting it well, but I am no longer content with receiving my parents' praise for what I did simply because it was me who did it. I want them to praise me because what I did was "something worth-while," because they value what I am beginning to discover is the most precious result of my labors: "the love of a good job well done" (288). My actions betray an unspoken craving to "stand conspicuous in this scheme of things" (289)—not merely to find enjoyment in what I accomplish, but for it to be recognized by others as in some sense an outstanding achievement.

Such an aim on my part, and on the part of my classmates, presupposes values that are not of our own making, with respect to which what we make is judged admirable, our work said to be exemplary. Our quest for fame requires others for its realization: our "desire for admiring attention" implies "an audience fit to render it" (288). For the audience to be one that is "fit" to applaud our deeds, its judgments must be, and be thought to be, objective. They must be based on some standard of worth recognized and accepted by our community or a relevant elite. We have come to realize that our fame depends on "a scheme of things with a worth beyond any single occasion," a worth beyond our own worth (288). Our concerns have regressed to self-concern, but for that concern to be fulfilled we must satisfy conditions set for us by others. We must be other-regarding in order to be self-regarding.

We third-graders did not undertake our Parents Day project for the praises showered on us, but we basked in the praise when it came. It is easy enough for the praise to become a goal, however, and it would be a legitimate teaching strategy to organize a subsequent class project around this feature. A contest of any sort will do. The sixth-grade science fair, for instance, is a competition among individuals in which success is measured by criteria independent of the preferences of the participants. When I enter an exhibit of my research project on the limestone springs in our area, my parents' praise of what I've done no longer suffices. They remain sources of support, encouraging and helping train me for the rigors of the competition, but the praise that counts is that of the judges whose objectivity is assured by their not being my parents or my teachers. Those of us who have a colored ribbon hanging from our poster displays stand conspicuous in the science-fair scheme of things. We may have selfishly sought this fame, but we earned it by bringing our imagination and technical skills into line with the standards of excellence stipulated by the fair and by established methods of scientific research.

Competitions can be among groups rather than individuals, of course: athletic games, debates, academic quiz shows, and marching band contests are familiar occasions in which our success requires team effort. I may have scored the only goal in our soccer game, but without the deft cross by another striker I would not have had a shot on goal, and without the shutout efforts of our goalkeeper one goal would not have secured a victory. I would not stand out as the hero of the game without the unsung heroics of my teammates. Individual and group efforts are also measured against external standards in noncompetitive contexts. The success of a speech or a new dramatic production, of a piano solo or orchestral performance, is assessed by the intensity of the audience's applause, the numbers attending, the judgment of a mentor or instructor, and the reviews that appear in the newspapers.

In all these instances, we students find ourselves living in a normative world not of our own making, and discover the satisfaction that comes when our creative efforts exemplify those norms. Too much help by our parents will undermine this opportunity for growth in virtue. Our fame must be deserved, the fruit of our own efforts, our own self-transcendence. By avoiding the pitfalls of excessive support, parents can sometimes manage to negotiate the difficult path leading from their primary role as sources of encouragement to their being included among those authorized by the wider society to make objective judgments about what is or is not praiseworthy. When we look to our parents for judgments we think will be later echoed by official judges, we honor them for their ability to legitimate our budding sense of how important it is that our achievements have objective worth.

The desire for fame becomes pathological when we attempt to control those who bestow it, transforming them into a hierarchy of evaluators with ourselves located at the apex. We claim that what we do is always and obviously of central importance, and that "the world has then no justification except as a satisfaction of such claims" (288). We require a sycophantic audience, a gaggle of fans who will applaud whatever we do. Rock stars and television personalities often attempt to justify their fame by the applause of those who applaud them not for what they have done but because they are famous, who think their fame is self-justifying. Tyrants assure themselves an audience fit to their requirements by the manipulation of public opinion and the threat of retaliatory violence against any who would have the temerity to show their disapproval. We sixth-graders are familiar with both kinds of fame among our peers, often embodied by a popular student whose coterie of friends express their adulation for her or him by drawing a sharp line between themselves and those they shun as unfit for inclusion in their praise group, with a special disdain reserved for those who want desperately to be included.

The importance of precision's concern for systemic order is evident in the contrast between legitimate and pathological versions of a desire for fame. A well-ordered system is defined by the rules that create and sustain it. So persons should not be honored by the system unless their successes were achieved in accord with its rules. For example, athletes who are discovered to have used illegal drugs to enhance their natural abilities are rightly stripped of the honors they have received, since the justification of the honoring was the excellence of their rule-governed achievements. The adulation of success achieved in disregard for accepted standards is a romantic response, an adulation blithely undisciplined by the demand that it be arrived at properly. In this sense, Vince Lombardi's famous insistence that winning isn't the most important thing but the only thing is not merely cynical but immoral. The desire for fame, understood as a level of moral development, is sanctioned by its conformity to the parameters and boundary conditions for success defined by the community within which it is pursued. It isn't whether we win that should bring us fame but how we play our winning game.

Level 4: Loving Virtuous Individuals. We may appreciate our admirers at first merely because they appreciate us, or because they have the authority to recognize the quality of our achievements. Eventually, however, we may come to admire these admirers for themselves, for their intrinsically admirable qualities, and for the objective worth of the goals they admire. Instead of valuing others as instruments by which we can attain our ends, we recognize their worth as akin to our own. Their virtues are an expression of the same qualities of humanity as ours are.

Love is how this recognition is lived. Initially and most naturally, says Whitehead, we love those closest to us. We come to love our parents by inverting their love for us, loving them because we recognize ourselves in them, loving them as we love ourselves, honoring them not only as our caretakers but also as fellow human beings. It is natural for the circle of those we love to widen as we mature until it also includes not only our brothers and sisters but also aunts and uncles, neighbors and friends, mentors and role models. But as this circle widens, it remains constrained by its particularity. Our love is "the love of particular individual things," a passing beyond ourselves "but with explicit, definite limitation to particular realities" (289). We love this person and that person, not anyone or everyone; our heart like our arms can only reach so far.

It is crucial to our moral development that exemplary persons be included among those we love, that we come to admire virtuous individuals, men and women living or dead who often function for us as surrogate parents: people we honor and seek to emulate. We take athletes and soldiers, coaches and priests, teachers and civic leaders as role models, trying to exemplify their actions or character or ideals in our lives. We imagine ourselves being Bret Favre as he and his Green Bay Packers win another snowy victory in frigid Lambeau Field, or Roald Amundsen as against all odds he wins the race to the South Pole and brings his expedition safely back home. We cry even now over the untimely death of JFK or Mozart or Jimmy Dean or Antigone, bemoaning a world in which such injustices are allowed even while celebrating a world in which their achievements have made a difference. Having read the King Arthur legends, we are ready to pull some version of Excalibur from the stone of our complacency and join in the quest for a new kind of Holy Grail. We love our heroes for who they are, not for how they can help us—although by imagining ourselves as them or as their comrades, we discover new ways for being who we are and new standards by which we might be measured.

Teachers should all the time be introducing us to new heroes and new kinds of heroes, to those whose virtue is not always as well-known as it ought to be. The heroes of pop culture and professional sports need no classroom to be identified, and we are quick to honor soldiers, police officers, and firefighters as people engaged in socially important but dangerous occupations. But other kinds of jobs are also heroic because difficult, even though they are not dangerous: scientists, homemakers, caregivers, mom-and-pop store entrepreneurs. Biographies of exemplary people should be assigned frequently, stories and whole novels about them read, videos watched, field trips arranged to the places where they are publically honored, websites about them visited, local people who lead lives virtuous in all sorts of ways invited to talk with the class.

For Veterans' Day, we ninth-graders are asked to bring pictures to class of our family members and neighbors who are veterans, and to write up accounts of their war experiences, all of these materials then made into a PowerPoint slide show which we present in the school's assembly. We go on later to create a similar compendium of "Our School's All-Time Greats." A family genealogy project in our civics course involves us tracing back our ancestors three or four generations, then interviewing our living grandparents and great-grandparents about what they did when they were our age, what challenges they met, what aspirations they had. These stories, shared with others in the class, honor our fathers and mothers by locating them in a family history, a story worth telling to others, a story the last chapter of which is about ourselves. We are our parents' story continued, as our parents are continuations of our grandparents' stories. Our ancestors—beloved for the unique people they were and for their genetic and cultural influence on who we are and wish to become—are, and we among them, participants in a story greater than any one of us.

The aesthetic aspects of romantic pedagogy, delighting in particulars for what they are rather than for their relevance to general truths or goods, are first-level involvements. They gained a hint of transcendence in the second level and were deployed self-centeredly in the third. Now here in this fourth level the aesthetic delight has deepened into love and has turned us away from ourselves toward others, whom we love for the virtues they embody, for the moral character that has become who they essentially are.

This new kind of love involves something crucial that has not yet been discussed, however. Loving virtuous individuals involves more than admiring and emulating them, more than loving them as we would love ourselves and manifesting that love by being as much like them as we can. It involves wanting them to flourish. We find our good in fulfilling their good. "In the extreme of love, such as mother's love, all personal desire is transferred to the thing loved, as a desire for its perfection" (289). To desire that our loved ones flourish means to be concerned not merely for the here and now but also for the long-term quality of their existence and hence for the character of the environing conditions that foster that quality.

This kind of love for an individual means that "the potentialities of the loved object are felt passionately as a claim that it find itself in a friendly Universe" (289). We insist that the world be such that its harmonies do not exclude, nor merely tolerate, but actively support the achievements and possibilities of those we love. We want things like they would be "if right could triumph in a beautiful world, with discord routed." Our love for a beloved one is "the passionate desire for the beautiful result, in this instance" (289). The perfection of the beloved individual requires perfection of the community, the systemic order, that nurtures it. Romance requires precision for its enhancement, as precision requires romance for its recognition of intrinsic value. In loving particular individuals, we begin to realize this interdependence and so are carried beyond the usual conflict between self and society, between romance and precision, to the verge of generalization.

Level 5: Patriotism. Our love for virtuous individuals—for mothers and fathers, heroes and saints, mentors and leaders—can now modulate into love of country. Love of other individuals leads us to a love for the community of which they are members. Previously our appreciation of communities of whatever sort had been for utilitarian reasons. We recognized that they provide the basic environment for securing the lives of loved ones and for assuring proper opportunities for their development. Moral maturity involves more than this, however. It means coming to love a community—our neighborhood or city, our tribe or nation—for its intrinsic worth.

Patriotism is the expression of this love, the loyalty we give to our traditions and to the political institutions by which they are embodied. It is loyalty to a common good that is more than any individual's preferences, that links us together with more predecessors and successors than those who appear in our family tree, widening the range of those whom we call our ancestors and our descendants. Patriots are loyal to a *patris*, to their fatherland, their motherland. As our heroes are surrogate parents, so also are our communities. Patriotism is one of the many ways in which we honor our fathers and mothers.

Whitehead finds an example of this way of honoring in the farmers of the Roman Republic, in particular the patriotism of one of its generals, Regulus, who chose freely to return to Carthage and certain death. He did so in order to keep the promise he had made when a prisoner there, that if he were sent to Rome bearing Carthage's peace terms, he would return should Rome reject them, which rejection Regulus then counseled Rome to make. He voluntarily faced the extinguishing of his life, for in his love of country he had found "something in the world which could not be expressed as sheer personal gratification." Like mother love, his commitment to another was unlimited; unlike it, his commitment was to a community rather than an individual. In thus sacrificing himself, "he achieved magnificence" because by what he did "his personal existence rose to its full height" (290).

The magnificence of the Roman Republic, the "general health of [its] social life" (289), lies in the fact that Regulus's commitment was not unusual. His conduct "evoked widest consent" because any of his fellow citizens were prepared to do the same. There is a distinctive grandeur to those Roman farmers, says Whitehead, who "generation after generation, amid all the changes of history" (290), assented to the worth of what Regulus did, as attested by their continual retelling of his story and by their own equally self-sacrificial deeds for the sake of that same patrimony.

Whitehead resists the tendency we all have to absolutize the ideals to which our nation adheres, to treat its values as having timeless universal significance. He argues that one of the banes of human history has been the "exaggerated claims" made on behalf of "moral codes." It is the "dogmatic fallacy" at "its worst" to insist that what we take as good is "incapable of improvement" because grounded in some absolute reality—a God, a Saint, a Despot, the Ancestors, Historical Necessity—the authority of which cannot therefore be questioned (290). On the contrary, "all realization of the Good is finite, and necessarily excludes certain other types" of good (291). Moral codes are relative to "the social circumstances of the immediate environment," so conduct that in one context produces "harmonious satisfaction" is in another context "destructively degrading." Values and ideals, virtues and moral practices arise from parochial conditions to which they are specifically tailored. "Thus the notion that there are certain regulative notions, sufficiently precise to prescribe details of conduct, for all reasonable beings on Earth, in every planet, and in every star-system, is at once to be put aside" (291).

Patriotism, understood in a way that preserves the concrete facticity of both the individual patriots and the national perfection that they are committed to achieve, is one of the most difficult and sophisticated modes by which to live a moral life because it invests a limited sense of good with a significance so far-reaching that those limits can easily be forgotten. Regulus provides us with a paradigmatic standard for patriotism, but our task is not to emulate what he did for the sake of Rome in his time and with respect to its ideals. Our task, instead, is to enact what we decide we should do in our time for the sake of our own country and with respect to its quite different ideals. "The moral code is the behaviour-patterns which in the environment for which it is designed will promote the evolution of that environment toward its proper perfection" (292).

Those genealogical studies we undertook last year could be expanded into a study of the periods in American history when our parents and grandparents were high school sophomores like ourselves. Tracing our family lineages on back to immigrant arrivals would be particularly interesting, since it would turn out that our ancestors had come to this country at different times and for differing reasons, some seeking freedom from persecution and some in bondage to their persecutors, some arriving very recently and some settled in the area long before the coming of Europeans. Turning these family stories into aspects of a single story about the origins and development of the United States would rescue our history class from being a dreary recitation of names and dates. We would be attempting an account of how various the people were who became we the people, how it could actually be that *e pluribus unum*.

Patriotism is not uncritical allegiance, however. It can never be my country right or wrong, because our loyalty is not simply to a nation as such but also to its ideals. We love America because of the hope for it articulated by the Mayflower Compact, the Declaration of Independence, and the Gettysburg Address, a hope we find brokenly but nonetheless genuinely incarnated in civil society and in the Constitution, the various laws passed by federal and state legislators, and decisions promulgated by the courts. We should love our country despite its flaws, and give proof of that love through our serious and sustained efforts to overcome those deficiencies.

Among our national heroes are those who gave the last full measure of their devotion to correcting the wrongs they saw marring the American dream. From Jefferson through Lincoln to FDR, from Jonathan Edwards through Jane Addams to Martin Luther King Jr., patriotism has been constantly expressed by reformers insisting that American practices be measured against American ideals, our "is" brought closer to our "ought." From their example, we come to learn that the virtue of our nation depends on individuals who are not self-regarding, who are motivated by ideals other than personal gain, ideals of a common good—individuals who devote their lives to these possibilities and find them worth struggling to realize no matter what it costs them personally in pain or loss. We begin to recognize that what we hope for is as important as who we are. As Whitehead puts it, "Such conformation of purpose to ideal beyond personal limitations" is a moral practice by which "the wise man can face his fate, master of his soul" (291).

We are now at the level of generalization: loving both ideals and particulars, and being skilled in the ways by which to incarnate those ideals in those particulars. Our senior class need not set out to save the world or even to improve the quality of our town, although there are obvious ways in which these lofty goals can be given local civic expression. It would be a helpful beginning simply for us to explore possibilities for improving what goes on in our class, perhaps enhancing its physical features, perhaps improving how lessons are conducted. In doing so, we learn to craft shared ideals that we can all use in working together to improve the character of our classroom community. Because we have in common a love for that community, we dedicate ourselves to doing what we can to bring what it actually is a bit closer to what we agree it ought to be.

These are issues about which we already think ourselves well informed, about which we are passionate and often dogmatically opinionated. Flushing out our various ideals for bettering things and then creating a forum in which these differences can be discussed is a good way for us to appreciate the complications of any reform—giving clear articulation to vague notions of what a better situation might look like, accurately understanding the views with which we disagree, exploring alternatives not initially imagined by any of us, working out compromises that might actually work, figuring out how to implement change within constraints of time, money, skill, and commitment. These are the lessons of citizenship in a democracy, ideally expressed. They are therefore precisely the way by which we can learn how our nation's ideals inform but never mirror its reality, and how this is an occasion not for passive acceptance or debilitating cynicism but for creative action. We honor our parents and our nation by doing our best to live up to their hopes for us, to their dream that we might grow up in a way that fulfills our culturally defined potentialities.

Level 6: Adventurous Ideals. The next widening and intensifying step in our moral maturation, the deepening of generalization, is for us to recognize the fragility of our achievements. It is good that we strive to do good, and it is wonderful that sometimes we succeed, that our family or neighborhood or nation or world in many important ways is a better place than it once was because of our actions. But these good things are incomplete. They are all the time requiring repair or renovation, constantly needing to be revised or replaced. We need to be sufficiently sensitive to the changing nature of things to be able to understand the reason for the demise or the failure or the misdirection of our efforts. We need to see clearly what was done and to see it in comparison to what could have been done, then to recognize that what could have been done might yet still be done in some new way.

A sports season is a good, even if trivial, example of the function of ideals in the struggle for their realization. When our college soccer team loses its opening game, the coach does not dwell on the loss except to help us see where we made mistakes, where we could have done better. Our team then practices with the correction of these inadequacies at the top of our agenda, and the next game then tests whether we have improved, whether we have learned the lessons of our defeat. The initial loss is indeed a loss, a blot on our record, a negative that cannot be erased. But the possibility for victory we took into that game remains a possibility, reaffirmed for the second game and pursued with the insights gained from the team's initial failure to achieve it. Victory is not an idle dream. It is a realistic goal shaping our approach to each game throughout the season, a goal always changing in its details but sustained as a source of motivation and focus right through to the final game. Obviously, we would celebrate the success of a soccer team that managed to win all its games, to realize its ideals every time it faced an opposing team, but we would also admire a team that played each game with fresh resolve, constantly renewing its victory aims, even if like Charlie Brown's baseball team it were never to win.

Tests administered as part of a course of study should have this same character. They should not merely measure our achievement level at a particular point in the course, but also be diagnostic of how we can improve. The tests should be like athletic contests: each a preparation for the next, each both a measure of what we have done and a way for us to learn how to do better. We enroll in a self-instructional course in which we can take the exam over a particular unit whenever we wish. The professor then goes over the results with us, figuring out why we had come up with wrong answers and not neglecting to explore why the right answers were right. We then go study some more, until we are ready to retake the exam. This cycle of test and critique continues until we achieve a satisfactory grade, at which time we can proceed to the next study unit.

Obviously, this testing strategy need not be limited to self-instructional courses: all subjects are fundamentally cumulative. Unless the first things are well-learned the later ones will be poorly grasped, for the chain of our knowledge is no stronger than its weakest link. The wisdom of competency-based education is its recognition of this fact, its insistence that a well-shaped bell curve on a professor's grade distribution for an exam is no virtue, that granting course credit for work that falls short of reasonable proficiency is equivalent to a social promotion in grade school. The inadequacy of competence-based learning is its assumption that a course of study can be analyzed into a finite number of specifiable competencies and that their mastery is an attainable goal. Such a view misses the fact that what we know of any subject worth studying is always less than we should know, that mastery of the subject is an ideal not a goal. Knowing that we don't know is the necessary first step to knowing something new, and wisdom comes when we learn that there is no final step to our cumulating knowledge, even though there are many valuable intermediate stopping points. Good professors, like good coaches, are those who encourage us to take both our successes and our failures as diagnostic learning experiences in an open-ended developmental adventure.

Success and failure are relative measures: our aim should always be toward the better. We can never honor our father and mother in some definitive manner. They deserve more honor than we can give, and today's honoring cannot rest on the laurels of yesterday's. Yet the honor we give them each day is precious, and if we are sensitive to how our efforts are received, why they sometimes succeed but sometimes don't, then we will find different and maybe even better ways of honoring them as we and they grow older.

Being Good

In an important sense, the whole ascent we have been tracing articulates Whitehead's notion of Peace. He will at times say of some moral sensibility appropriate to one of the levels we have so far discussed that it is as aspect of Peace or even its essence. But I have chosen to restrict Peace to this last level, of which the earlier six are intimations, each more explicitly so.

Level 7: A Sense of Peace. What Whitehead means by Peace is, to say the least, very elusive. It will help in understanding him to consider once again the other four qualities that along with Peace comprise the conditions of civilized existence. Recall that Beauty is a matter of Appearance, of possibilities, ideals, and values, and it finds concrete expression through Art. Truth is a matter of the conformation of Appearance to Reality, of ideals to fact. Sometimes ideals are only fanciful dreams; there is no chance whatever that the lion and the lamb will ever lie down together in peace. Sometimes values are lies; it is simply false that Aryans are a superior race or that women are unable to think rationally. Thus Beauty need not conform to reality, but it has "no secure efficacy" if it "hides within itself the dislocations of falsehood" (292), if its attractiveness obscures its falsity, its irrelevance to existing realities. Furthermore, a "feeling of dislocation" with regard to such relevance "is the final destructive force, robbing life of its zest for [A]dventure. It spells the decadence of civilization, by stripping from it the very reason for its existence" (293).

A necessary condition for our civilization to thrive is that our ideals are in some sense attuned to the way things actually are, that our dreams are realizable. It is crucial that a dream "has not built itself up by the inclusion of elements that are foreign to the reality from which it springs," that it is "a generalization and an adaptation of emphasis; but not an importation of qualities and relations without any corresponding exemplification in the reality" (293). The past is our resource for improving the future: our oughts are a function of our is. We change our circumstances not by rejecting them and starting over afresh, but by reshaping what we have. In order to overcome the inadequacies of our situation, its discords cannot merely be "dismissed into irrelevance"; a way must be found instead to "rescue discords from loss" (294). If the good we want is pie in the sky, our efforts will yield nothing tangible. If the pie we want is a pie able to feed our actual needs, it must be an actuality made from antecedent actualities, made new in part but not in whole. Our ideals must hug close the reality they would make over into something better. Their Beauty must be a Truthful Beauty.

As a young person, I have a dream about what I might do when I grow up, how I might best live my life, what sort of person I might become. If this dream is merely fanciful, having no grounding in the realities of who I now am and what the world around me is like, my efforts are not likely to be effective. If I'm going to be the next Einstein or Shakespeare, I'd better have excellent mental capacities and an interest in honing them to a sharp mathematical or poetic edge. If I'm going to be the new Pelé or Patton, I'd better have good motor skills and an interest in honing them to the sharp edge strikers need. And of course it's also the case that scientists and artists need healthy bodies and soccer players and military officers quick minds. Without the proper capacities, without appropriate motivation and self-discipline, without relevant familial, educational, and cultural support systems, my dream will have little to no traction.

There are some who defy all odds and achieve the seemingly impossible, but they do so by taking unusual advantage of given realities while sidestepping what they cannot adapt to their aims. The impossible often seems so because it is a possibility especially difficult to tether down, the skills needed to wrestle actuality out of it exceeding rare. Most of us require realities that are more obviously supportive to our aspirations, so that we tend to like the things for which we are adept at acquiring the needed skills, and we tend to acquire the skills for what we like. We need to tailor our dreams to the realities of our situation in order to then be able to tailor those realities so that they better fit our dreams.

It's when I dream an impossible dream but think it readily possible, when my aims are fundamentally at odds with my capacities or those of my support systems, that things seem out of joint. I think myself inept, my life worthless, my ambition irrelevant. Or I avoid such despair by thinking myself a victim, believing the cards are stacked against me, my life ill-fated. Under such conditions, my zest for attempting to actualize my dream withers. Why try if things indeed are not as they seem, if my hopes are delusions, my ideals wishful thinking, my striving for the better something only fools do. Hence it is important that I cultivate the artistry by which to craft truthful appearances, by which to imagine possibilities for change that are in fact harbored in the way things are.

Such truthful appearances are not easy to craft, however, for they are not easy to distinguish from false ones. Claiming of a possibility—an artistic insight, a scientific hypothesis, a lesson plan, a market strategy—that it nestles close to reality, that it reveals a truth about that reality of which we were previously unaware or to which we were indifferent, is a contingent and always debatable judgment. Were the closeness self-evident, there would be no need for us to learn how to think creatively, to be able to make relevant judgments of importance. If, however, the possibilities that guide our actions are achievable possibilities that depend on what we do for whether or not they will be achieved, if the inventions or discoveries we make need not have been invented or discovered, then we agents, we who sow dreams and seek to bring them to harvest, need to be good at what we do. We need to develop into good dreamers of realizable dreams, good cultivators of harvestable crops, good custodians of the seed corn from which new dreams can sprout in anticipation of further harvests in the years to follow.

So here is a necessary condition for the sense of Peace: a belief in the pragmatically possible, in workable ideals. There is a second necessary condition, however, which is found in Whitehead's answer to the question of "whether there exists any factor in the Universe constituting a general drive towards the confirmation of Appearance to Reality," a drive which is "a factor in each occasion persuading its aim at such truth as is proper to the special appearance in question" (293). It is not enough that we recognize our ideas are worth actualizing. We need also to recognize that we are not alone in our struggle to actualize them, that we are part of "an Adventure in the Universe as One," an adventure embracing all particular drives toward various conformations of various Appearances to Reality, but which "as an actual fact stands beyond any one of them" (295).

Our ideals and undertakings are not isolated even though they are contextually grounded and so necessarily parochial. Although they are family or neighborhood or national concerns, they are at the same time aims and efforts that belong to a vast community of aims and efforts. We are, all of us, to some extent and with some degree of self-awareness, struggling to realize what we think is the best future possible for ourselves and those we love, for our family, our school, and our society, for humankind and for all creation. We are part of an adventure that goes on everywhere and has gone on seemingly forever, an adventure in the universe of all its constituents, seeking to make possibilities into actualities, to transcend the given facts toward the creation of new facts, many adventures comprising one grand adventure. We honor our fathers and mothers by understanding ourselves as jointing with them in the never-ending effort to actualize possible goods that constitutes the creative advance of the universe, and our zest for striving as we do is undergirded by realizing that this is so.

So the sense of Peace that sustains our zest for creative adventure has two preconditions: that our ideals be practical and that we recognize we are not alone in what we do but are part of a vast community of similar adventurers. However, there is a third precondition: our acceptance of the final Truth to which Adventure leads, that of Tragic Beauty. The pursuit of ideals is not only a high-risk adventure in which we are all the time suffering setbacks and needing to refashion our plans and rethink our purposes. We must also recognize that it is an effort doomed to failure. We must recognize "the tragic issues which are essential in the nature of things" (286).

Youth, the stage of moral development with which we began, is "Life as yet untouched by tragedy" (287). Tragedy is the recognition that "Decay, Transition, Loss, Displacement belong to the essence of the Creative Advance" (286). Thus it is that "at the heart of the nature of things, there are always the dream of youth and the harvest of tragedy" (296). This trajectory is a fact about the World, always a fact, not occasionally or unfortunately but essentially a fact. A fact located not at the periphery but at the core of the cosmos, at the heart of the very nature of things. Our aim is toward the pragmatically better but our journey always runs afoul of problems we are unable to resolve. The resulting failure is tragic because success was not impossible, because although our strengths offered a possibility of fulfilling our aim, our limitations undercut our attempt to do so. Always the fecund dream, the transcendent aim; but also always the fracturing evil, the tragic harvest. We achieve a sense of Peace when, coming to realize this fact, we are then able to grasp its importance and to respond appropriately.

After all, failed ideals are still ideals. "Each tragedy is the disclosure of an ideal:—What might have been, and was not: What can be. The tragedy was not in vain." It is an intuition that "sees the tragedy as a living agent persuading the world to aim at fineness beyond the faded level of surrounding fact" (286). Note that for Whitehead the "living agent" disclosing an unrealized ideal is tragedy. The novel possibilities we take as adumbrating ends worth seeking, as goals orienting our actions, motivating what we do, are not manna from heaven, not divine gifts from beyond or even from within history. They are the flotsam and jetsam remaining after the sinking of our dreams.

The tragedy of our failures—the hope dashed, the gaping fissure opened, the opportunity misused or disdained, the cowardly compromise or self-serving injustice accepted—can be the catalyst by which hope is salvaged from the surrounding wreckage and used in an attempt to fashion some finer fact. The tragedy of Tragic Beauty is that we failed to get the job done. The possibility could have become a reality, but we fell short in our attempt to make it happen. The beauty of Tragic Beauty is that it is also truthful, that it was a reasonable goal and so remains, despite the failure, a viable possibility.

We experience a tragic loss, but we discover in this experience a possibility that redeems the loss. That other ship didn't make it through the rock-bound strait, but the passage is navigable and so let's give it a try ourselves. Those soldiers thought they had made the world safe for democracy, but although the fledgling democracies have stumbled into chaos and fled into tyranny, democracy is still the better way and we should take up their cause anew, chastened by their naivety but encouraged by their dream. And so it always is: the dream ending in tragic failure but the dream still potent, our decision to carry on motivated by a conviction that those who died for it should not have died in vain.

"The Reality which the Adventure transmutes into its Unity of Appearance," the tragic fact that harbors a cause we embrace as worth our allegiance, is "the final Beauty with which the Universe achieves its justification" (295). The world as we find it is a meaningful world because, although each ideal is always lost in the attempt to incarnate it in the world, that ideal always remains available for some renewed attempt. Peace, which is Tragic Beauty appreciated, believed in, and acted on, is the way by which "Beauty has always within it the renewal derived from the Advance of the Temporal World" (295). Peace infusing the strivings of all the world's creatures "is the immanence of the Great Fact" uniting the exuberant dreams of Youth with "this final Beauty which constitutes the zest of self-forgetful transcendence belonging to Civilization at its height" (295–96).

It should be clear now why Whitehead says, as I indicated at the beginning of this chapter, that Peace "calms destructive turbulence and completes civilization" (285). Our attempts to perfect reality, to achieve goals to which we are firmly committed, will typically intensify when thwarted. A failed idea can be simply a marginal improvement we will have to do without, or a slight decline in our quality of life we will have to accommodate. Failure, however, is often more fundamental—an unresolved problem that spirals into a crisis and then a catastrophe, a threat to the continued existence of the things that give our life meaning or a direct threat to that existence itself. So we redouble our efforts and grow more frantic when they also prove inadequate. Desperate times call for desperate measures, and so the finer qualities of civilized behavior give way to the shortsighted aims and extremist actions of an attempt to save ourselves at whatever price.

A sense of Peace rescues us from such a downward spiral by keeping our focus on the worth of the ideals by which we have been guiding our actions rather than on the success or failure of those actions. We can weather the storm by remaining calm, sustained by our sense of fellowship with all those others who like us have been caught by the threatening waves and looming rocks endemic to this world and, whether weathering the storm or destroyed by it, have remained faithful to their ideals. Peace is the conviction that Beauty, although necessarily Tragic, is also Truthful, and so justifies our zestful persistence in Adventures by means of Art's boundary-transgressing inventiveness toward novel reworkings of Reality.

The purple color of Whitehead's prose (and mine) may seem too bold for the pastels of academe, but not if we remember that tragedy is a synecdoche for all the ways in which we inevitably fall short of our goals. Whitehead's point is captured in Browning's claim that "a man's reach should exceed his grasp, / Or what's a heaven for?" ("Andrea" 97–98). Heaven is a star by which we navigate the open sea, not an ultimate destination. There are always ports of call with their momentary satisfactions, each a pragmatic goal that tests our skill and judgment to secure, but soon we are on our way elsewhere. If we must be assured safe passage to a final resting place before we will embark, then either we will never journey anywhere significant or we will assure our destruction by deluding ourselves into thinking that the sea poses no threat or that our boat and its helmsman have no flaws. We should always be reaching for something beyond the visible horizon, even though as we set a course in its direction it always recedes, eluding our grasp. Our efforts are not in vain if their importance lies in the worth of our aim. That our successes will be at best partial and transient should detract in no way from the worth of our undertaking them. The temporary harbors we reach on our journey and the expertise by which we negotiate the treacherous obstacles to reaching them are achievable good achieved. The good which they serve, the more fundamental good, is the journeying, the recognition that it is more important to be embarked on a worthwhile venture across the open sea than to arrive safely at our destination.

Our teachers can't teach us to ground our purposes in a sense of Peace, but they can discomfort us with respect to our current moral condition until we learn to reach deliberately for ends beyond our grasp and to take the paltry handful of reality we actually end up grasping as a resource for extending our reach anew. Our teachers should offer us neither moral comfort nor moral condemnation. Their task is constantly to be a Socratic goad, disclosing the inadequacy of our present goodness and through it the lure of some better good, and disclosing the inadequacies and the lures that have shaped our predecessors' endeavors and given our own their significance. Like them, we need to learn the importance of always trying to be better, always collaborating with others in this endeavor, always with that goodly company only somewhere along the way toward fulfilling our promise as human beings.

Our moral development as students can be measured by observing the sophistication of our responses to morally problematic situations. Yet what should be important for us and our teachers is not the quality of the results, but rather whether we learn to recognize the limitations of both our successes and our failures, and learn through this mix of inadequacies the habits by which one grows morally. The question is whether we have developed a character marked by self-transcending openness. The worth of our education is to be found in the extent to which this quality of character is being developed—in our capacity for continued moral and intellectual improvement, in our teachers' capacity for pedagogical improvement, and in the wider communities' functional capacity for reform, for furthering the common weal. Capacity not success. Insofar as we want to learn to be good persons, good scholars, and good citizens, we should locate that good not in our actual achievements but rather in our increased capacity to improve.

Whitehead says, in summarizing his argument, that "the secret of the union of Zest with Peace" is our appreciation of the fact that the suffering of tragedy "attains its end in a Harmony of Harmonies" (296). Peace is the realization that the only Harmony of Harmonies, the only ultimate perfection, is an ideal—an ideal not of some final achieved perfection, however, for there can be none, but an ideal of the endlessly recurrent drive toward the particular perfections that give our lives their meaning.

The ultimate good is a civilizing ideal. Not an end but a way of pursuing ends, not a value but a virtue, a manner of morally maturing. It is an Adventure from the dreams of Youth to the harvest of Tragedy, from the Beauty of the possibilities Art unveils to the Truth of our actual achievements, achievements that unavoidably fall short of the initial dream. Peace is the recognition that this process, the Tragic Beauty of this Artful Adventure, is the ultimate Truth about the world, the Final Fact—and is therefore its own justification. Peace is the recognition that by incarnating this ideal in the hows and whys of our lives "the World receives its persuasion towards such perfections as are possible for its diverse individual occasions" (296).

CHAPTER SEVEN

Recollecting

After explicating in the first chapter of this book Whitehead's three stages of education, I attempted in the subsequent five chapters to expand and deepen what the stages mean by drawing analogies between them and triads of concepts from some of Whitehead's metaphysical writings. Each analogy has been unique, an attempt to look afresh at romance, precision, and generalization from the standpoint of the ideas developed in a book of Whitehead's not written with education in mind. My focus has not been to on developing an overall argument about the stages, nor about Whitehead's metaphysics, although I have suggested strands of continuity from chapter to chapter and presumed the analogies to be analogous.

In this concluding chapter, I change focus, recollecting how the cumulative effect of the five different analogies enhances our understanding of each of the three stages of education. I follow these refocusing recollections of romance, precision, and generalization with a similar one concerning the metaphysical perspectives that stimulated the fashioning of those analogies. In each of the four cases, I proceed by six numbered sets of paragraphs where each number stands for the chapter of this book contributing the features I'm recollecting, concluding with a few additional paragraphs that I've labeled with this present chapter's number to indicate their function as a general concluding recollection.

I call what I'm doing in this chapter a process of recollection because I'm not summarizing the prior chapters but collecting some of their salient features into new versions of what I've said, complete with some fresh allusions and applications they have suggested. I'm interpreting my interpretations, assessing their significance and import, just as we always do when recollecting what we have previously thought or done.

Romance

1. Our education should begin with romance, the salient feature of which is an appreciative openness to the world around us. Both the appreciation and the openness are natural proclivities, although our teachers must often work against habits learned elsewhere that have accustomed us to dampen down such spontaneities. Their pedagogical challenge is to kindle where needed our delight in the things we come upon, to encourage us to enjoy this object or person, that occurrence or happenstance, for what it is. These things appear before us, and we embrace them delightedly.

The things of the world are connected, however, and so each new thing we encounter is steeped with import. It points beyond itself, luring us away from its solitary immediacy toward neighboring things that it also is or implies, including possibilities it might harbor or could even become. In this sense, romance is discursive: our experiences fit together, they tell a story. We enjoy not merely this or that but the adventure of which they are components. Appreciative openness is a process of discovery, an exploration of what we experience that begins with what is nearby and leads us somewhere else. Imaginative curiosity should reign supreme in a romantic learning environment, with us as its loyal subjects.

2. Appreciation of this sort pays no attention to truth. It's concern is with things as they seem to be, not as they really are. Colors and sounds attract our interest without our needing to know what they are colors of or by what means the sounds were made. We sigh comfortably at the rustle of a wind in the willow and are awestruck by the gale-force winds of a nor'easter, without feeling any need to know the causes or consequences of either. It is enough to enjoy the moment and leave the explanations for some other time. And we can assist Mr. Toad in his escape from prison or warn Ulysses that the storm is driving him dangerously close to Scylla, without caring one whit that what we are imagining is true. It is enough that our fancy has been tickled.

This attitude is aesthetic; it is the way of approaching experience we associate with the arts, with music and painting, poetry and fiction, dance and theater. What is valued is the beauty of the sounds or images, of the bodily movement or the developing storyline. We create beautiful objects as well as enjoy them, and we easily imagine the beauty of natural objects as the work of unseen agencies whose artistic powers are proof of their divinity. So our teachers encourage us to find beauty everywhere and follow it wherever it may lead, from perception to imagination and back to perception, blurring the difference between the tangible and intangible. Romance invites us to experience the mystery of the supposedly mundane, the exhilarating wonder that lurks at the heart of the everyday.

3. Perceptive experiences are not passively received. We do not merely open our eyes and accept information transmitted to us from external realities. We are not copying machines by which images of the external world are impressed onto receptor plates in our brains. Likewise, our response to those images, our delight or our revulsion, is not an overlay we impose on them, a subjective response we make for reasons that have to do with us rather than the images. Quite the contrary; for what we feel is the impinging world, its intrusive insistence, and we abstract the perceptual qualities from these feelings and take them as the way the world is. We feel appreciatively the presence of our surroundings and derive from that feeling the soothing colors and textures that we say account for our delight. Our concern may not be with truth, but our aesthetic enjoyments have objective roots.

Romance is an active stage of learning. Through spontaneous processes of symbolic reference, we engage the world by touching, tasting, smelling, listening, and looking. We appreciate by appropriating, as a baby seeks to know what spoons and toys and someone's finger are by trying to put them in its mouth. The discursive character of curiosity, the way things always lead on to further things, requires our engagement. It makes no sense, if we are to learn anything, for us to sit passively at our classroom desks. We need to be up and about, doing something, interacting with things in order to discover what they have to offer. The intrinsic value of the world emerges for us in our adventurous aesthetic explorations of its presence and import. We interpret the world as we go.

4. Romantic curiosity is holistic. When our concerns are aesthetic, they are focused on how things fit together, how they harmonize. Our discursive exploration of these harmonies overruns any barriers impeding our progress. Our efforts know no bounds. They are endlessly expansive, extrapolating at every opportunity from the known into what might lie beyond it. Because we are impatient with limits, we find no problem with vague generalities and fuzzy logics, implicit assumptions and intuited meanings. If we contradict ourselves, then so be it; like Emerson's great minds, our aim is to encompass all things. We speculate about possibilities we cannot specify and entertain notions too inchoate to explain. Teachers

need to refrain from too quickly tethering our imagination, throwing cold water on our bubbling expectations, insisting that we move right along to the next topic or the next step in the lesson plan.

The way of romance is playfulness. Ideas are to be enjoyed, and this means paying no attention to their usefulness, their relevance to practical or intellectual outcomes. When our friends wonder what good it does to study Minoan history or French existentialism, they presume that for learning to be good it must be practical, a matter of the relevance of all those hours in the library to our chances of ending up with a well-paying job and becoming a responsible spouse and parent and citizen. Such concerns are beside the point, however, if our interest refuses to abide by any normative preconditions. We will follow the idea wherever it leads, and find our good in the delight we take in doing so.

5. Fickle, transient, and irresponsible it may be, but romance justifies its concern for things in the totality of their real and imagined interconnections by claiming that this totality is the experiential foundation for all knowledge and action. Our delight in any particular thing is our recognition that it matters. In having a care for it simply for what it is, however, we come to appreciate its unique importance in contrast to all the other unique things there are, and thus learn to appreciate how the value of the whole depends on the value of each of its unique details. For both aesthetic appreciation and creation, the one and the many are not at odds even though their compatibility is complex and unstable. This instability is what fosters our inquietude in the presence of a work of art. Indeed, for anything whatsoever our naively immediate sense that it matters carries us into an appreciation of how all things matter, a realization of the essentially sacral character of each individual and of the totality they comprise. Consistency is a hobgoblin if ever it belittles this boundless concern and demands that we put an end to the agitated explorations it nurtures.

Assemblage is thus a romantic task: trying to make sure that nothing is left out of what we take to be the complete expanse and specificity of things. In a totality that is genuinely relational, all its components are equally important; for all of them we should have the same unlimited care. It is a familiar artistic insight, however, that any specific context gives a relatively greater importance to one or another of its particular elements. A splotch of fire-engine red leaps from a canvas composed in shades of blue and green but contributes quietly to the intricate subtleties of one in which all the colors are shades of red. This tension between two different kinds of unbounded value, between the importance of the individual and the importance of the whole, is another way to indicate why aesthetic appreciation is disturbingly discursive. Figuring out how to help us discover, then appreciate, and then finally creatively appropriate this tension is what makes teaching an art, and indeed a ministry, rather than a science.

6. Delight deepens into care, care into love, and our love for a finite thing leads us to be concerned for the conditions that permit it to flourish. The conditions, however, are also finite and so our concern for a particular set of conditions leads to a concern for the world, for the conditions that nurture the emergence of contexts that support the flourishing of their components. Such practical concerns for appropriate contexts deepen into a sense of their intrinsic worth, and so into a care for them as such, and into boundless love. Thus our love for a single precious individual matures ideally into a love for the world, for all that is and was, and for all that might have been and might yet be. The unique one and the one whole are both sacred because they matter, and we love what matters and seek its perfection in blithe disregard for accepted procedures and self-evident truths. Romance is a form of irrational exuberance, the passionate work of fools—or of geniuses.

The vitality of a civilization is a function of the extravagant variety of the ideals it makes available for its members to entertain and pursue. The reservoir of idle dreams, impractical possibilities, and discarded hopes that romance nourishes are a heritage of inestimable worth. Teachers who provide us with an education that leaves us unaware of that reservoir of romance, or merely leaves us unpracticed at delving into it, betray their civilization. For they rob both us and our successors of the capacity for novel adaptive invention without which no social order can long endure.

7. Thus we can see that romance has a trajectory. It lifts our eyes to the near horizon and whispers of possibilities that lie beyond it if we would dare to seek them. The things we immediately experience are linked in intrinsically complex ways with other things, such that it is somewhat arbitrary to say where one stops and another begins. They are each unique, but they are wholes that are composed of elements and that are themselves elements of other wholes. So appreciating something we come upon whets our curiosity about its connections, but whether we are led to ever more detailed analyses of its components or to ever broader syntheses of the wholes of which it is a part, our stopping places are always temporary. We never reach a least component or a final whole.

This romantic trajectory does not fit easily into the framework of formal education, which is designed to accommodate the needs of the stage of precision. Romance is an attitude not a method. A teacher can encourage our curiosity and create situations that foster it, but there is no content to impart to us and so no way to test the extent of our romantic competence. Hence, probably the best way to further our development in this indispensable first stage of learning is for teachers to be curious themselves, to appreciate real and imagined things in a manner so genuine and intense that it is infectious.

Teaching contagiously is more than role modeling, of course, for it requires goading and cajoling, praising and suggesting, and sometimes it is effectively transmitted by irascible demands and a grumpy display of disappointment. The ways of good teaching when the kindling and nurturing of romance is the aim are too dependent on the unique character of the student and the teacher to be stated in anything other than exceedingly vague generalities. We appreciate good teaching when we experience it, but we cannot clearly specify its conditions or the standards for assessing it. Which is altogether fitting, since romantic pedagogy like romantic learning is improvisational; it cannot be explained, although it can be acquired.

There is a second trajectory to romance, let us not forget, a qualitative rather than quantitative one. It leads from curiosity to care and then to love, love first for particular things and then for their contexts as well. The quantitative recurrences of romance, as the helix of learning carries us beyond early childhood and K-12 schooling into collegiate, graduate, and adult forms of learning, grow increasingly sophisticated. They remain fundamentally the same, however: modes of aesthetic appreciation and creation. The shift from enjoyment to love is a different kind of movement. It alters the fundamentals, transforming them from an aesthetic to an ethical kind of appreciation. When we recognize that something matters, not merely for us but in itself, we are recognizing that we have a responsibility to protect and nurture its proper development. As indifference is transmuted into obligation and obligation modulates into love, we want to do what we ought not out of respect for the ought, as Kant argued, but out of respect for the object of our love—which is a unique person or thing but at the same time everyone and everything, understood both as a multitude of unique particulars and as the integrated whole they comprise. To love a single daffodil is to love all of God's creation and to embrace the deep ecology that honors it. Likewise, our love of the whole world ends in our tender embrace of a crying child and our sorrow that an idea of ours is dying because we do not know how to express it properly.

If fostering quantitative romance is a difficult pedagogical task, fostering qualitative romance is pedagogically impossible. For we do not choose to love what we love; it comes to us unbidden and sometimes unwanted. And yet love is not an alien intrusion into our appreciative adventuring. We appreciate something because of its inherent worth, and the transformation of appreciation into love is thus a flowering of that sense of worth. Our teachers, when they care for what they find enjoyable and love those things for which they care, will influence us in this transformative way. Some of us, of course, will remain stolidly indifferent to any such influence and others will recover from it eventually, but many of us will become transformative influences on others, in some cases even though we ourselves remain untransformed.

These complications are why neither a teacher's effectiveness nor the worth of a student's education can be measured. Just as no one knows another's innermost thoughts, so we can only surmise but never fully know the extent to which the seeds of romance have blossomed into the hundred thousand loves that comprise a person's soul. Teaching is an adventure because our teachers never know if they have done their pedagogical work well or even done it at all. Fortunately, if they love their work they can trust it will make a difference for how we students do our work. And love and trust are good enough in matters as fragile, as transient and therefore as precious, as are teaching and learning.

Precision

1. Precision is an intellectual virtue: being able to express an idea or describe a fact clearly and distinctly. Saying exactly what we mean is how we avoid the confusions that result from the fuzzy meanderings that plague the romantic stage of education. In order to understand something, we need to distinguish it carefully from other things with which it might easily be confused, to specify its boundaries and its essential features. It is important for me to know that I have three children not merely some, and that Susan is neither James nor is she Karen.

Precise knowledge cannot be acquired or utilized helter-skelter. We must proceed in a proper manner, starting with basics and building up more complex facts and ideas on those foundations. A good method is key, a plan or recipe stipulating the steps to follow in order to arrive at an acceptable result. The steps indicated by the GPS program tell us how to get to our destination, the mac and cheese recipe tells us step by step how to bake a casserole our kids will eat. When we organize detailed facts or ideas into systems, we are able to understand and make use of them more effectively because we can see how they work together, how the details function. We see how the trees have created the forest; we hear the sonata modulating from G major to B-flat minor; we understand why the pistons in going up and down make the vehicle move forward.

2. Theories provide systematic frameworks within which to locate what we are experiencing. If our experiences fit with the framework, we take the experiences as factual and the framework as true. If they fail to fit, we discard one or the other of them as false, as an error in our data collection or a misreading of that data. We can use theories also to predict what we will experience by extending the scope of their framework to include possible future events. The formula $3 \times 3 = 9$ is a rule derived from a theory about the relationship among numbers that allows us to predict how many additional chairs we will need if Tom, Dick, and Harriet each bring in three more members for our club. Theories that are successful predictors we take as trustworthy guides. By helping us anticipate what will happen, we are able to adapt to it, to have the nine chairs ready for the next meeting. Or by altering current conditions, we are able to prevent it from happening at all, as when we can only find six chairs and so limit our recruitment efforts to only two new members each.

Theories are closed systems. They achieve the benefits of precision by limiting knowledge to the facts and ideas that fit the system. What lies outside it—anything that might be thought to dwell beyond its boundaries or fail to accord with its rules—is not merely false but meaningless, not a merely imagined fact but something unimaginable, an impossibility. We can imagine Arthur pulling Excalibur from the stone or a unicorn grazing in our garden, although it is not true that either event has ever happened or is likely to happen; but a round square cannot possibly exist, and it would be silly to think we could travel back in time to when our grandparents were young adults, and by introducing them to one another, contribute to our own eventual birth. Learning to avoid these confusions and to be critical of those who don't is a boon to us as well as to them. Political discourse, for instance, is rife not only with claims that have no factual basis but with those that cannot be true and yet are believed because it would be pleasant were they so.

3. Thinking and acting within a closed system can be stifling, breeding rigid habits, making us unwilling and even unable to deal with surprises, with things that although they don't fit our theories cannot be ignored. It's difficult to hold fast to a flat earth theory as we watch a departing ship's sails slowly drop below the horizon, or to deny global warming as

we inspect the receding line of stakes marking the century-long shrinkage in the extent of a mountain glacier. We need to learn to think critically about the systems we accept as trustworthy, to apply the tools of precision in determining whether our theories are sufficiently adequate and how they can be adjusted to include what can no longer be excluded, but in a way that doesn't undermine their systemic coherence. We discover that a spherical earth is not incompatible with our experience of the endless flat expanse of a Kansas wheat field, and that global warming is not refuted by the heavy amount of snowfall at our home last winter but rather helps explain it.

Conceptual analysis is critical thinking systematically pursued. It provides us with the flexibility, the adaptive prudence, we need to maintain the efficiency of proven systems. It is a style of thinking that involves a method for recognizing errors we would prefer to ignore and for anticipating errors we can be too focused on present concerns to bother ferreting out. Theories like machines are constantly in need of repair, and so just as they provide us with effective methods for achieving our purposes, we also need an effective method for predicting when they will need to be repaired or remodeled or replaced by a better machine. Problem-oriented approaches to learning are excellent methods for teaching conceptual analysis, most obviously in science laboratories and field trips but also by means of case studies, computer simulations, and role-playing scenarios. For in all these situations, students encounter not simply the theory in all its theoretical glory but also situations in which the theory runs into difficulties, real or only apparent, that call for reconsidering the relevant factors and making whatever adjustments turn out to be needed.

4. We think precisely in order to achieve practical results; we justify our theories by their payoff, by whether they work. If pragmatism is king, then the skills we need are more than analytic ones. They include the clever use of our methods, theories, and factual information so that they get us where we need to go. Common sense is our primary source of useful theories because the frameworks it offers have been verified time after time: hammered into shape on the anvil of situational demands, tempered in the fires of unexpected exigencies, and well-honed on the sharpening stone of generations of critics with firsthand knowledge of how they could be improved. Our teachers should justify the theories and methods about which they are instructing us by telling the story of how those tools proved superior to predecessor theories and methods. Selections from the history of a discipline should be an essential feature

of lesson plans and syllabi, lest the justification for what we are taught be taken as resting on the *ex cathedra* authority of the teacher's bold claim that this is obviously what we must study in this course on this subject at this educational stage in our development.

If the problem of romance is the transience of its enjoyments, the problem with precision is the blindness bred of its success. Even common sense is dulled when the fields it has plowed have seemingly forever offered it no resistance, have never contained a rock that turned its blade. If the toolbox of effective techniques has sufficed long enough, the importance of keeping them in good repair, much less of adding new tools, is easily forgotten. The citizens of Ann McCaffrey's Pern neglected the recruitment and training of active contingents of dragonriders when no destructive thread had fallen for 250 years, and so were defenseless when it suddenly began falling once again. A precisely focused but shortsighted sense of what is important is no better than a vague amorphous sense. Both are eventually ineffectual. We should be taught to use our newly acquired tools confidently, but with an acute sense of their limitations. Trust but verify.

5. The best way to be precise about a fact is to quantify it. We quantify something, however, by stripping away its value. We can specify with mathematical precision the metric dimensions and spacing of the floor joists in our new house or the parameters of our retirement fund's investment strategy, but we cannot quantify their importance. Or rather we can only do so by defining importance as utility, understanding it solely in terms of its functional contribution to attaining a specifiable goal. The importance of the goal, however, cannot be similarly specified, unless it is a means to another goal, and so on. Ultimate ends, essential goods, normative measures, and other intrinsic values are left unanalyzed so that, whatever they happen to be, we can get about the business of achieving them with an optimal expenditure of time, energy, and money. The value of proceeding in this manner, of course, is among the intrinsic values left unanalyzed.

Precision is a creature of perspectives. When we become attracted to a possibility, desiring it because we care for what it would enhance, we orient ourselves and our context with respect to its realization. Wanting a pebble as a keepsake from my vacation at the shore, I no longer let my gaze wander but instead focus it on pebbles. I'll be most likely to succeed in my quest if I have clearly in mind what sort of pebble I'm after, one with a distinctive color and smoothly ovoid shape. I walk a route along the beach that maps it into sectors through which I search without inadvertently going back over the same area. And each time I find a possibility that I then discard as inadequate, I adjust more precisely the qualities I'm seeking. In doing these things, I create a scalar perspective, a closed structure with a trajectory that narrows relentlessly toward the point of its success, where I find at last just what I want, even though at the beginning, before the increasing specification of my search, my goal had been relatively ill-defined. The origin of my quest lay in a romantic value, the end for the sake of which my perspective arose, and the task at hand was to canalize that value, that enthusiastic caring, to bound its boundlessness, so that it became the engine driving my actions along the perspective's trajectory. In this way, systematic thinking is a powerful tool for achieving good. But it is a tool relative to the ends and contexts that it is designed to serve, and it typically serves us ill when it is extended beyond that limited domain. Not everyone dreams of finding a keepsake pebble or writing the Great American Novel or curing cancer; few who dream of doing such things ever do, and it would be silly to think everyone ought to try, that our humanity or masculinity or moral integrity is somehow at stake.

6. The ends served by a wisely deployed perspective, a systemic framework for understanding and action, are parochial but they are not subjective. They may serve our private aims but they do so by adhering to objective procedural standards. One of us seeks an understanding of how female frogs can distinguish those of its own species among the males croaking in a frog chorus, while another of us wants to determine if the existence of mesons entails the existence of anti-mesons. We both use the same basic methods of scientific inquiry, however, and our conclusions will be faulted if it were shown that we had departed from those established methods. We humanities students need to learn that this distinction applies to us as well, that we can disagree about whether *Robinson Crusoe* is a great novel but we cannot be taken seriously if we claim that our differing judgments are subjective, are merely matters of personal taste.

A pragmatic excellence is achieved by formulating and implementing a system that effectively serves our own interests, but our efforts are more worthy, their excellence more intrinsic, the greater the scope of the interests served. Teachers have a responsibility when teaching us the techniques that lead to a standard excellence to inspire us to strive for more than that, for an enhanced pragmatic excellence. The expansion of what we care about from ourselves to those we love, and then the expansion of those we love to yet other persons and to other creatures and ultimately to the whole cosmos, is the highest excellence to which precision aspires: to work with others, on their and our behalf, so as to craft in an efficacious way the greatest practical good possible under existing conditions.

7. So precision requires a confluence of three factors: a practical aim, the viewpoint this creates, and a criterion of relevance able to organize experience accordingly. We orient ourselves toward a desired outcome and pay attention only to those features of our surroundings that we think will be helpful in achieving our objective. Thus like romance, precision also has a trajectory, but because the trajectory works itself out within a closed rather than open system, it succeeds if it moves from start to finish as efficiently as possible. Romance succeeds by complicating things, enlarging the possibilities for what might ensue, and wandering down interesting byways as opportunity permits. Precision, in contrast, is always looking for the shortest distance between two points, the quickest route rather than the most scenic. For it, the value lies in reaching one's destination not in the journey undertaken.

Formal education is tailored to fit precision, organizing the learning process into units that are linked together sequentially. Each unit—a class session, a topic, a course—traverses material defined as relevant to the unit's goal and is completed by demonstrating knowledge of the outcomes that goal defines. Sometimes our movement from an educational unit of one species to that of a higher kind—from grade school to junior high, from high school to junior college, from undergraduate to graduate school—is accomplished by our completing a specified number of units, often grouped further into various subspecies. Occasionally, however, shifting up the hierarchy of kinds requires us to demonstrate knowledge of the lower species of unit as a whole. Since the ends are what is important, and the processes important only if they serve those ends effectively, it is possible to accelerate our movement through a species and up the hierarchy of species by skimming through or even skipping over the standard sequence and proceeding quickly or immediately to the test by which our knowledge of a unit or group of units can be exhibited.

The organization of knowledge into academic disciplines, and hence of college and university curricula into majors and minors, general education courses and electives, implements all of this quite effectively. The system becomes ineffective when we move from one unit or group of units to another without having actually demonstrated the knowledge legitimating that move, such as when it is discovered that Johnny can't read or Mary has received a social promotion. The cure is found in improving the accuracy of the legitimating tests, testing the teachers' ability to prepare students who can pass those tests, and assessing the worth of the schools by how well these improvements translate into improvements in the flow of students through the school system.

What is amiss here is the narrowing of education to the values and functions appropriate to the stage of precision. The narrowing is self-reinforcing, since the propensity of a closed system is to dismiss as irrelevant whatever doesn't fit into its approach. The immediate attraction pedagogically of precision is that it is comparatively straightforward. Precision-defined systems call for lesson plans and course syllabi detailing expected outcomes and the steps by which to get there. Once in place, these plans created by the teacher for our course can be used over again in the following semester's course, tweaked as experience suggests, emphasizing some outcomes more than others, replacing those found to be less relevant with new ones, and altering the specifics of the exams to better measure our grasp of what has been taught or simply to make it difficult for our friends to use our exams from last semester as crib sheets. The comforts of a teacher's consistently increasing expertise in these matters contrasts sharply with the frustrations of teaching at the romance stage where what is learned cannot be measured quantitatively, where plans therefore must be vague and flexible and learning encouraged obliquely.

Precision has the resources for overcoming its deficiencies. Its methods can and should include methods of self-criticism and boundary modification. Disciplines also break through their traditional boundaries by two or more of them combining to form a new discipline or by a discipline splintering off from a parent discipline. Biochemistry, American studies, and comparative literature are examples of the former mode; psychology, which was once an aspect of philosophy, is an example of the latter mode, and is itself now little more than the empty skin shed by a series of its more specialized successors. Disciplines are also constantly borrowing methods and content from each other, sometimes without attribution, and disciplinary collaboration is typical, especially with respect to practical undertakings that require a variety of expert information and techniques, and sometimes even require the creation of new approaches reached by an imaginative leap from the clash of competing but obviously inadequate traditional disciplinary approaches.

The way in which our romantic love can mature into an exuberant embrace of the whole wide world and of all its creatures great and small is paralleled in the way love of our expertise can mature into a love of Earth's ecosystem and of the vast cosmos in which it spins. The transition from a commitment to a discipline in which we have a proven record of success to a concern for issues that our discipline has uncovered but cannot by itself master is a trajectory most familiar to us when a famous scholar begins to write and speak about matters that outrace the scholar's competence. Think of the entomologist who formulates the new discipline of sociobiology; or the historian of ancient Greece who writes a philosophy of history in which civilizations rise and fall in order to make possible the emergence of a single global religion; or the professor of applied physics who begins elaborating a metaphysics in which eternal things are derivative abstractions from the processes by which spatiotemporal realities are fashioned. E. O. Wilson, Arnold Toynbee, and Alfred North Whitehead loved their specializations, but they came to love the whole world more.

Generalization

1. As a first approximation, we can say that generalization is a stage of learning in which we return to the concerns of romance equipped with the skills of precision. Where in the stage of romance we were actively engaged with the world but for no purpose other than to enjoy the delights it offers us, now we have the tools provided by precision by which the fruit of that engagement can be mastery. Both romance and precision are concerned with particulars, the one appreciatively the other practically. As romantics, we flit from one particular to another, drinking our fill of each, having no care for what comes next until it is upon us. Precision involves us in developing systems that organize the facts effectively for our purposes, although our interest is not in the systems as such but in the facts they gather for our convenience.

Generalization moves beyond both precision and romance by cultivating a way of proceeding in which facts are subordinated to the interpretive theories they ground. We learn to see the forest and not just the trees, to be alert for patterns, trends, and hierarchies of dependence, and to be guided by them in our judgments. We are initially captivated by the grandeur of the trees and the mystery of their having congregated where they did. Then we focus in on the particular trees and how they are both unique and interrelated. By means of the theories that generalize this information, we are now able not merely to appreciate the trees but the forest as well, doing so by understanding it in all its temporal and spatial complexity, and being able to deal with it accordingly.

2. Our attempt to understand the things in which we delight is necessarily incomplete, however. We have not captured all the forest's grandeur and mystery by what we understand of it. Generalization is thus not merely a return to romance but a critical return, one that identifies the limitations of the systems we devise and discloses some of the things they have denied, thereby pointing a way to craft a more adequate understanding. Mastery is helical; it involves constantly transforming our expertise. Art, in the broad sense of any open perspective in contrast to precision's closed ones, is the instrument for accomplishing these transformations. It works by enhancing an experience through associating it with a great variety of other experiences that are related to it in any of a number of cognitive and affective ways. The intensity of our response to a work of art, its ability to command our attention in a manner at once unsettling and satisfying, is due to this concentration of meaning.

Teachers should encourage us to approach works of art in ways that help us experience their transformative power. For instance, Caspar David Friedrich's famous painting, *The Chasseur in the Forest*, shows us not only trees and the patterns of their confluence but also the foreboding import of human intrusion. The painting depicts a single intrusive act, evidenced by an ax and tree stump, but because this act is one already completed, no longer a fresh wound but already a permanent scar, the painting also evokes a history of intrusion and foreboding that are primordial in their antiquity and horizonless in their scope, boundless in the intensity of values lost and transgressions still unpunished. We shudder at what we feel in what we see. The unity of an aesthetic object, unlike a systemic object, explodes the framework by which we initially encounter it. It exposes us to unfamiliar emotions and thoughts, fresh possibilities for our consideration, novel curiosities for our exploration, depths we had never plumbed because we were not before aware of them.

3. Our actions are symbolically conditioned. Especially when those symbols are functions of open systems of interpretation such as works of art, they liberate us from the blind necessities of instinct and habit, allowing us to develop an individual style, our own way of making sense of our experiences, in order that we might thereby be able to identify our genuine interests and act on them. These symbol systems also bind us

together, because in breaking through conventional meanings they reveal deeply rooted cultural meanings of which we were unaware. In freeing us from the claims of the present social order that has so obviously shaped how we think and act, they have exposed us to the claims of the past on which rest both our present world and our ability to transcend it. We discover that our individual melody is a variation of our devising on a cultural fugue we have been singing since birth. They know not what they do, those who insist that math and science are essential to the education of our country's rising generation but that the arts are frosting on the cake that can be neglected or dispensed with in times of budgetary constraints.

The more we have freed ourselves from blind acceptance of our cultural heritage the better able we are to reform the symbols comprising that heritage, to engage in the helical tasks of generalization. The greater the cultural resources, the greater our ability to become our own persons. A strong culture requires strong individuals; strong individuals require a strong culture. Self and society, the particularity precision values and the holism romance celebrates, are not incompatible polarities even if they are often at odds. Their interactions are a standard nonzero practice, for each is crucial to the enhancement of the other. The art of a free society lies in the adaptive power of individuals who find the formation of their private good in the contribution they can make to the reformation of the common good. The aim of our teachers should be to aid us in learning this art. Unfortunately, nowadays such an aim seems rarely to be understood much less embraced by those with the administrative or political authority and financial resources to shape the direction of education.

4. The logic of discovery is an achievement of generalization, the crafting of a manner of thinking in which speculation is subjected to orderly method. Theories, systemic ideas, and other general principles of understanding need not be subservient to the facts on which they rest. If acceptable frameworks of interpretation are limited to those that have worked, then they will be useless when any significant change occurs in the conditions of workability. Speculations are frameworks ungrounded in fact, and on the whole they are therefore useless. But change is constant and the emergence of a crisis, of a major problem that cannot be resolved by established techniques, is no time to begin the task of inventing new techniques from scratch. A well-stocked reservoir of idle, irrelevant, and discarded speculations are just what is needed. The speculative ideas, it turns out, are never as ungrounded as they seem. They are not mere fancies but hypotheses that didn't work, prophecies that weren't fulfilled,

once-failed or unverified predictions. A hypothesis is an idea that is partly grounded in established facts and theories but that reaches beyond them, identifying further possible facts that if actually facts would turn the hypothesis into a workable interpretation, a better version of an existing theory or its more adequate replacement. Generalization is a method for devising with the help of old hypotheses new ones that have a reasonable chance of working.

This interplay of speculative innovations with established methods opens the possibility for responses to change that are not radical, that tinker with an old way of understanding in order to fashion an improved version of it, to shift from version 1.0 to 1.01 and on to 1.99 without having to take the decisive step to version 2.0—but, when having to do so, manage to preserve most of version 1.0 and its variations, making 2.0, as the software developers say, backward compatible. This self-repairing dynamic is what Whitehead calls the Way of Rhythm: it preserves the general structures by varying the specialized ones. The Ways of Transience and Blindness, of romance and precision, are thereby integrated. The revolutionary destructive power of the one and the slow decay endemic to the other are avoided by making them symbiotic features of adaptive systems. We need to learn how to be at the same time conservatives who believe in the importance of innovative improvements and reformers who believe in the importance of preserving old accomplishments.

5. These various ways in which romance and precision are reconciled find yet another expression in the notion of rationalization. The clash of polar opposites is overcome by recognizing that both a thing's self-identity and its difference from other things are only partial. The red ball is different than the blue ball, but both are spherical and both colored; this red ball is a unique object, but it would still be a ball if it were blue and still be red were it a block. Generalizations thus proceed by analogy, finding unnoted similarities in what are said to be different and unrecognized differences in what we take as similar. They do not identify universal and necessary relationships, however, because analogies illuminate forms of process and are therefore impermanent and regional. The colored balls are currently in my grandchildren's toy box, but long before the kids grow up the balls will probably suffer irreversible damage and be discarded or in some other way will become irretrievably lost. Analogies are temporary scaffolds for understanding and action, approximations that work for a limited time and a particular purpose, but then become irrelevant or prove false.

We need to learn from our teachers how to interpret our experiences through a practice of analogical thinking that gives equal attention to pluralities and unities, to facts and theories, and that is able to move freely from one to the other. We will thereby learn how to check the adequacy of a theory by recourse to the sufficiency of the facts from which it was abstracted, and to assess the adequacy of the facts by recourse to the scope of the theories they justify. The clichéd example in logic books that all swans are white turns out to be a hasty generalization by Europeans from the swans with which they were familiar: these swans on our streams and lakes are white, so all other swans must be similar to them. A global survey of swans identifies many that are totally or partially black, which means that the generalization has to be corrected to the more modest claim that some swans are like our white ones—those found in the northern hemisphere. A philosophically informed pedagogy has a special task in this analogical badminton: to bridge the differences among the modes of thought, to find and explore the limits of insightful and fruitful analogies among art, science, religion, politics, morality, and mathematics.

6. The reconciliation of romance and precision is illustrated by how patriotism is love for a nation that is in one sense a love of its history and in another sense a love of its ideals. Our love is for an actuality that never quite lives up to its essential meaning. Patriots who love a nation only for what it has been are blindly conservative, presuming that what should be and what is are unambiguously identical. Patriots who love a nation only for its ideals are blindly utopian, presuming that what should be and what is are unambiguously different. A genuine patriot recognizes the ambiguity, and loves the nation for what this means: a nation that has both succeeded and failed to live up to its ideals, that has managed to overcome horrendous deficiencies but that needs desperately to do so again, that has already accomplished many great things but that still needs to accomplish many more great things. From this love of something ambiguous flows our commitment to using our nation's ideals to guide our efforts to improve its practices and the worth of its accomplishments. Always we will partially succeed and partially fail, for our efforts are necessarily open-ended, a helix of reconciling labors that can never come to rest because they are approximate and so must constantly be renewed in order to be sustained. American History textbooks need to be patriotic in this sense, not in the sense notoriously insisted on by the Texas Board of Education and all the school boards that place orders for the books it mandates.

It follows that our interest should always be in what is pragmatically possible, in workable ideals. Those no-nonsense realists who deny the worth or even the reality of ideals, and those starry-eyed dreamers who think they can make their ideals historically actual, are in their differing ways both purists, demanding the unconditional victory of either the many or the one, of difference or of identity. It is the pragmatists, the denizens of ambiguity and hence of analogy, who are the effective agents of the world's creative advance. They accept the tragic truth that our ideals are always betrayed by our actions but that what remains after our failure are ideals still worthy of our commitment and so resources for further undertakings. Our failures are always redeemable.

7. The difficulty in teaching students how to function at the third stage of education is that it lacks a point of equilibrium. Generalization lives by creating tensions that it resolves only by creating new tensions. Patterns of interdependence among the particulars comprising experience are discerned and their implications exploited, but in a way that uncovers further particulars that require reworking the patterns. Romance invites our restless hearts to find rest in the mystery of the one, whether it be the singular uniqueness of what is before us or the holistic uniqueness of all that encompasses us. Precision orients our restless thoughts and undertakings toward a multiplicity of specific resting places: this problem solved, that safe harbor attained, the truth of this or that ascertained. Generalization turns every resting place into the basis for some new departure, recognizing that there can be no rest in a restless universe, that patterns are necessarily partial and no goals can ever be final.

Whitehead's identification of rational thinking with the use of metaphors and analogies explains this inherent instability. No matter how illuminating the metaphor, it fails to capture fully the comparison to which it calls attention, for when something is like something else it is so only in regard to certain features. Were the two alike in all ways, they would not be two things at all—they would be, as we say, one and the same. But nothing is just one thing, because what it is depends on the things around it: the things of which it is composed, and the composites of which it is a component.

Notoriously, metaphorical thinking is a very difficult conceptual practice, difficult to appreciate and difficult to master. Textbooks are studiously prosaic in their presentation of material, and students whose reading experience is limited for the most part to textbooks have had insufficient practice in interpreting poetry and metaphorically rich prose.

For instance, William James says that for those he calls "rationalists" the universe comes "in many editions" but only "one real one, the infinite folio, or *edition de luxe*, eternally complete." Whereas for pragmatists, he argues, there is "only one edition of the universe, unfinished, growing in all sorts of places, especially in the places where thinking beings are at work" (*Pragmatism* 116). As attentive readers, we should have no problem seeing this as a contrast between closed and open editions, the complete one the rationalists embrace and the one still in the making that James champions.

We might wonder, however, how those inadequate "many editions" of the rationalists differ from James's single edition, since they are all in the making and for any of them to attain completeness is an impossibility. We wonder if perhaps pragmatists should be described as also fashioning many editions of the universe, differing from the rationalists only by denying there is a *de luxe* edition that is the standard by which the adequacy of the incomplete versions can be measured. James supports our speculation a few paragraphs later: "For pluralistic pragmatism, truth grows up inside of all the finite experiences. They lean on each other, but the whole of them, if such a whole there be, leans on nothing. All 'homes' are in finite experience; finite experience as such is homeless. Nothing outside of the flux secures the issue of it" (117). Thus James has clarified his initial metaphor by offering us two more: editions are like walls of a house, supported only by each other; editions are like our homes, each a place of refuge and renewal for us, although these refuges themselves have no place of refuge.

So we ask ourselves whether James's "editions" metaphor rings true, whether it works. But this question, like James's clarification, is itself a metaphor. Indeed, like his it is two of them. We need to deal therefore with the ambiguity inherent in how our question has been formulated in order to decide whether we can reduce the ambiguity inherent in James's claim enough to answer our question. Or perhaps it would be a mistake to give a prosaic answer to a poetic claim. After all, it is not that James clothed his claim in a metaphor and our task is to strip that covering away in order to get at the naked truth. Rather, the truth requires the metaphor, and to remove it would be to lose the truth it alone can convey.

The traditional way for students to learn to appreciate metaphors and thereby to learn how to think analogically, to think, that is, philosophically, is to grow up reading authors who are good metaphorists. In the last half-century or so, however, our culture has celebrated media other than books, and more and more of us now come into the schools metaphorically unpracticed, and often make it all the way through to college graduation without any but the most rudimentary exposure to nonprosaic writing. It is difficult for our teachers to play catch-up, although not impossible. The most effective strategy seems to be focusing on romance, as Frank McCourt did in getting his students excited about poetry by having them recite cooking recipes, since enjoying a good metaphor can as well as not begin by enjoying a bad one or enjoying recipes as though they were metaphorical, just like loving to read good books can as well as not begin by learning to love reading any sort of books, even comic books.

Metaphors are not limited to verbal modes of expression, of course. Whitehead's examples are from painting and architecture as much as they are from poetry. The power of aesthetic meaning in any medium, its open-ended intensity, lies in the way it reaches beyond its prosaic meaning to a more profound meaning with which it resonates and hence which it invokes. The cathedral spires at Chartres are long and pointy; looking at them, our imagination quivers with the wealth of meanings toward which they direct us. Freudian phalluses and Star Wars spaceships may come to mind, but the religious meanings of infinity predominate. They pour out unbidden, and not only because the cathedral is obviously a place of Christian worship. They do so because the cathedral and its spires suggest other mysteries as well, having to do with myths of ancestral origin and cultural destiny, with life's restlessness and the hope of ultimate rest. Of course, I speak metaphorically in claiming that a cathedral spire can be a metaphor. But how else could I ever make my point?

Søren Kierkegaard says faith is the task of a lifetime (*Fear and Trembling* 7), and so similarly is becoming adept at generalization. Why this is so should now be obvious: whatever thrives amid contrasting tensions and open-textured patterns always finds its accomplishments at risk. Appropriately, therefore, generalization is the practice of the art of life, for like life it thrives only insofar as the tensions that define it do not collapse. We are alive insofar as we are constantly running the risk of losing ourselves for the sake of the possibilities that are our heart and soul. Denizens of academic institutions who are alive in this sense are genuinely students and teachers, who because they can find no peace in their educational aspirations are filled with the "zest of self-forgetful transcendence" (*Adventures* 296) that Whitehead calls Peace.

Metaphysics

1. Whitehead says nothing metaphysical during his discussion of romance, precision, and generalization in *The Aims of Education*. It goes without saying, however, that the stages of education have metaphysical import, as the preceding chapters have indicated. An adequate metaphysical system should be applicable to every aspect of our experience, and education is certainly one of those aspects. To be adequate, however, a metaphysics should not merely apply to education but should be influenced by it. Whitehead never developed an explicit metaphysics of education, never sketched for us the flight of his philosophic airplane from concrete learning experiences to the abstractions of cosmology and then back to the solid ground of educational practices. So we have to make that flight ourselves. I've been suggesting some of its features.

The most obvious link between Whitehead's philosophy of organism and what he has to say about the rhythm of education is the importance of relatedness. Things are fundamentally interrelated, mutually dependent. They can neither exist nor be understood apart from their relationships: the past from which they arise, the present in which they come to be and thrive and perish, and the future for which they make a difference. Romance is the condition for the emergence of precision, and without precision generalization cannot emerge, nor will romance once more be relevant except through generalization. Moreover, this sequence is not one of fixed stages. Romance weaves its spell in increasingly sophisticated ways until its limitations have become important. Precision develops its special virtues in response to those inadequacies, and continues to refine them until they prove inadequate. Generalization uses the virtues of romance and precision to foster a harmony that moves beyond them both, but the achievement is inherently unstable. And similarly for each shift through a cycle of stages and for the helical shift from cycle to cycle, whether the stages and cycles be educational, psychological, societal, or sacral, whether they are physiochemical, organismic, planetary, galactic, or cosmic.

2. We are vividly aware of these forms of process in our everyday experience of a world marked by lots of changing details that rest on a bed of fundamental continuities. We trust this picture of things because it makes sense of them. It orients us amid objects, persons, and events, allowing us to frame reasonable purposes and plausible means for achieving them. These pictures, these commonsensical and scientific frameworks of understanding, are closed systems, however. They suppress aspects of

our experience in order to make sense of it, so when these systems no longer serve us well we need a way to access what has been suppressed, hoping to find there resources for improving our systems of understanding. In *Adventures of Ideas*, Whitehead assigns this redemptive role to Art, which fashions open systems that unloose those closures, disclosing depths of reality beyond the power of speech to express or reason to understand.

Reality is more than our systems of truth can encompass; our theories are necessarily imperfect because the real world is far too interrelated to be systematized. It is not that there are certain mysteries fundamentally beyond our ken, however, ineffable realities that always and necessarily transcend our grasp of them. Understanding is never more than partial, but it is adjustable. What is transcendent is always relative to some system that has omitted it. No specific thing is beyond all understanding, but for any attempt at understanding there must be some things that get left out. We can examine the statue from the front or from the back, the side or the top, but we cannot examine it from all those perspectives all at once. We can imagine round objects or square objects but not round squares. Thus, Art is not a technique for getting us in touch with realities science cannot reach; it is a technique for reaching beyond the confines of any particular scientific picture of reality to aspects it has omitted. Romance explores the same world precision busily structures, ferreting out interesting things in which precision has shown no interest.

3. The interplay of science and art reflects the interplay of our two modes of perception, which Whitehead explores in *Symbolism*: one, like art, primarily concerned with vague feelings of the impinging world, the other, like science, concerned with vivid sense-data. Because both modes of perceptions are interpretations of reality, because neither mirrors that reality, they need to be constantly coordinated in order to be useful guides for understanding and action. Because they are both interpretations, however, this correlation is inherently inadequate, an interpretation of interpretations, so critical assessment is constantly needed to adjust the effectiveness of the correlations. These adjustments cannot be merely ad hoc, focusing only on immediate stop-gap improvements. Long-term assessments and adjustments are also required, leading to the development of the cultural habits by which we can anticipate significant changes and alter our modes of response accordingly. The height of the critical process is the art of life, which prevents us from growing blind to the limitations of even our most successful habits, from trusting uncritically the truths we think self-evident.

The continuities in our lives are crucial. If the present and immediate future were not largely more of the same, if experience were a random flux of one damn thing after another, we could never envision goals and plot how best to pursue them. Each moment would be disorienting, life impossible. Order is necessary for us simply to survive, much less to live a meaningful life, just as order is necessary for there to be any things at all. So the problem is not order but unbending order. The inadequacy of our interpretations is evidence of our limitations, the fallibility of our understanding and the fragility of our achievements, but it is also evidence of our strength, our capacity to critique and reform our means and ends. We are able to live well by learning from our failures, yet not merely by happenstance but by learning how to learn from them. The creative advance of the cosmos is a function of entities fashioning flexible continuities. Inadequacy and frailty are the engines of reality, the fundamental forms of its process.

4. Boundary-defined systems are pragmatic forms by which we are able to identify ends that are in our interest and pursue them by means of standardly accepted methods. Boundary-bursting systems are not end-oriented; they are patterns of behavior uninterested in our interests, expressions of our idle curiosity that, precisely because they have no practical objective, often lead to unexpectedly relevant facts and truthful novel ideas. In *The Function of Reason*, Whitehead identifies these two forms of process as two forms of reason, one associated with well-ordered stability, the other with destabilizing innovation. They are obviously at odds, so it is a striking innovation for humans to have discovered a way to reconcile them: by finding a place for curiosity in our practical pursuits. The role played by imagination in pragmatic activities—formulating novel possibilities for systematizing some aspect of experience—rescues them from the closure seemingly endemic to boundary formation. And similarly, the role played by methodological focus in our speculative explorations rescues them from their tendency toward silly incoherence. Generalization's reconciliation of romance and precision is a special instance of the reconciliation necessary for any form of process to prove itself cosmically fit.

The Way of Rhythm explicitly extends the reconciling pattern of this discovery to biological organisms which, because for Whitehead they are paradigmatic, means extending it to all actualities. The key to this reconciliation is holding the general form constant while varying the particular content, the changes in content eventually modifying the form. The continuity of form constrains the content changes, those changes modify the form in a manner that preserves rather than destroys its continuity. So the right balance between the polar opposites is built into the process rather than imposed by something outside it. These systems are self-repairing, in ways so exquisitely sensitive to context that innovations characterizing their evolution are unique and therefore unpredictable, although in retrospect fully intelligible. The cosmos is governed by a single overarching cosmic form of process, but it points to no ultimate end, no cosmic apotheosis. It describes instead an open-ended endeavor: effective local achievements occurring in regimes of inevitable inadequacy.

5. Whitehead summarizes these metaphysical considerations with respect to their human relevance by arguing in *Modes of Thought* that all the ultimate notions by which we seek to understand reality are versions of the same polarity: concrete-abstract, particular-general, many-one, fact-idea. They are all reconciled by finding their value to lie neither in the one nor the other pole but in a judgment that reveals their interdependence. The judgment that "this is important" requires us to appreciate both the many concrete particular facts that ground this judgment and the one abstract general idea that gives them meaning. A group makes it possible for its members to fashion their own unique selves, and then gives that uniqueness significance; unique individuals provide a group with the critical flexibility by which it can respond inventively to its unique context and so survive to foster successor individuals.

Rationalization is judgment-making: fashioning meaningful interpretations by collecting a number of facts together by means of an appropriate unifying concept. This uniting of form and contents is unstable, however, because the facts don't all fit well and none of them fit perfectly. The value the unity creates, the purpose it serves, is worth our effort if it enhances both the vibrant uniqueness of its various components and the stabilizing function of the organizing form. When it is no longer worth our effort, the unity must be dissolved and a new one devised. We should be engaging in this judgment-making effort, this attempt to rationalize our experience, at all times and in all the modes of our thought about facts and importance, for it is the source of that ultimate good sense by which we are able to exist as civilized persons. We flourish quite literally by metaphors: by the understandings they tenuously permit and the practical accomplishments they fleetingly enable.

6. Working out these tensions between fact and ideal, particulars and wholes, is what drives the character of our moral development. We return to *Adventures of Ideas* for an account of this crucial helix. We begin

with the enjoyment to be found in each moment's experience. We learn from that experience how to broaden and deepen what we value so that it includes other and more complex moments as well, under unifying notions other than our own enjoyment. The process is open-ended, for whatever level of moral maturity we may reach, there are particulars we have overlooked and values we have understood too superficially. Moral perfection is not attainable, however, for we do not fit its requirements, imperfect creatures that we are, having only a partial grasp of what is the case and what the possibilities are for interpreting its intrinsic worth.

Moral maturity is found in this recognition of not only our finitude but the finitude of all things. Our moral aspirations are rooted in a standpoint we can modify but not ever overcome; our achievements are as partial as are our skills at bringing them to fruition. Yet it is because of those aspirations that we can achieve anything at all, for in the development of moral character, as in the making of all things, value arises when a unifying ideal is brought together with the particulars of a concrete situation, resulting in a new creation—whether for the better or the worse. To understand ourselves as sharing our creaturely condition with all other entities—harboring ideal ends, seeking to actualize them, falling short—is to understand the nature of reality as a creative interplay of Youth and Tragedy. To find this truth enough to give our lives meaning—to be able to say that "this is important" of our efforts to frame worthy ideals, even though they are problematic and transient, and to say it also of our struggle on behalf of those ideals, even though what we achieve is at best partial and unsustainable—is to gain the sense of Peace that is the capstone of civilized existence.

7. I have been interpreting as incisively pragmatic the metaphysics Whitehead develops in the four books we've been considering. Like most pragmatists, Whitehead as I'm interpreting him insists on the temporal character of reality: all actual things are concrete particulars that come into existence, endure for a finite period, and then cease to exists. Anything not temporal, anything general or recurrent or everlasting, anything eternal or necessary or universal, is not actual but an abstraction from actualities. An interpretation is a way of unifying particulars; it is a function of the interpreter's particular standpoint. A particular actuality, an object or event or person, is a way of unifying facts and possibilities into a standpoint; it is an interpretation of its contingent situation. Consequently no interpretation can be complete, nor any concrete reality

perfect. Actualities are finite achievements that are ontologically fragile, epistemologically fallible, and ethically biased. Despite these limitations, actualities are achieved, complex systems fashioned, a cosmos sustained. In the absence of perfection, there is nonetheless a vital continuing creative advance into the future.

Conclusion

I have attempted over the course of this book to develop analogies between the three stages of education Whitehead discusses in the first two chapters of *The Aims of Education* and the triplets of ideas found in four of Whitehead's metaphysical writings. I have also argued that the triplets are analogous to each other as well as to the educational stages, and that these analogies yield an insight into a consistent theme in Whitehead's thought: that of the cosmological centrality of open systems. Events are acts of unification that reveal their inadequacy in their success. This success is transmittable to successor events only insofar as acts of unification are adaptively self-repairing efforts, efforts oriented not simply toward achievable repetition but also toward sustainable improvements on past successes.

By making this open-endedness central to an adequate interpretation of Whitehead's metaphysics, focusing on incompatibilities and their transformation into contrasts, on forms of process, unstable unities, evolving helixes, and the power of tragic beauty, my interpretation of Whitehead and of the reality he struggles to interpret is strongly temporalist. It affirms a reality for which the only literal sense in which something is real is that it becomes and perishes.

John Dewey once argued that Whitehead's metaphysics is an incoherent mix of "morphological" and "genetic-functional" generalizations, the former a "system of independent definitions and postulates," the latter arising from "experimental observational inquiry" ("Whitehead's Philosophy" 174–75). Unsurprisingly, he suggests that Whitehead should embrace the latter, the pragmatic, approach. I have followed Dewey's advice in this book. I think my interpretation is truer to Whitehead than more morphological interpretations and is the way in which his thought is truer to reality. It also makes Whitehead's metaphysics more accessible to nonspecialists, and hence more conducive to the comparisons I have developed in this book between the ways we learn and the ways the world works.

The relevance of this book for teachers and professors is not as a how-to handbook of useful pedagogical strategies, lesson plans, or course templates. Teaching is an art not a technique. The value of transmitting to students a body of facts, theories, and methods, whether traditional or innovative, is not self-justifying. Nor is the more subtle task of infecting students with profound convictions, whether one's own or those of a group. So neither transmission nor infection can be the foundation or goal of learning. They are intermediate enterprises justified by appeal to metaphysical presuppositions already in place. I have attempted to contribute some insights into these presuppositions, into what the aim of education should be and from what platform of understanding it should be launched.

The conclusion that slowly emerges over the course of this book is that the aim of education—the goal and foundation of learning—should be to create conditions that will enhance the possibilities for ourselves and our teachers to become practiced in thinking approximately, to develop effective habits of rationalizing the polarities that everywhere abound. We all need to become accustomed to envisioning possibilities worth actualizing and methods for actually actualizing them, while at the same time recognizing that even our best efforts won't quite hit the bull's-eye, that at best they will be on target. And so we also need to become accustomed to recognizing that falling short of our goals is endemic to having them, and that this is not only a tragic truth but a beautiful one. For if approximation is the foundation of every good ever achieved, then it is itself the greatest good.

The clichés of academic life offer intimations of this metaphysical insight. Discouragement is the specter haunting every class we teach or take, every idea we explicate or data set we interpret, every paper we write or exam we design. We never quite get it right, we often get it quite wrong, and yet we are soon at it again, whether from duty or inclination, fearful of the consequences of failure or confident that next time we will do better or even well. The world begins anew with each class, each paper, each semester. Anew is never de novo, however, but afresh: coming once again to an old task with the wreckage of our shortcomings a fundamental resource that emboldens us to be hopeful about the task we now face.

On the impractical foundation of an insufficient good, we think it sufficiently practical to take aim toward a pragmatically possible better. When this is our habitual response, the helix of learning is activated, and the aim of education achieved. Approximately.

Works Cited

Allan, George. *Rethinking College Education*. Lawrence: University Press of Kansas, 1997.

———. *The Patterns of the Present: Interpreting the Authority of Form*. Albany: State University of New York, 2001.

Augustine of Hippo. *The Confessions of Saint Augustine*. 401. Trans. Edward B. Pusey. Intro. Fulton J. Sheen. New York: Modern Library, 1949.

Bentham, Jeremy. *The Principles of Morals and Legislation*. 1781. Buffalo, NY: Prometheus, 1988.

Bergman, Gregory. *The Little Book of Bathroom Philosophy: Daily Wisdom from the Greatest Thinkers*. Beverly, MA: Fair Winds, 2004.

Bhagavad-Gita (The Song of God). First century BCE. Trans. Swami Prabhavananda and Christopher Isherwood. New York: Mentor, 1954.

Bizet, Georges. *Carmen*. 1875. Lib. Henri Meilhac and Ludovic Halévy. Deutsche Grammophon: London Symphony Orchestra, Claudio Abbado conductor, 2005. Audio CD.

Bradley, Marion Zimmer. *The Mists of Avalon*. New York: Alfred A. Knopf, 1983.

Browning, Robert. "Andrea del Sarte." 1835. *Robert Browning's Poetry (Norton Critical Edition)*. Ed. James F. Loucks and Andrew M. Stauffer. 2nd ed. New York: W. W. Norton, 2007.

Campbell, Joseph. *The Hero with a Thousand Faces*. 1949. 3rd ed. Novato, CA: New World Library, 2008.

Chevalier, Tracy. *Remarkable Creatures*. New York: Dutton, 2010.

Coleridge, Samuel Taylor. "Kubla Khan." 1816. *The Major Works*. Ed. and Intro. H. J. Jackson. 2nd ed. New York: Oxford University Press, 2000. 103–4.

Crews, Frederick C. *The Pooh Perplex: A Freshman Casebook*. 1963. Chicago: University of Chicago Press, 2003.

———. *Postmodern Pooh (Rethinking Theory)*. 2001. Evanston: Northwestern University Press, 2006.

Croce, Benedetto. *Philosophy, Poetry, History: An Anthology of Essays*. Trans. and Intro. Cecil Sprigge. New York: Oxford University Press, 1966.

———. *My Philosophy: Essays on the Moral and Political Problems of Our Time.* Trans. E. F. Carritt. New York: Collier, 1962.

cummings, e. e. "I thank You God for most this amazing." 1950. *100 Selected Poems.* New York: Grove, 1994. 114.

DeFoe, Daniel. *Robinson Crusoe.* 1719. Ed. Thomas Keymer and James Kelly. New York: Oxford University Press, 2007.

Descartes, René. *Discourse on Method.* 1637. Trans. and Intro. Laurence J. Fafleur. Indianapolis: Bobbs-Merrill, 1956.

Dewey, John. "Whitehead's Philosophy." *Philosophical Review* 46(2) (1937): 170–77. Rpt. in *John Dewey: The Later Works, 1925–1953, Volume 11: 1935–37.* Ed. Jo Ann Boydston. Carbondale: Southern Illinois University Press, 1987. 146–54.

Emerson, Ralph Waldo. "Self Reliance." 1841. *The Essential Writings of Ralph Waldo Emerson.* New York: Modern Library, 2000. 132–53.

Friedrich, Caspar David. *The Chasseur in the Forest.* 1814. Oil on canvas. Private collection. http://www.caspardavidfriedrich.org.

Geoffrey of Monmouth. *The History of the Kings of Britain.* ca. 1136. Trans. Lewis Thorpe. London: Penguin, 1966.

Gould, Stephen Jay. *Time's Arrow, Time's Cycle: Myth and Metaphor in the Discovery of Geological Time.* Cambridge: Harvard University Press, 1987.

Harrison, Robert Pogue. *Forests: The Shadow of Civilization.* Chicago: University of Chicago Press, 1992.

Hegel, G. W. F. *The Phenomenology of Spirit.* 1807. Trans. and Intro. J. B. Baillie. 2nd ed. New York: Macmillan, 1949.

Hirsch, E. D., Jr. *Cultural Literacy: What Every American Needs to Know.* Boston: Houghton Mifflin, 1987.

Homer. *Odyssey.* Late eighth century BCE. Trans. Robert Fagles. New York: Penguin Classics, 1999.

Horace. *Odes.* 23 BCE. *Horace: The Odes and Epodes.* Trans. C. E. Bennett. Cambridge: Harvard University Press, 1988.

Hutton, James. *Theory of the Earth: With Proofs and Illustrations.* 1788. 2 vols. Weinheim: H. R. Engelmann, 1959.

James, William. *Pragmatism.* 1907. Ed. and Intro. Bruce Kuklick. Indianapolis: Hackett, 1981.

Kant, Immanuel. *Foundations of the Metaphysics of Morals.* 1785. Trans. and Intro. Lewis White Beck. Indianapolis: Bobbs-Merrill, 1959.

Kaufman, Kenn. *Kaufman Field Guide to Birds of North America.* New York: Houghton Mifflin, 2000.

Kierkegaard, Søren. *Fear and Trembling: Dialectical Lyric by Johannes de Silentio.* 1843. Ed. and Trans. Howard V. Hong and Edna H. Hong. Princeton: Princeton University Press, 1986.

Kuhn, Thomas. *The Structure of Scientific Revolutions*. 1962. 3rd ed. Chicago: University of Chicago Press, 1996.

Larkin, Philip. "Church Going." 1954. *Collected Poems*. Ed. and Intro. Anthony Thwaite. London: Marvell, 1988. 97–98.

Lawhead, Stephen R. *The Pendragon Cycle*. 4 vols. New York: Avon, 1987–94.

Levi, Primo. *The Periodic Table*. 1975. Trans. Raymond Rosenthal. New York: Schocken, 1984.

Locke, John. *An Essay Concerning Human Understanding*. 1790. 2 vols. Ed. Alexander Campbell Fraser. New York: Dover, 1959.

Lyell, Charles. *Principles of Geology*. 1842. 3 vols. Chicago: University of Chicago Press, 1990–92.

MacIntyre, Alistair. *After Virtue: A Study in Moral Theory*. 1981. 3rd ed. South Bend: University of Notre Dame Press, 2007.

Malory, Thomas. *Le Morte D'Arthur*. 1485. 2 vol. Ed. Janet Cowen. Intro. John Lawlor. London: Penguin, 1969.

Maslow, Abraham. *Motivation and Personality*. 1954. 3rd ed. New York: Harper & Row, 1987.

McCaffrey, Ann. *The Dragonriders of Pern*. New York: Del Rey, 1988.

McCourt, Frank. *Teacher Man: A Memoir*. New York: Scribner, 2005.

Newton, Isaac. *Principia Mathematica*. 1687. *The Principia: Mathematical Principles of Natural Knowledge*. Trans. I Bernard Cohen and Anne Whitman. Berkeley: University of California Press, 1999.

Oakeshott, Michael. *On Human Conduct*. 1975. New York: Oxford University Press, 1990.

Perry, William G., Jr. "Examsmanship and the Liberal Arts: A Study in Educational Epistemology." *Examining in Harvard College: A Collection of Essays by Members of the Harvard Faculty*. Cambridge: Harvard University, 1963. Rpt. in *The Norton Reader*. Ed. Linda Peterson, John Brereton, and Joan Hartman. New York: W. W. Norton, 1996. 543–53.

———. *Forms of Intellectual and Ethical Development in the College Years: A Scheme*. New York: Holt, Reinhart, and Winston, 1970.

Peterson's Field Guides: Rocks and Minerals. Auth. Frederick H. Pough. New York: Houghton Mifflin Harcourt, 1958.

Piaget, Jean and Barbel Inhelder. *The Psychology of the Child*. 1966. New York: Basic Books, 2000.

Plato. *Meno*. Ca. 390–380 BCE. Trans. G. M. A. Grube. *Plato: Complete Works*. Ed. John M. Cooper. Indianapolis: Hackett, 1976. 870–97.

———. *Phaedo*. Ca. 380–360 BCE. Trans. G. M. A. Grube. *Plato: Complete Works*. Ed. John M. Cooper. Indianapolis: Hackett, 1976. 49–100.

———. *Sophist*. Ca. 365–360 BCE. Trans. Nicholas P. White. *Plato: Complete Works*. Ed. John M. Cooper. Indianapolis: Hackett, 1976. 235–93.

———. *Statesman.* Ca. 365–360 BCE. Trans. C. J. Rowe. *Plato: Complete Works.* Ed. John M. Cooper. Indianapolis: Hackett, 1976. 294–358.

———. *Symposium.* Ca. 385–360 BCE. Trans. Alexander Nehamas and Paul Woodruff. *Plato: Complete Works.* Ed. John M. Cooper. Indianapolis: Hackett, 1976. 457–505.

Ridley, Matt. *Genome: The Autobiography of a Species in 23 Chapters.* New York: HarperCollins, 2000.

Santayana, George. *Scepticism and Animal Faith.* New York: Dover, 1923.

Shakespeare, William. *Hamlet.* 1600. *The Norton Shakespeare.* General ed. Stephen Greenblatt. 2nd ed. New York: W. W. Norton, 2008. 1683–1784.

———. *Tempest.* 1611. *The Norton Shakespeare.* General ed. Stephen Greenblatt. 2nd ed. New York: W. W. Norton, 2008. 3055–3115.

Sir Gawain and the Green Knight. Late fourteenth century. Trans. Simon Armitage. New York: W. W. Norton, 2008.

Stewart, Mary. *The Crystal Cave.* New York: William Morrow, 1970.

de Troyes, Chrétien. *The Complete Romances.* Late twelfth century. Trans. and Intro. David Staines. Bloomington: Indiana University Press, 1991.

Whitehead, Alfred North. *Adventures of Ideas.* 1933. New York: Free Press, 1967.

———. "The Aims of Education." 1916. *The Aims of Education*, New York: Free Press, 1929/1967. 1–14.

———. *The Aims of Education.* 1929. New York: Free Press, 1967.

———. *The Function of Reason.* 1929. Boston: Beacon, 1958.

———. *Modes of Thought.* 1938. New York: Free Press, 1968.

———. *Process and Reality: An Essay in Cosmology.* 1929. Corrected Edition. Ed. David Ray Griffin and Donald W. Sherburne. New York: Free Press, 1978.

———. *Religion in the Making.* 1926. Intro. Judith A. Jones. New York: Fordham University Press, 1996.

———. "The Rhythmic Claim of Freedom and Discipline." 1923. *The Aims of Education*, New York: Free Press, 1929/1967. 29–41.

———. "The Rhythm of Education." 1922. *The Aims of Education*, New York: Free Press, 1929/1967. 15–28.

———. *Symbolism: Its Meaning and Effect.* 1927. New York: Fordham University Press, 1985.

Whitman, Walt. "When Lilacs Last in the Dooryard Bloom'd." 1865. *Leaves of Grass and Selected Prose.* New York: Modern Library, 1950. 259–66.

Whyte, Jack. *The Camulod Chronicles.* 7 vols. New York: Tom Doherty Associates, 1996–2008.

Index